C++ Programming:

From Problem Analysis to Program Design, Second Edition Lab Manual

by Judy Scholl

THOMSON

COURSE TECHNOLOGY

Australia • Canada • Mexico • Singapore • Spain • United Kingdom • United States

THOMSON

COURSE TECHNOLOGY

C++ Programming: From Problem Analysis to Program Design, Second Edition Lab Manual
by Judy Scholl

Product Manager:
Alyssa Pratt

Senior Acquisitions Manager
Amy Yarnevich

Development Editor:
Lisa Ruffolo

Senior Marketing Manager
Karen Seitz

Associate Product Manager:
Mirella Misiaszek

Editorial Assistant:
Amanda Piantedosi

Production Editor:
Brooke Booth

Cover Designer:
Steve Deschene

Compositor:
GEX Publishing Services

Disclaimer
Course Technology reserves the right to revise this publication and make changes from time to time in its content without notice.

ISBN 0-619-21676-X

TABLE OF CONTENTS

INTRODUCTION

The objective of this lab manual is to give students step-by-step examples to become familiar with programming concepts, design, and coding. This text is designed to be used with *C++ Programming: From Problem Analysis to Program Design*, 2e, but it also can be used to supplement any CS1 C++ textbook. This manual is written to be used in a classroom lab environment.

FEATURES

To ensure a successful experience for instructors and students alike, this book includes the following features:

- **Lab Objectives** – Every lab has a brief description and list of learning objectives.
- **Materials Required** – Every lab includes information on hardware, software, and other materials you will need to complete the lab.
- **Completion Times** – Every lab has an estimated completion time, so that you can plan your activities more accurately.
- **Activity Sections** – Labs are presented in manageable sections. Where appropriate, additional Activity Background information is provided to illustrate the importance of a particular project.
- **Step-by-Step Instructions** provide steps to enhance technical proficiency.
- **Review Questions** help reinforce concepts presented in the lab.

SOFTWARE REQUIREMENTS

- Computer running Windows 98, Windows ME, Windows 2000, or Windows XP
- Microsoft Visual C++ .NET

COMPLETING THE LAB ASSIGNMENTS

Some lab assignments require written answers to complete an exercise, while others are programming assignments that require you to work with a C++ compiler.

- To complete the written assignments, remove the pages that your instructor assigns, and then write your answers directly on the pages of the Lab Manual.

- To complete the programming assignments, use the compiler that your instructor recommends or requires. Print all the documentation assigned, including program code, program prompts, input and output displayed on the screen, input files, and output files. You can submit your written answers and the printed documentation with a lab cover sheet for grading.

  If your instructor requires an electronic copy of your work, e-mail the completed assignment to your instructor or include a floppy disk with your work. (Note that all the files associated with a C++ program do not fit on a single floppy disk.) Your instructor will tell you what is needed, but be sure to submit the .cpp, .exe, and any .h files that you create, as well as any input and output files. Also include your name or ID in the titles of all your files.

- To provide program documentation, compile and run your program, copy the prompts, input, and output (if appropriate), and paste them as a block comment at the end of your program.

  In Windows 2000, click the Mark button on the toolbar of the output window. (The toolbar appears by default; if the output window does not have a toolbar, follow the instructions for Windows XP.) Drag to select the text you want to copy, and then click the Copy button. Open your program in a text editor, such as the program editor in your SDK, click at the end of the program, and type /* to begin a block comment. Press Ctrl+V to paste the text in the program file, and then type */ to end the block comment.

  In Windows XP, right-click the title bar of the output window, point to Edit, and then click Mark. Drag to select the text you want to copy, and then press Enter. Open your program in a text editor, such as the program editor in your SDK, click at the end of the program, and type /* to begin a block comment. Press Ctrl+V to paste the text in the program file, and then type */ to end the block comment.

  After you paste the comment in the program, either print the program file from your text editor or submit the program file to your instructor electronically.

ABOUT THE AUTHOR

Judy Scholl has been a Professor of Computer Science at Austin Community College in Austin, Texas since 1988. She currently teaches programming languages and Web authoring courses. She received her Ph.D. from the University of Texas at Austin.

ACKNOWLEDGMENTS

I would like to thank the reviewers for the endless hours they spent reviewing my chapters, including Richard Albright of University of Delaware, Julie Anderson of Capitol College, and John McGaha of Metropolitan Community College. I would also like to thank Marianne Broughey and John Freitas, QA testers, and especially Lisa Ruffolo, Developmental Editor and Jennifer Muroff, Senior Editor, for their patience and help. Without the support of my husband, Jack, and my children Jenny, Jeremy, Joni, and Jaime, I could never have completed this project. And to Jaime, who is still living at home, "Jaime, I love you. You do have a mom."

Judy Scholl

1 An Overview of Computers and Programming Languages

In this chapter, you will:

○ Learn about different types of computers

○ Explore the hardware and software components of a computer system

○ Learn about the language of a computer

○ Learn about the evolution of programming languages

○ Examine high-level programming languages

○ Discover what a compiler is and what it does

○ Examine how a high-level language program is processed

○ Learn what an algorithm is and explore problem-solving techniques

○ Become aware of structured design and object-oriented design programming methodologies

○ Become aware of Standard C++ and ANSI/ISO Standard C++

CHAPTER 1: ASSIGNMENT COVER SHEET

Name _____   Date _____

Section _____

Lab Assignments	Assigned	Grade
Lab 1.1 Learning about Different Types of Computers		
Lab 1.2 Exploring the Hardware and Software Components of a Computer System		
Lab 1.3 Storing Information Electronically		
Lab 1.4 Processing a High-Level Language Program		
Lab 1.5 Programming with the Problem Analysis-Coding-Execution Cycle		
Lab 1.6 Object-Oriented Programming (Critical Thinking Exercises)		
Total Grade		

See your instructor or the introduction to this book for instructions on submitting your assignments.

LAB 1.1 LEARNING ABOUT DIFFERENT TYPES OF COMPUTERS

Computers and software can help you perform many tasks, such as maintaining a bank account and writing assignments or reports. Software is developed using programming languages. This book uses the C++ language to develop programs to accomplish specific tasks.

Computers have evolved from their introduction in the 1950s, when there were very few computers, through the 1960s, when manufacturers produced very large, expensive computers, to the 1970s, when people began to use cheaper, smaller computers. Today computers are affordable and faster. Regardless of the type, mainframe, midsize, and microcomputers share some basic elements, including input, output, storage, and performance of arithmetic and logical operations.

A mainframe computer was once one of the largest, fastest, and most powerful computers available. However, a mainframe in 1960 was less powerful than today's microcomputer. A midsize computer was less expensive, less powerful, and smaller than a mainframe, and was created as a more affordable alternative to mainframes. Today the microcomputer is called the personal computer. Personal computers are usually sold with descriptions of their features to help non-specialist consumers match the features with their needs.

Objectives

In this lab, you become acquainted with the different types of computers that have evolved and identify how these types are used.

After completing this lab, you will be able to:

- Identify and define the different types of computers.

- Identify the different uses of the different types of computers.

Estimated completion time: **10–15 minutes**

Learn about Different Types of Computers

Match the following terms with the appropriate definitions.

1. _____ 1950s

2. _____ 1960s

3. _____ 1990s

4. _____ Mainframe

5. _____ Midsize computer

6. _____ Microcomputer

a) Personal computer

b) Computers became affordable for non-specialists

c) A computer less expensive and smaller than a mainframe that allowed more companies to afford computers

d) When computers were introduced to very few people

e) When large companies began to use computers

f) One of the largest, fastest, and most powerful computers until recently

LAB 1.2 EXPLORING THE HARDWARE AND SOFTWARE COMPONENTS OF A COMPUTER SYSTEM

A computer is an electronic device made up of physical components (hardware) and programs (software). Major hardware components include the following: central processing unit (CPU), which contains the control unit (CU) and arithmetic logic unit (ALU); main memory (MM), also called random access memory (RAM); input/output devices; and secondary storage. Main memory is directly connected to the CPU. Main memory is an ordered sequence of cells, called memory cells. Each cell has a unique location in main memory, called the address of the cell. The ALU carries out all arithmetic and logical operations. The accumulator (ACC) holds the results of the operations performed by the ALU. All instructions (programs) and data must be loaded into main memory before they can be executed, or performed. Programs and data are transferred to secondary storage when they are not being executed.

Programs are commands that perform input (get data), output (display results), storage, and performance of arithmetic and logical operations. There are two types of programs, system programs and application programs. System programs control the computer and monitor activities of the computer. Application programs perform a specific task, often for the user. Examples include word processors, spreadsheets, and games.

Objectives

In this lab, you become acquainted with common computer terminology regarding hardware and software components.

After completing this lab, you will be able to:

- Identify and define hardware components.

- Distinguish between types of programs.

- Recognize addressing, storage, input, and output.

Estimated completion time: **15–20 minutes**

Explore the Hardware Components of a Computer System

Match the following terms with the appropriate definitions.

1. _____ Accumulator

2. _____ Address

3. _____ Arithmetic logic unit

4. _____ Computer

5. _____ CPU

a) An electronic device that can perform commands to input, output, or store data, and can calculate arithmetic and logical expressions

b) Computer components including the central processing unit (CPU), main memory (MM), input/output devices, and secondary storage

c) The brain of the computer, containing several components such as the control unit (CU), program counter (PC), instruction register (IR), arithmetic logic unit (ALU), and accumulator (ACC)

d) Controls a program's overall execution

e) Points to the next instruction to be executed

6. _____ CU

f) Holds the instruction that is currently being executed

7. _____ Hardware

g) Holds the results of the operations performed by the arithmetic logic unit

8. _____ Input devices

h) The component of the CPU that performs arithmetic and logical operations

9. _____ Instruction register

i) A unique location in main memory

10. _____ Output devices

j) Stores information permanently

11. _____ Program counter

k) Devices including the keyboard, mouse, and secondary storage

12. _____ Secondary storage

l) Devices including monitor, printer, and secondary storage

Explore the Software Components of a Computer System

1. _____ Application program

a) Computer instructions to solve a problem

2. _____ Program

b) Programs run by the computer

3. _____ Software

c) Monitors the overall activity of the computer and provides services

4. _____ System program

d) Performs a specific task; examples include word processors, spreadsheets, and games

Answer questions about the computer used in the computer lab:

1. What is the operating system of the computer you use?

2. How much memory does the computer you use have?

3. What type of CPU does the computer you use have?

4. How much secondary storage does the computer you use have?

LAB 1.3 STORING INFORMATION ELECTRONICALLY

A computer is an electronic device that processes digital signals, which represent information with a sequence of 0s and 1s—binary code. These digital signals are called the language of a computer, or machine language. The digit 0 or 1 is called a binary digit, or bit. A sequence of eight bits is called a byte.

Additionally, all data is stored and manipulated as binary codes. Inside the computer, every character is represented as a sequence of bits, each having a unique representation. Encoding schemes need either one or two bytes to store characters, depending on the scheme. Although most computers perform the same kinds of operations, the machine language of one computer is not necessarily the same as the machine language of another computer.

Machine language coding, or programs written in binary code, are very difficult to write and are also error-prone. Assembly languages, instructions written as an easy-to-remember form called a mnemonic, were developed to make programming easier. Assembly language instructions must be translated into machine language before being executed. A program called an assembler translates the assembly language instructions into machine language.

The next step toward making programming easier was the creation of high-level languages that were closer to natural languages. To run a program written in a high-level language, the instructions must first be translated into machine language using a program called a compiler. To run on a computer, C++ instructions first need to be translated into machine language.

Objectives

In this lab, you become acquainted with electronic signals and the representative code used to interpret these signals.

After completing this lab, you will be able to:

- Identify machine representation of computer code.

Estimated completion time: **20–25 minutes**

Storing Information Electronically

Fill in the blank with the appropriate term.

1. The two types of electrical signals are _____ and _____.

2. _____ signals represent information with a sequence of 0s and 1s.

3. The digits 0 and 1 are used to represent _____.

4. The digits 0 and 1 are called _____ or the shortened term _____.

5. The sequence of 0s and 1s is referred to as _____.

6. A sequence of eight bits is called a(n) _____.

7. The most common encoding scheme on personal computers is _____ _____ and abbreviated as _____.

8. Refer to the appendices in your text: The character represented by the decimal number 97 is _____.

9. Refer to the appendices in your text: The character represented by the decimal number 65 is _____.

10. C++ differentiates between uppercase and lowercase characters. True or false?
   _____.

11. Early computers using machine language that used binary code made programming prone to errors. True or false? _____.

12. Assembly language used _____ to make instructions easy to remember.

13. A program that translates assembly language instructions into machine language is called a(n)
   _____.

14. A program that translates instructions written in a high-level language into machine code is called a(n) _____.

Give the decimal representations of the following integers and characters:

1. 'A'   _____

2. 4   _____

3. '4'   _____

4. 'a'   _____

5. '\n'   _____

6. '\0'   _____

7. 0   _____

8. '0'   _____

LAB 1.4 PROCESSING A HIGH-LEVEL LANGUAGE PROGRAM

C++ is one of many programming languages that are high-level languages, which makes it closer to a natural language than a machine language or an assembly language. There are five steps necessary to execute a program written in a high-level language.

1. You use an editor to create a program that is called the source program while following the rules, or syntax, of the high-level language.

2. Verify that the program obeys the rules of the programming language. When the program is syntactically correct, the compiler translates the program into a machine language program called an object program.

3. To write a high-level program, use a software development kit (SDK). The SDK contains several programs, which perform a specific application that leads to creating an executable program. You must bring the code for the resources that you use from the SDK into your program to produce a final program that the computer can execute. This prewritten code resides in a place called the library. A program called a linker combines the object program with the programs from libraries.

4. Next, load the executable program, using a program called a loader, into main memory for execution.

5. Execute the program.

Objectives

In this lab, you become acquainted with the different programs in the SDK that are needed to process a source program written in a high-level language program.

After completing this lab, you will be able to:

- Identify the process needed to convert a high-level language program to an executable program.

Estimated completion time: **15–20 minutes**

Processing a High-Level Language Program

Match the following terms with the appropriate definitions.

1. _____ Alternative names for linking

2. _____ Compiler

3. _____ Editor

4. _____ Library

5. _____ Linker

a) The program used to create a program in a high-level language

b) The program created using an editor that follows the rules or syntax of a high-level language

c) The machine language version of the source program created by the compiler

d) The program that checks for correctness of syntax and translates a program into machine language

e) A set of programs to help write a high-level program that produces a final executable program

6. _____ Loader

    f) The location of prewritten code used as a resource with the source code that has been successfully compiled

7. _____ Object program

    g) A program that combines the object program with the programs from libraries that creates executable code

8. _____ Programs contained in an SDK

    h) A program that loads an executable program into main memory

9. _____ Software Development Kit (SDK)

    i) An editor, compiler, linker, and loader

10. _____ Source program

    j) Build, rebuild, and make

LAB 1.5 PROGRAMMING WITH THE PROBLEM ANALYSIS-CODING-EXECUTION CYCLE

To become a good programmer, you must learn good problem-solving techniques. To develop a program to solve a problem, you start by analyzing a problem, outlining the problem requirements, and designing steps, called an algorithm, to solve the problem. Next, you implement the algorithm in a programming language. You follow the four steps listed in Lab 1.4 to run the program and verify that the algorithm works. Lastly, you maintain the program by using and modifying it if the problem domain changes.

Running a program successfully does not necessarily mean that the program runs correctly. You need to test your program with sample data or perform some mathematical analysis to test whether it runs correctly. If it does not, then you must examine the code, the algorithm, or even the problem analysis.

Dividing a problem into smaller subproblems is called structured design. In structured design, you analyze a subproblem, and then produce a solution for the subproblem. The process of implementing a structured design is called structured programming, top-down design, stepwise refinement, or modular programming. To develop a program to solve a problem, you start by analyzing the problem. Next, you code the program, and then execute it. Structured programming breaks a problem into smaller problems, and applies the problem analysis–coding–execution cycle to each small problem.

Objectives

In this lab, you learn problem-solving and design steps to solve problems.

After completing this lab, you will be able to:

- Analyze problems and produce the steps necessary to solve the problem.

Estimated completion time: **45 minutes**

Programming with the Problem Analysis-Coding-Execution Cycle

Answer the following questions or complete the steps for problem solving.

1. What are the three steps required in problem solving in the programming environment?

2. Insert the problem analysis–coding–execution cycle steps in the following diagram. Include arrows that indicate the flow when an error occurs and when there is no error.

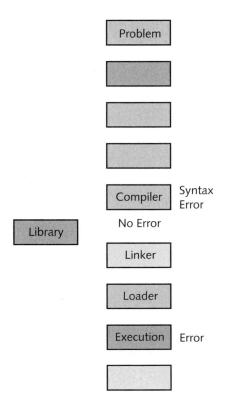

3. What is the most important step in program development? Why?

4. What are three other names used to represent structured design? What is the basis for structured design?

5. Once a problem has been divided into subproblems, what step must occur next?

6. Converting your design into a high-level language only occurs after your design has been checked to be logically sound. What steps do you take once you have created your source code from your design?

7. Even if a program executes successfully, how do you know that it is correct?

8. Consider the problem of converting miles to kilometers. To find the equivalent kilometers, the number of miles is divided by 0.62. Write the steps involved in calculating the mileage conversion when the number of miles is 12.

9. Consider the problem of calculating a paycheck. The pay is calculated by multiplying the number of hours worked by the rate of pay. All hours greater than 40 are calculated at time and a half. Correct any steps below that are in error.

   a. Get the number of hours worked.

   b. Get the rate of pay.

   c. Get the amount of pay.

   d. Find the amount of pay at the base salary.

   e. Find the number of overtime hours.

   f. Find the number of hours at regular pay.

   g. Find the amount of pay at overtime rate.

   h. Calculate the paycheck using the following equation:

   pay = hoursWorked * rateOfPay + overtimeHours * pay * 1.5

LAB 1.6 OBJECT-ORIENTED PROGRAMMING

In contrast to structured design programming, a methodology called object-oriented design (OOD) starts solving problems by identifying objects and then determining how the objects interact with one another. A programming language that uses OOD is called an object-oriented programming (OOP) language.

Each object consists of data and operations on those data combined into a single unit. To create operations, you write algorithms and implement them in a programming language. You use methods to implement algorithms. In C++, the mechanism that allows you to combine data and operations on the data into a single unit is called a class. C++ was designed especially to implement OOD. Furthermore, OOD works well and is used in conjunction with structured design.

The programming language C++ evolved from C. For approximately 20 years, several C++ compilers were available with slight differences, meaning that C++ programs were not always portable. In mid-1998, ANSI/ISO C++ standards were approved.

Objectives

In this lab, you learn how to solve problems using the object-oriented design methodology.

After completing this lab, you will be able to:

■ Identify objects and the relevant data and possible operations performed on that data.

Estimated completion time: **15–20 minutes**

Object-Oriented Programming

Answer the following questions or complete the steps for solving problems.

Identifying objects or components is the first step in problem solving in OOD. Use an OOD design rather than a structured programming design for an OOD program that performs the following tasks:

■ Get baseSalary

■ Get noOfServiceYears

■ Calculate bonus using the following formula:

   if (noOfServiceYears is less than or equal to five)

   bonus = 10 x noOfServiceYears

   otherwise

   bonus = 20 x noOfServiceYears

■ Get totalSale

1. *Critical Thinking Exercise*: What are the objects?

2. *Critical Thinking Exercise*: For each object, specify the relevant data and possible operations to be performed on that data.

3. Which organizations approved the standardized syntax of C++? Why?

2 Basic Elements of C++

In this chapter, you will:

- O Become familiar with the basic components of a C++ program, including functions, special symbols, and identifiers
- O Explore simple data types and examine the `string` data type
- O Discover how to use arithmetic operators
- O Examine how a program evaluates arithmetic expressions
- O Learn what an assignment statement is and what it does
- O Discover how to input data into memory using input statements
- O Become familiar with the use of increment and decrement operators
- O Examine ways to output results using output statements
- O Learn how to use preprocessor directives and why they are necessary
- O Explore how to properly structure a program, including using comments to document a program
- O Learn how to write a C++ program

CHAPTER 2: ASSIGNMENT COVER SHEET

Name _____   Date _____

Section _____

Lab Assignments	Assigned	Grade
Lab 2.1 Identifying Basic Elements of a C++ Program		
Lab 2.2 Identifying Data Types		
Lab 2.3 Using Arithmetic Operators and Operator Precedence		
Lab 2.4 Using cin, Allocating Memory, and Writing Assignment Statements		
Lab 2.5 Using cout, the endl Manipulator, and Common Escape Sequences		
Lab 2.6 Using Preprocessor Directives, the string Data Type and Writing a C++ Program using Good Programming Style and Form (Critical Thinking Exercises)		
Total Grade		

See your instructor or the introduction to this book for instructions on submitting your assignments.

LAB 2.1 IDENTIFYING BASIC ELEMENTS OF A C++ PROGRAM

A computer program is a sequence of statements whose objective is to accomplish a task. These statements in C++ are grouped into functions. Some functions, called predefined or standard functions, are provided as part of the system. Other functions are written by programmers. Each C++ program must have one and only one function named main. The following is a sample C++ program that displays "Welcome to C++ Programming" on the screen.

```
#include <iostream>
using namespace std;

int main()
{
cout <<"Welcome to C++ Programming" << endl;
return 0;
}
```

To write meaningful programs, you must learn the special symbols, words, and syntax rules of any programming language. You must also learn semantic rules, which determine the meaning of the instructions. Additionally, you should learn the tokens, which are the smallest units of a program written in any programming language. C++ tokens are divided into special symbols, word symbols, and identifiers.

Some special symbols in C++ are:

+   -   *   /

.   ;   ?   ,

<=   !=   ==   >=

Some word symbols (reserved words or keywords) in C++ are:

```
int, float, double, char, void, public, return
```

Identifiers are names of things. A C++ identifier can only consist of letters, digits, and the underscore character (_). Identifiers cannot start with a digit and are case sensitive. Identifiers can be of any length. However, each computer system has a maximum significant number of characters, which restricts the length of an identifier.

Two predefined identifiers are cout, which is used when generating output, and cin, which is used to input data. Predefined identifiers can be redefined, but it would not be wise to do so.

Objectives

In this lab, you become acquainted with tokens, which are the special symbols, word symbols, and identifiers used in C++ statements.

After completing this lab, you will be able to:

- Recognize special symbols.
- Recognize word symbols.
- Recognize identifiers.
- Recognize invalid symbol representations.
- Write a simple C++ program that displays a message to the screen.

Estimated completion time: **10–20 minutes**

Identifying Basic Elements of a C++ Program

Indicate whether each of the following representations is a special symbol, word symbol, or identifier, or is invalid.

Token	Special Symbol	Word Symbol	Identifier	Invalid
1. ABC				
2. xy!				
3. double				
4. $2ft				
5. &&ab				
6. ab*				
7. return				
8. c3po				
9. void				
10. 123z				
11. FLOAT				
12. date				
13. qr&				
14. first name				
15. *				
16. R2D2				
17. 5day				
18. !=				
19. +xy				
20. hello				

Question	**Answer** **(Circle the correct answer)**

21. Given: T   F

    `int number;`

    `int` is a keyword.

22. Given: T   F

    `date today;`

    `date` is a keyword

23. Given: T   F

    `int date;`

    `int` is a keyword

24. The syntax to declare a name constant is   T   F

    `const dataType identifier = value;`

25. The order-of-precedence rules for arithmetic   T   F
    operators are semantic rules.

26. The semantics of the following statements are the same.   T   F

    `2 + 3 * 5`

    and

    `(2 + 3) * 5`

27. Write the statements needed for a C++ program that will display "Hello World" on the screen.

LAB 2.2 IDENTIFYING DATA TYPES

The objective of a C++ program is to manipulate data. C++ categorizes data into different types, and only certain operations can be performed on particular types of data. Every data type has a different set of values associated with it. The data type also determines the amount of memory used, and consequently, how a value or other data is represented.

Three C++ data types are simple, structured, and pointers. Simple data types are categorized as integral, floating-point, and enumeration. Integral types are integers or numbers without a decimal part. Floating-point are decimal numbers. Enumeration types are user-defined and will be discussed in Chapter 8.

Integral data types are further classified into nine categories: `char`, `short`, `int`, `long`, `bool`, `unsigned char`, `unsigned short`, `unsigned int,` and `unsigned long`. Each type is associated with a different set of values. This chapter focuses on `int`, `bool`, and `char` integral types. Positive integers do not need a plus (+) sign in front of them. No commas are used with an integer.

The `int` data type is used to represent integers between –2147483648 and 2147483647, and the data type `short` is used to represent integers between 032768 and 32767. Different compilers may allow different ranges of values.

The `bool` data type has only two values: true and false. (The data type `bool` is not available on all systems.) The central purpose of the `bool` type is to manipulate logical (Boolean) expressions.

The `char` data type deals with small numbers, and is used to represent characters and special symbols. The `char` data type is used to represent integers between –128 and 127. Additionally, the `char` data type can represent every key on your keyboard and every printable character. When using the `char` data type, you enclose each character represented within single quotation marks. In C++, the `char` data type uses the American Standard Code for Information Interchange (ASCII) character set, which contains 128 values. Each character is listed in a predefined order, which is called a collating sequence. The collating sequence is used when you compare characters. Some character representations require the backslash character combined with another character. These representations are still considered to be single characters.

The floating-point data type is represented in the form of scientific notation called floating-point notation. C++ has three data types to represent numbers with decimals. The data type float uses 4 bytes, which holds numbers between −3.4E+38 and 3.4E+38, and has a maximum number of significant digits of six or seven. The data type `double` uses 8 bytes, which holds numbers between −1.7E+308 and 1.7E+308, and has a maximum number of significant digits of fifteen. On newer compilers, the data types `double` and `long double` are the same. The maximum number of significant digits is called the precision. For your exercises in this Lab Manual, mostly use the `double` type instead of the `float` type because certain compilers might give you a warning message when using the `float` type.

The data type `string` is a programmer-defined data type. To use this data type, you need to access program components from the library. A string is a sequence of zero or more characters enclosed in double quotation marks. Every character has a relative position in the string. The length of a string is the number of characters in it. The data type `string` may not be available in Standard C++. To process strings effectively, C++ provides the library string, which contains various operations to manipulate a string.

Every character in a string has a relative position in the string. The position of the first character is 0, the position of the second character is 1, and so on. The length of a string is the number of characters in it. Remember that a space is a character.

Objectives

In this lab, you become acquainted with the simple data types—int, bool, char, floating-point, and the user-defined string type.

After completing this lab, you will be able to:

- Identify integral, Boolean, character, floating-point, and string data types.

Estimated completion time: **15–20 minutes**

Identifying Data Types

Identify which simple data type or string type could be used to represent the value.

Value	Integral	Floating	Boolean	Character	String	Invalid
1. –2147483648						
2. true						
3. 1						
4. 0						
5. '?'						
6. "Hello"						
7. "123"						
8. '1'						
9. 66						
10. 7.8E3						
11. 0.1E-6						
12. ""						
13. ' '						
14. '+'						
15. "int"						
16. "false"						
17. +36						
18. 0.0						

Value	Integral	Floating	Boolean	Character	String	Invalid
19. 127.0						
20. false						

Question   **Answer**
                                       (Circle the correct answer)

21. The following numbers are examples of integral numbers: **T**   **F**
    4.1

    4.2

22. The data type `int` is a simple data type.   **T**   **F**

23. The data type `double` is a complex data type.   **T**   **F**

24. A simple data type can be assigned one and only one
    value, while a complex data type can be reassigned values. **T**   **F**

LAB 2.3 USING ARITHMETIC OPERATORS AND OPERATOR PRECEDENCE

In computer programming, there are five arithmetic operators: + addition, − subtraction, * multiplication, / division, and % remainder (modulus operator). Arithmetic expressions and precedence are evaluated as they are in mathematics with multiplication, division, and modulus having the same precedence and a higher precedence than addition and subtraction, which have the same precedence. However, the symbols—the operators—used in evaluation have minor differences. For instance, in mathematics "a times b" can be written as a × b, ab, a(b) (a)b, or (a)(b). In C++ "a times b" can only be written using the * operator. Parentheses can be used, such as a*b, (a*b), or (a)*(b), but they do not indicate multiplication.

The numbers or variables in the expression are called operands. Operators that have two operands are called binary operators. Operators that have only one operand are called unary operators. When evaluated, mixed expressions with mixed operands change integers to floating-point numbers. Additionally, you can use the cast operator to explicitly convert data types.

Integer division truncates the result. For example, in integer division, the expression 5/2 results in 2 (with no decimal). In floating-point division, the expression 5.0/2.0 results in 2.5. In a mixed expression of either 5/2.0 or 5.0/2, the result is 2.5.

The modulus operator works with integers to find the whole number remainder. Using the same example 5%2, the remainder is 1, not 0.5. The remainder of ¾ is 3, not 0.75.

The operators *, /, and % have the same level of precedence, meaning that the operation occurs as it is encountered, left to right (unless overridden by parentheses), when evaluating the expression. The operators + and − have the same level of precedence, and that level is below the level of the operators *, /, and %.

Since the `char` data type is also an integral data type, C++ allows you to perform arithmetic operations on `char` data. The character '8' differs in representation from the integer 8. The integer value of 8 is 8, whereas the integer value of the character '8' is 56.

If all operands (that is, numbers) in an expression are integers, the expression is called an integral expression. If all operands in an expression are floating-point numbers, the expression is called a floating-point or decimal expression. An expression that has operands of different data types is called a mixed expression. When evaluating an operator in a mixed expression, keep the following guidelines in mind:

- If the operator has the same types of operands, the operator is evaluated according to the type of operands.

- If the operator has both types of operands, then during calculation the integer is changed to a floating-point number with the decimal part of zero and the operator is evaluated. The result is a floating-point number.

Operators having the same level of precedence are evaluated from left to right.

A value of one data type can be automatically changed to another data type, as in a mixed expression. This process is called implicit type coercion. To avoid implicit type coercion, C++ provides for explicit type conversion through the use of the cast operator, also called type conversion or type casting. Type casting does not change the actual value of a variable. Type casting changes the value of an expression. The cast operator takes the following forms with the first example being more stable:

- `static_cast<dataTypeName>(expression)`

- `dataType(expression)`

Objectives

In this lab, you learn the mathematical representation in C++ of arithmetic expressions and precedence. Additionally, you learn to evaluate expressions using type conversion (casting).

After completing this lab, you will be able to:

- Evaluate arithmetic expressions using addition, subtraction, multiplication, division, and remainder.
- Use type conversion (casting) in arithmetic evaluations.
- Evaluate arithmetic expressions by precedence.
- Evaluate mixed arithmetic expressions.

Estimated completion time: **20–30 minutes**

Using Arithmetic Operators and Operator Precedence

Evaluate the following expressions or indicate that they are invalid if an illegal operator is used with the incorrect operand:

Expression	Result
1. 20 % (4 – 2)	
2. 20 / 4.0 * 6.4 / 2	
3. 4 % 5	
4. 3.0 * (6 / 24)	
5. 3 – (3 + 3.0) * 10 / 3	
6. 12.0 % 4	
7. 7 * 6 / 21 / 3.0	
8. 11 % 4 * 3.0	
9. 17 % 4 / 3	
10. 5 % 6 / 4	
11. 5 / 4.0 * 5	
12. 6 + 2 / 4	
13. (2 – 3 + (2 * (3 / 3) % 1))	
14. 5 % 4	
15. 5 – (2.0 + 5) * 10 / 2	

Expression	Result
16. static_cast<float>(4)/3	
17. static_cast<int>(3.7)+5.3	
18. static_cast<int>(3.7+5.3)	
19. static_cast<double>(5/2)	
20. static_cast<char>(65)	

Question	Answer (Circle the correct answer)

21. The explicit conversion of one data value to another data value is called type _____.

    a. casting
    b. coercion

22. The implicit conversion of one data value to another data value is called type _____.

    a. casting
    b. coercion

23. The following is an example of type casting:

    T   F

```
static_cast<double>5
```

24. The following is an example of type coercion:

    T   F

```
static_coercion<double>5
```

25. Given the following code, type casting occurs:

    T   F

```
int number;
double value = 8.6;
number = value;
```

26. Given the following code, type coercion occurs:

    T   F

```
int number;
double value = 8.6;
number = value;
```

LAB 2.4 USING CIN, ALLOCATING MEMORY, AND WRITING ASSIGNMENT STATEMENTS

Data must be loaded into main memory before it can be manipulated. Storing data into the computer's memory is a two-step process.

1. Instruct the computer to allocate memory.

2. Include statements in the program to put data into the allocated memory.

When you allocate memory, you use a name to identify each memory location that is being allocated. Additionally, you indicate the type of data that is to be stored in those memory locations. A memory location whose value cannot be changed is called a named constant. It is customary to use all uppercase characters for memory location identifiers (names) that are named constants. This is not required but sets them apart from memory locations whose values can be changed. Named constants do not change their values and must be initialized at declaration. You declare a memory location as a named constant with the following syntax:

```
const dataType identifier = value;
```

In C++, `const` is a reserved word that specifies that the value stored in the memory location is fixed and cannot be changed. It is customary to use all uppercase characters for memory locations that are named constants, but it is not required.

In C++, memory locations that can be changed are called variable memory locations or variables. Variables can be initialized at declaration and can be given different values through execution. You declare a variable with the following syntax:

```
dataType identifier1, identifier2, …, identifierN;
```

Data is stored in variables either through an assignment statement or through an input statement. Assignment statements use the = assignment operator. C++ evaluates the expression to the right of the assignment operator, and then stores the result in the memory address identified by the variable to the left of the operator. The expression on the right must evaluate to a value compatible with the data type of the variable on the left. The first time a value is placed in the variable is called initialization. Tracing values through a sequence of statements, called a walk-through or desk checking, is a valuable tool to learn and practice.

Memory that has been reserved and not assigned a value contains the sequence of bits that remain from system functions or prior use. You must therefore either assign a value or read a value into a variable after you declare it; otherwise the program uses the leftover bits as the value of the variable.

When the computer receives data from the keyboard, the user is said to be acting interactively. Putting data into variables from the standard input device is done by using `cin` and the stream extraction operator >>. By using more than one variable with `cin`, more than one value can be read at a time. When reading multiple values, these values must be separated by at least one blank or tab, or entered one per line.

Variables can obtain values either through input or through assignment. Inputting data offers the program more flexibility and requires a prompt to the user to enter the data. Assignments are used in calculations.

The increment operator, ++, and decrement operator, --, are used in assignment statements or with the variable name alone to increase or decrease a variable by one. Increment and decrement operators each have two forms, pre and post. The syntax of the increment operator is:

Pre-increment: `++variable`

Post-increment: `variable++`

If ++x is used in an expression, first the value of x is incremented by 1, and then the new value of x is used to evaluate the expression. On the other hand, if x++ is used in an expression, first the current value of x is used in the expression, and then the value of x is incremented by 1. When the increment and decrement operators with a variable are used in a stand-alone statement, it does not matter if you use the pre-increment or post-increment format.

Objectives

In this lab, you learn that allocating memory with both variables and named constants results in the programming assigning a name and type to the memory location. You must initialize named constants when you declare them; initialization is optional for variables. Additionally, you learn that the value of variables can be changed through assignment or inputting data. When changing a variable by the value 1, you can use increment and decrement operators.

After completing this lab, you will be able to:

- Allocate memory with both variables and named constants.

- Assign values to variables when expressions are evaluated.

- Assign values to variables through input.

- Use the decrement and increment operators.

Estimated completion time: **30 minutes**

Using cin, Allocating Memory, and Writing Assignment Statements

Describe the following declarations, assignments, and input statements. Indicate the value in memory after each statement is executed. Write "invalid" if the statement is not executable.

cin, memory allocation, and assignment statements	Show the variable name and value of each statement
1. `int a, b = 9;` `a = b;`	
2. `int d = 2, x = 3, y = 1;` `y + 4 = d - x;`	
3. `short number = 10;` `number = 0;`	

4. `short number = 0;`
 	
`number = 10;`
 	
`number = number + 5;`	

5. `double value = 12.0;`
 	
`value = 10.0;`
 	
`value = value + 0.5;`	

cin, memory allocation, and assignment statements	Show the variable name and value of each statement
6. `const int b = 9;`	

7. `double x = -14.5, y = 22.5;`
 	
`int d = 3;`
 	
`y = d - x + y;`	

8. `double ans = 4;`	

9. `int n;`
 	
`cin >> n;`
 	
//Assume the user enters 3.24	

10. `char a;` `cin >> a;` Assume the user enters 'b'	

11. `double x;`
 	
`cin >> x;`
 	
//Assume the user enters 3.24	

12. `double a, b, c = 0.0;`	
13. `int d = 2, x = 3, y = 4;` `4 = d - x + y;`	
14. `double def = 123.5; int y;` `y = def;`	
15. `int b = 9.0;`	

16. `int num1= 8, num2 = 3, temp = 0;`
 	
`temp = num1;`
 	
`num1 = num2;`
 	
`num2 = temp;`	

cin, memory allocation, and assignment statements	Show the variable name and value of each statement

17. `int num;`
 	
`cin >> num;`
 	
`//Assume the user enters 8`
 	
`num++;`	

18. `int c = 8;`
 	
`++c;`
 	
`c--;`	

19. `double x = 5.0;`
 	
`int y = 4;`
 	
`x = x + y / 4;`	

20. `double x = 5.0;`
 	
`int y = 4;`
 	
`y = x + y/4;`	

21. `int count = 0;`
 	
`cout << ++count << endl;`
 	
`cout << count++ << endl;`
 	
`cout << count << endl;`	

Question	Answer (Circle the correct answer)

22. There is no difference between the following two statements:
```
count++;
++count++;
```
    T   **F**

23. Given:
```
int num1 = 2;
```
The following statements are equivalent statements:
```
num1 = num - 1;
num1--;
```
    T   **F**

24. The statement **num-** subtracts 1 from num and the statement **num--** subtracts 2 from num.
    T   **F**

25. Given:
```
int count = 5;
--count++;
cout << count << endl;
```
The number 5 will be displayed.
    T   **F**

LAB 2.5 USING COUT, THE ENDL MANIPULATOR, AND COMMON ESCAPE SEQUENCES

In C++, to output on the standard output device (usually the screen), you use `cout` and the stream insertion operator, <<. C++ evaluates the expression used with the stream insertion operator and prints its value at the current cursor position on the output device. You use a manipulator to format the output. The `endl` (the lowercase letter el, not the number 1) manipulator moves the cursor to the beginning of the next line and is called a newline character. You can accomplish the same action using the newline escape sequence \n as a character by itself or within a string. You can use multiple stream insertion operators in a single cout statement. Do not use a line wrap if an output string is too long. Close the string, go to the next line, use another insertion operator, and start a new string. If you break a string this way, remember to include blanks if appropriate.

There are many escape sequences in C++ that allow you to control the output. The following are some of the commonly used escape sequences:

\n	Newline	Cursor moves to the beginning of the next line
\t	Tab	Cursor moves to the next tab stop
\b	Backspace	Cursor moves one space to the left
\r	Return	Cursor moves to the beginning of the current line (not the next line)
\\	Backslash	Backslash is printed
\'	Single quotation	Single quotation mark is printed
\"	Double quotation	Double quotation mark is printed

Comments appear in a program as explanations to the programmer and are ignored by the compiler.

Objectives

In this lab, you learn to use `cout` and the insertion stream operator to display expressions or manipulators on the screen.

After completing this lab, you will be able to:

- Display expressions on the screen.
- Use the endl manipulator.
- Use common escape sequences.

Estimated completion time: **30–40 minutes**

Using cout, the endl Manipulator, and Common Escape Sequences

Describe the following declaration, assignment, input, and the output statements or write C++ code to implement the comment statements. Describe what is contained in memory and show what is displayed to the screen after each `cout` statement is executed.

```
1. const double PI = 3.1416;
   double radius = 2.5;
   cout << "The area of the circle is " << PI * radius * radius << endl;
```

2. Write the appropriate C++ statement to match the description in each of the following comments:

   // declare an integer variable for the width of a rectangle

   // declare an integer variable for the length of a rectangle

   // prompt the user for the width and length

   // input the width and length values

   // output the area of the rectangle found by multiplying length times width

3. Indicate the purpose of the declaration statements and each pair of input and output statements.

```
   double balance;
   double deposit;
   double checks;
   cout << "Enter your beginning checkbook balance: ";
   cin >> balance;                //assume 536.25 is entered
   cout << "Enter your deposits for the month: ";
   cin >> deposit;                //assume 64.75 is entered
   cout << "Enter your checks for the month: ";
   cin >> checks;                 //assume 425.50 is entered
   cout << "Your ending check balance is: " << balance + deposit - checks
   << endl;
```

4. Write the appropriate C++ statement to match the description in each of the following comments:

    // declare three double variables called num1, num2, num3

    // declare a variable called average

    // ask the user to input values separated by a space for 3 values

    // input the values into num1, num2, num3

    // assign average the value of num1, num2, and num3 divided by 3

    // output a statement with a message describing the values input and the average

5. When a value is assigned in memory, whatever value was previously in memory is replaced by the new assigned value. This is called destructive replacement. If you want two memory locations to exchange values, you need to save a value in a third location to prevent losing the original value. The following code shows how to swap two values in memory. Explain the purpose of each of the following lines:

```cpp
int num1 = 10, num2 = 5, temp;
cout << "num1 is " << num1 <<", num2 is "<< num2 << endl;
temp = num1;
num1 = num2;
num2 = temp;
cout << "Now the numbers swap and num1 is " << num1 <<", num2 is "
     << num2 << endl;
```

6. Write the appropriate C++ statements to match the descriptions in the following comments:

   // declare two integer variables feet and inches

   // ask the user how many feet and inches tall they are (no fraction)

   // input the feet and inches

   // assign inches the value of inches plus feet times 12

   // output with an appropriate message the number of inches the person is tall

7. Write the output of the following code:

```cpp
int x = 2, y = 3, z = 5;
cout << "This is my report in columns\n"
     << '\t' << x << '\t' << x * x << endl
     << '\t' << y << '\t' << y * y << endl
     << '\t' << z << '\t' << z * z << endl;
```

8. Write a C++ statement to match the descriptions in the following comments:

   // output a heading that has your name used as a possessive noun (use a single quote)

   // followed by the words favorite movie

   // output a newline that shows your favorite movie title in double quotes

LAB 2.6 USING PREPROCESSOR DIRECTIVES, THE STRING DATA TYPE, AND WRITING A C++ PROGRAM USING GOOD PROGRAMMING STYLE AND FORM

C++ provides a collection of libraries, called header files, with functions and symbols needed to run programs. To indicate which header file to use, you insert the pound symbol (#), the preprocessor directive *include,* and the name of the header file between left and right angle brackets <>. There is no semicolon with preprocessor directives. Preprocessor directives are placed as the first lines of a program.

Standard C++ and ANSI/ISO Standard C++ differ in the declaration of header files. This book follows the rules for ANSI/ISO Standard C++. In ANSI/ISO Standard C++, header files do not have file extensions. Additionally, the cin and cout identifiers are declared within a namespace. One way to use the identifiers `cin` and `cout` declared in the namespace std is to refer to them as std::cin and std::cout throughout the program. Another option is to include the statement using namespace std; after the preprocessor directive.

Programs that have structure are easier to understand and modify. C++ programs consist of preprocessor directives and program statements creating the C++ source code. Source code must be saved in a file with the extension .cpp. When compiled successfully, the compiler generates the object code saved in a file with the extension .obj. When the object code is linked with system resources, executable code is produced and saved in a file with the extension .exe. (These extensions are system dependent. The SDK that you use might use different naming conventions.)

C++ programs must contain the function main and follow syntax, or grammar, rules. All function statements consist of a heading and a body. The statements are in the body and are enclosed in curly braces. The heading indicates if the function returns a value and, if it does, what data type the value is. Additionally, the function contains declaration statements and executable statements. Declaration statements are used to declare elements such as variables. Executable statements perform calculations, manipulate data, create output, accept input, and so on. C++ programs follow not only C++ syntax but also semantics, which is the set of rules that apply to the statements and operations. For ease of use, programs should be well documented both with comments and meaningful identifier names and have an easy to read format. Use comments to document a program and explain its purpose, identify who wrote the program, and explain the purpose of particular statements. A single-line comment begins with // anywhere in the line. Everything encountered on that line after // is ignored by the compiler. Multiple-line comments are enclosed between /* and */.

In skeleton form, a C++ program looks like:

preprocessor directives to include header files

using statement

declare named constants

int main()

{

        statement1

        .

        .

        .

        statement*n*

        return 0;

}

Some characters have defined uses in a C++ program. Spaces are used as separators. Spaces must never appear within a reserved word or identifier. The semicolon is a statement terminator. Brackets are delimiters and have other uses in addition to enclosing the body of a function, which will be discussed as necessary. Commas are used to separate items in a list.

Using meaningful identifier names is another way to document the program. Although not required for a program to run, use lowercase letters for variable names, uppercase letters for constant names, begin a class name with an uppercase letter, and join multiple words for a name using the underscore character (_). For example, a typical variable name is hat_size or hatSize, while a typical constant name is CIRCLE_RADIUS. The examples in this book follow these standards.

Good documentation uses clearly written prompts that are executable statements that tell users what to do when they interact with a program. A prompt should not only tell the user what to enter but also state the limits of the input.

In addition to simple assignment statements, you can use a compound assignment statement for more concise notation. The compound operators are +=, -=, *=, /=, and %=.

Objectives

In this lab, you learn to write complete programs with ANSI/ISO Standard C++ header files.

After completing this lab, you will be able to:

- Read a complete program and determine the output.

- Write a complete program including preprocessor directives for iostream and string header files.

- Use a readable format in a C++ program.

- Use meaningful identifiers.

- Use comments for documentation.

Estimated completion time: **60–80 minutes**

Using Preprocessor Directives, the string Data Type, and Writing a C++ Program using Good Programming Style and Form

1a.   Read the following C++ program. The line numbers are for descriptive purposes only and are not part of the actual program. Write the appropriate comment for lines 1, 3, 5, 6, 7, 20, 23, 26, 29, 32, 34, 37, 39, and 42. Next to each **cout** statement, show what is to be displayed on the screen. In the memory chart, show what value is contained in memory as the variable values change.

```
1. // Enter your name as a comment for program identification




2. // Program assignment StuInfo1.cpp
```

3. // Enter your class section and time

4.

5. // Describe the purpose of this program

6. // Describe what input is expected

7. // Describe what output is expected

8.

9. // header files

10. #include <iostream>

11. #include <string>

12. using namespace std;

13.

14. int main()

15. {

16. // Declare variables:

17. string firstName, lastName, classification, major;

18. double gpa;

19.

20. // Describe the use of the prompt line

21. cout << "Please enter your first name and last name separated by a space.\n"

22.   << "Limit your input to 2 names. ";

23. //Describe the use of the input statement

24. cin >> firstName >> lastName;
25.
26. // Describe the use of the prompt line

27. cout << "Please enter your classification:\n"
28.   << "freshman, sophomore, junior, senior, special, or graduate: ";
29. //Describe the use of the input statement

30. cin >> classification;
31.
32. // Describe the use of the prompt line

33. cout << "Please enter your major (one word only): ";
34. //Describe the use of the input line

35. cin >> major;
36.
37. // Describe the use of the prompt line

38. cout << "Please enter your grade point average: ";

39. //Describe the use of the input statement

40. cin >> gpa;

41.

42. // Describe the use of the output line

43. cout << "\nYou have entered the following information:\n"

44.   << "\nClassification:\t" << classification

45.   << "\nMajor:\t\t" << major

46.   << "\ngpa:\t\t" << gpa << endl;

47.

48. return 0;

49. }

1b.   Step through the code by hand. Then use the following memory table to show what occurs in memory when the C++ code is executed.

To fill out the memory table, use two lines for each variable. On one line, enter declaration information. Write the name of the declared variable, its data type, and the line number at declaration. On the next line in the memory table, enter test data for that variable. The variable firstName is entered as an example.

Variable Name	Data Type	Value in Memory	Line Number at Declaration	Line Number When Initialized
firstName	string	?	17	
		Mary		24

In the following space, show what is displayed on the screen after executing the output message.

1c.   Use your SDK to enter the program with your comment changes. For readability, preserve the blank lines that separate parts of the program. Do not enter the line numbers; they are for description purposes only. Save the program as **StuInfo1.cpp** in the Chap02 folder on your Student Disk. Compile, link, and execute the program.

To compile your program, check with your instructor regarding the specific instructions for the SDK that you are using. Correct any errors until your program successfully compiles.

To link your program, check with your instructor regarding the specific instructions for the SDK that you are using. Correct any errors, recompile and relink until your program successfully links.

To execute your program, check with your instructor regarding the specific instructions for the SDK that you are using. Check your output for accuracy. If necessary, correct any errors, recompile, relink, and reexecute until your output is accurate.

Make necessary changes until your program is successful. Select and copy everything that appears on your screen. Paste the copied text into a comment block at the end of your program. Then compare the output of the actual program to the output you predicted.

2a.   Using Exercise 1 as an example, create the design for a program that prompts the user to select a lunch from several sandwich choices.

The user should be prompted with the following information:

- Identification of the program and an explanation of how to use it

- Sandwich choices: Ham, Beef, Reuben, PBJ, Cheese, or Vegetarian

- Bread choices: Rye, Wheat, White, Sourdough, or Pumpernickel

- Condiment choices: Mayo, Mustard, Ketchup, or none

- Drink choices: Coke, Diet, Tea, Coffee, or Water

- The price of a half sandwich or a whole sandwich: 3.99 or 5.99

Then the user enters his or her choice.

After all data has been entered, output the complete selection. Include comments to identify the program author, describe the program, and describe program statements. Additionally, remember to include all preprocessor directives that you need.

Write your design in the following space. Your design should be a list of C++ comments without any code.

2b.   Write a C++ program based on the design you created in Exercise 2a, and name it **Deli.cpp**. Step through the code by hand.

Use the following memory table to show what occurs in memory when the C++ code is executed. (Include line numbers as documentation only. Do not use line numbers when entering your final program.) To fill out the memory table, use one or two lines for each variable as needed. On one line, enter declaration information. Write the name of the declared variable, its data type, and the line number at declaration. On the next line in the memory table, enter test data for that variable. The variable sandwich is entered as an example; your design might use different line numbers.

Variable Name	Data Type	Value in Memory	Line Number at Declaration	Line Number When Initialized
sandwich	string	?	17	
		Ham		24

In the following space, show what is displayed on the screen after executing the output message.

2c.   Enter, compile, link, and execute **Deli.cpp**. Then copy the output and save it in a block comment at the end of your program. Save **Deli.cpp** in the Chap02 folder on your Student Disk.

The following is a copy of the screen results that might appear after running your program, depending on the data entered. The input entered by the user is in bold.

```
Welcome to the Sandwich Corral
You will be given choices for building your sandwich.
Please enter your selection after each prompt and then press
the Enter key.
Please enter your sandwich choice:
Ham, Beef, Reuben, PBJ, Cheese, or Vegetarian: Ham
Please enter your bread choice:
Rye, Wheat, White, Sourdough, or Pumpernickel: Rye
Please enter your choice of condiment (one only):
Mayo, Mustard, Ketchup, or none: Mustard
Please enter your drink choice:
Coke, Diet, Tea, Coffee, or Water: Water
Please enter 3.99 for a half sandwich or 5.99 for a whole
sandwich: 3.99

You have entered the following information:
Sandwich:       Ham
Bread:          Rye
Condiment:      Mustard
Drink:          Water

Tab:            3.99
```

3a.   *Critical Thinking Exercise*: Using Exercise 1 as an example, create the design for a program that prompts the user to enter two names. Display the two names the user enters—this is called echo printing. Then swap the values of the names. For example, the value name1 will become the value of name2, and the value of name2 will become the value of name1. (Consider the value of each memory location and how many memory locations are needed to accomplish this task.) Display the two names after they have been swapped.

Include comments to identify the program author, to describe the program, and to describe program statements. Additionally, remember to include all preprocessor directives that you need.

Write your design in the following space. Your design should be a list of C++ comments without any code.

3b.   Write a C++ program based on the design you created in Exercise 3a, and name it **Swap.cpp**. Step through the code by hand.

Use the following memory table to show what occurs in memory when the C++ code is executed. (Include line numbers as documentation only. Do not use line numbers when entering your final program.) To fill out the memory table, use two or three lines for each variable. On one line, enter declaration information. Write the name of the declared variable, its data type, and the line number at declaration. On the next line in the memory table, enter test data for that variable. On the third line for each variable, show where the value has changed if it changes. The variable name1 is entered as an example; your design might use different line numbers.

Variable Name	Data Type	Value in Memory	Line Number at Declaration	Line Number When Initialized or Changed
name1	string	?	17	
		Boubacar		21
		Celine		30

In the following space, show what is displayed on the screen after executing the output message.

3c.   Enter, compile, link, and execute **Swap.cpp**. Then copy the output and save it in a block comment at the end of your program. Save **Swap.cpp** in the Chap02 folder on your Student Disk.

The following is a copy of the screen results that might appear after running your program, depending on the data entered. The input entered by the user is in bold.

```
Enter two names separated by a space: Boubacar Celine

The first name is: Boubacar
The second name is: Celine

The first name is: Celine
The second name is: Boubacar
```

4a.   *Critical Thinking Exercise*: Imagine that you are a real estate agent and make your living from sales commissions. House commissions paid to sell a house through multiple listings are 6%. The listing agency receives 3% and the selling agency receives 3%. Of that 3%, each agency receives 1.5% and the selling agent or listing agent receives 1.5%. As a real estate agent, you want to know how much you will receive for a house that you either list or sell. For your records, identify the house by the owner's last name.

Design a program that asks the user for the name and selling price of the home. Calculate the amount paid by the home owner to sell the home and the amount of the commission you will receive. Use constants for the entire cost to sell the home and for the listing agent's commission rate.

Write your design in the following space. Your design should be a list of C++ comments without any code.

4b. Write a C++ program based on the design you created in Exercise 4a, and name it **Realtor.cpp**. Step through the code by hand.

Use the following memory table to show what occurs in memory when the C++ code is executed. (Include line numbers as documentation only. Do not use line numbers when entering your final program.) To fill out the memory table, use two lines for each variable. On one line, enter declaration information. Write the name of the declared variable, its data type, and the line number at declaration. On the next line in the memory table, enter test data for that variable. The variable name is entered as an example, but you may use different line numbers in your design.

Variable Name	Data Type	Value in Memory	Line Number at Declaration	Line Number When Initialized or Changed
name	string	?	24	
				31

In the following space, show what is displayed on the screen after executing the output message.

4c.   Enter, compile, link, and execute **Realtor.cpp**. Then copy the output and save it in a block comment at the end of your program. Save **Realtor.cpp** in the Chap02 folder of your Student Disk.

The following is a copy of the screen results that might appear after running your program, depending on the data entered. The input entered by the user is in bold.

```
Please enter the owner's last name: Garcia
Please enter the sales price of the home: 100000

The Garcia's home sold for $100000
The cost to sell the home is $6000
The selling or listing agent commission is $1500
```

3 Input/Output

In this chapter, you will:

○ Learn what a stream is and examine input and output streams

○ Explore how to read data from the standard input device

○ Learn how to use predefined functions in a program

○ Explore how to use the input stream functions get, ignore, putback, and peek

○ Become familiar with input failure

○ Learn how to write data to the standard output device

○ Discover how to use manipulators in a program to format output

○ Learn how to perform input and output operations with the string data type

○ Become familiar with file input and output

CHAPTER 3: ASSIGNMENT COVER SHEET

Name _____   Date _____

Section _____

Lab Assignments	Assigned	Grade
Lab 3.1 Examining Predefined Input Functions		
Lab 3.2 Examining and Formatting Output (Critical Thinking Exercises)		
Lab 3.3 Using the `getline()` Function with the string Type		
Lab 3.4 Using Files for Input and Output (Critical Thinking Exercises)		
Total Grade		

See your instructor or the introduction to this book for instructions on submitting your assignments.

Lab 3.1 Examining Predefined Input Functions

In C++, I/O is accomplished through a stream, which is a sequence of characters from the source to the destination. To receive data from the keyboard and send output to the screen, every C++ program must use the header file iostream, which includes a set of functions to perform specific I/O tasks.

You use the variable `cin` with the extraction operator >> to input data from the keyboard. Additionally, C++ allows the `cin` statement to read more than one data item by using the extraction operator several times. The extraction operator >> is binary and thus takes two operands. The left operand must be an input stream variable such as `cin`. The right operand is a variable. The extraction operator >> skips all whitespace characters. When reading a `char` variable, after the program ignores whitespace, it reads only the next character. When reading an `int` or a `float`, a program reads digits (including possible leading + or – signs) until it finds whitespace or a character. The `int` type also stops at a decimal point. If no decimal is entered for a `float` type, the value is converted to a `float` type when the receiving variable is of the `float` type.

The main function executes automatically when you run a program. Other functions execute only when they are activated or called. C++ comes with predefined functions and variables that are already included in header files. The iostream header file contains a variable declaration for `cin`. A useful predefined function found in the cmath header file is the `pow` function, which is used to calculate a base number raised to an exponent. To use a predefined function in a program, you need to know the name of the header file containing the specifications of the function and include that header file in the program. In addition, you need to know the name of the function, the number of parameters the function takes, and the type of each parameter. You must also be aware of what the function is going to do.

The variable `cin` has access to operators and functions that can extract data from the standard input device. You can use dot notation to associate the input stream variable name with the function name. The `get` function inputs the very next character, including whitespace characters, from the input stream and stores it in the memory location indicated by its argument. The `ignore` function allows the program to discard a portion of the input. The maximum number of characters to be ignored can be stipulated or input is ignored until a specified character is encountered, whichever comes first. Additionally, the `putback` function puts the last character extracted from the input stream by the `get` function back into the input stream. The `peek` function returns the next character from the input stream, but does not remove the character from that stream.

The variables `cin` and `cout` are data types of the istream and ostream classes found in the iostream header file. These variables also have special names, called objects.

After the program terminates, any values left in the input stream are discarded. Other than a `float` type accepting integer input, no other mismatch of data is allowed. When a C++ program attempts to read invalid data, input failure occurs, causing the input stream to enter the fail state. Once an input stream enters a fail state, all further I/O statements using that stream are ignored. The stream function `clear` can restore the input stream to a working state.

Objectives

In this lab, you become acquainted with using I/O streams and the predefined functions `get`, `ignore`, `putback`, and `peek`.

After completing this lab, you will be able to:

- Use the I/O predefined functions `get`, `ignore`, `putback`, and `peek`.

Estimated completion time: **60–75 minutes**

Examining Predefined Input Functions

In the following exercises, you indicate whether statements are true or false. Then you design and write programs that use predefined input functions.

Question	**Answer** (Circle the correct answer)	
1. When using `cin` and the extraction operator for multiple input items, the items are separated by commas.	T	F
2. When using `cin` and the extraction operator to input numeric data, the + operator is optional.	T	F

3. The statements:
 	
`cin >> x;`
`cin >> y;`
 	
require that items are input on different lines whereas the statement
 	
`cin >> x >> y`
 	
requires items are input on the same line.
	T	F

4. If the user is prompted to enter an integer value, press the Enter key, then enter another integer value, the `cin` statement to read those values is as follows: `cin >> x >> endl >> y;`	T	F
5. When using `cin` and the extraction operator, the newline character is treated the same as other whitespace characters.	T	F
6. When using the `get` function, whitespace characters are treated the same as other characters.	T	F
7. The `peek` function does not remove characters from the input stream.	T	F
8. To enter a newline character as part of a stream, you press the Enter key.	T	F
9. When input failure occurs, the program terminates.	T	F
10. The stream function `putback` lets you put the last character extracted from the input stream by the `get` function back into the input stream.	T	F

11a.   Create the design for a program that prompts the user to enter a first name, middle name or initial, and last name, with each name separated by a space. Display only the user's initials on the screen. (Use a combination of the get and ignore functions.)

Write your design in the following space. Your design should be a list of C++ comments without any code.

11b.   Write a C++ program based on the design you created in Lab 3.1, Exercise 11a and name it **Initial1.cpp**. Step through the code by hand.

Use the following memory table to show what occurs in memory when the C++ code is executed. (Include line numbers as documentation only. Do not use line numbers when entering your final program.) To fill out the memory table, use one or two lines for each variable. On one line, enter declaration information. Write the name of the declared variable, its data type, and the line number at declaration.

Variable Name	Data Type	Value in Memory	Line Number at Declaration	Line Number when Initialized

In the following space, show what is displayed on the screen after executing the output message.

11c. Enter, compile, link, and execute **Initial1.cpp**. Then copy the output and save it in a block comment at the end of your program. Save **Initial1.cpp** in the Chap03 folder of your Student Disk.

The following is a copy of the screen results that might appear after running your program, depending on the data entered. The input entered by the user is shown in bold.

```
Enter your first name, middle name or initial, and last name separated
by spaces:
Jane Ann Doe
Your initials are: JAD
```

11d. What would occur if the user begins the input with one or more spaces?

11e. What would occur if the names were separated by more than one space?

12a. Create the design for a program that prompts the user to enter a first name, middle name or initial, and last name, with each name separated by a space. Display the user's first name, middle name or initial, and last name on the screen. On another line, display only the user's initials. (Use a combination of the `get` and `putback` functions.)

Write your design in the following space. Your design should be a list of C++ comments without any code.

12b.   Write a C++ program based on the design you created in Exercise 12a and name it **Initial2.cpp**. Step through the code by hand.

Use the following memory table to show what occurs in memory when the C++ code is executed. (Include line numbers as documentation only. Do not use line numbers when entering your final program.) To fill out the memory table, use one or two lines for each variable. On one line, enter declaration information. Write the name of the declared variable, its data type, and the line number at declaration.

Variable Name	Data Type	Value in Memory	Line Number at Declaration	Line Number when Initialized

In the following space, show what is displayed on the screen after executing the output message.

12c.   Enter, compile, link, and execute **Initial2.cpp**. Then copy the output and save it in a block comment at the end of your program. Save **Initial2.cpp** in the Chap03 folder of your Student Disk.

The following is a copy of the screen results that might appear after running your program, depending on the data entered. The input entered by the user is shown in bold.

```
Enter your first name, middle name or initial, and last name separated
by spaces:
Jane Ann Doe
Your initials are: JAD
Your name is: Jane Ann Doe
```

12d.   What would occur if the user begins the input with one or more spaces?

12e.   What would occur if the names were separated by more than one space?

13a.   Create the design for a program that prompts the user to enter a first name, middle name or initial, and last name, with each name separated by a space. Display the user's first name, middle name or initial, and last name on the screen. On another line, display only the user's initials. (Use a combination of the `get` and `peek` functions.)

Write your design in the following space. Your design should be a list of C++ comments without any code.

13b.   Write a C++ program based on the design you created in Exercise 13a and name it **Initial3.cpp**. Step through the code by hand.

Use the following memory table to show what occurs in memory when the C++ code is executed. (Include line numbers as documentation only. Do not use line numbers when entering your final program.) To fill out the memory table, use one or two lines for each variable. On one line, enter declaration information. Write the name of the declared variable, its data type, and the line number at declaration.

Variable Name	Data Type	Value in Memory	Line Number at Declaration	Line Number when Initialized

In the following space, show what is displayed on the screen after executing the output message.

13c. Enter, compile, link, and execute **Initial3.cpp**. Then copy the output and save it in a block comment at the end of your program. Save **Initial3.cpp** in the Chap03 folder of your Student Disk.

The following is a copy of the screen results that might appear after running your program, depending on the data entered. The input entered by the user is shown in bold.

```
Enter your first name, middle name or initial, and last name separated
by spaces:
Jane Ann Doe
Your initials are: JAD
Your name is: Jane Ann Doe
```

13d. What would occur if the user begins the input with one or more spaces?

13e. What would occur if the names were separated by more than one space?

Lab 3.2 Examining and Formatting Output

C++ has various output functions and manipulators you can use to format output. The floating-point number default output is in scientific notation, which is difficult to read. The manipulator `setprecision` formats the number of decimal places of floating-point numbers according to the number in the argument and requires the header file iomanip. The manipulator `fixed` formats floating-point to decimal output rather than scientific notation. Once set, the fixed-decimal format will apply throughout the program unless disabled. You can disable the manipulator `fixed` using the stream member function `unsetf`. The manipulator `showpoint` shows a decimal point and trailing zeros when the decimal amount is zero. The manipulator `setw` outputs the value of the next expression in an output statement in the number of columns specified by the argument and requires the iomanip header file. If the number of columns specified by the manipulator `setw` exceeds the number of columns required, the field width expands to accommodate the size. *Note:* The manipulator `setw` controls the output of only the next expression. The manipulator `flush` outputs all data in the buffer without including a newline character.

To get more formatting control, use the `fill` function or the manipulator `setfill` to fill the unused columns with the character used as the argument in the function call. The `setfill` manipulator works like the `fill` function except that it follows the stream manipulator in the `cout` statement and requires the iomanip header file. The manipulators `left` and `right` will left-justify or right-justify the output in the column specified by `setw`.

Objectives

In this lab, you become acquainted with the output formatting functions and manipulators and the `flush` function.

After completing this lab, you will be able to:

- Write programs using the functions and manipulators `setprecision`, `fixed`, `showpoint`, `setw`, `fill`, `setfill`, `left`, and `right` for formatting output.

- Use the `flush` function to clear the buffer.

Estimated completion time: **50–60 minutes**

Examining and Formatting Output

In the following exercises, you select the correct answer to a question. Then you design and write programs that produce formatted output.

Question	Answer (Circle the correct answer)

1. Given the following statements:
 	
`int number;`
 	
`double value;`
 	
`cout << "Enter two numeric values: ";`
 	
`cin >> number >> value;`
 	
`cout << number << ' ' << value << endl;`
 	
if the user enters 8.5 6, which of the following is output?
	a. 8 .5
	
	b. 8.5 6
	
	c. there is no output; input failure occurs

2. Given the following statements:

   ```
   int number = 6;

   double value = 4.2

   cout << setprecision(3) << number <<
           << ' ' << value << endl;
   ```

   which of the following is output?

   a. 6 4.200

   b. 6.000 4.200

   c. 6 4.2

3. Given the following statements:

   ```
   int number = 6;

   double value = 4.2

   cout << showpoint << number <<
           << ' ' << value << endl;
   ```

   which of the following is output?

   a. 6 4.2

   b. 6.0 4.2

   c. 6 4.20

4. Given the following statements:

   ```
   int number = 6;

   double value = 4.2

   cout << fixed << number <<
           << ' ' << value << endl;
   ```

   which of the following is output?

   a. 6 4.2

   b. 6.00 4.20

   c. 6 4.20

5. An **endl** may be placed after the << insertion operator anywhere in the **cout** statement.

   T   F

6. Given the following statements:

   ```
   string begin = "abc", end = "xyz";
   cout << "1234567890\n"
           << setw(5) << begin << endl;
   ```

   which of the following is output?

   a. 1234567890
      abc xyz

   b. 1234567890
      abc   xyz

   c. 1234567890
      abcxyz

   d. 1234567890
      abc xyz

7. Given the following statements:

   ```
   string begin = "abc", end = "xyz";
   cout.fill('*');
   cout << "1234567890\n"
           << setw(5) << begin << endl;
   ```

   which of the following is output?

   a. 1234567890
      abc**xyz

   b. 1234567890
      abc****xyz

   c. 1234567890
      **abcxyz

   d. 1234567890
      abcxyz

8. The manipulator `setw` is used to output the value of   **T   F**
   an expression in specific columns.

9. Both the `flush` and `setw` manipulators position   **T   F**
   the cursor at the beginning of the next line on the
   output device.

10. Once the `setw` manipulator is used, the column   **T   F**
    width is set until `setw` is reset.

11a. *Critical Thinking Exercise*: (If you completed the program **Realtor.cpp**, which you stored in the
     Chap02 folder on your Student Disk, redesign that program in this exercise.) Create a new
     design for a program to produce a real estate report. As a real estate agent, you keep a record of
     homes you list, and you want to create a report that is easy to read. The report should also indi-
     cate the costs associated with selling the home, which includes the total commission, the listing
     agency commission, the selling agency commission, and the selling agent's commission.

The information needed to sell the home includes the following:

■ The last name of the owner of the house.

■ The selling price of the home.

The costs are based on the following information:

■ House commissions paid to sell a house through multiple listings are 6%.

■ The listing agency receives 3% and the selling agency receives 3%.

■ Of that 3%, each agency gets 1.5% and the selling agent or listing agent gets 1.5%.

Your data is the sales amount entered as a double number with no fractional decimal value. Your
calculations should consider the following:

■ Calculate the amount paid by the homeowner to sell the home and the amount of the commission you will receive as the selling agent (not agency).

■ Use a constant for the commission rate.

Display your output using the following guidelines:

■ Display your output in columns using the `setw` function.

■ Your first row of output should be headings. Use `setw(15)` for each item in the first row.
  When writing your string literals, be sure to include a blank at the end of the string to make
  sure that one string does not display directly next to another string.

■ The second row should list your variables. For the second row use a fixed format, two decimal places, and show the decimal point even when the fractional decimal value is 0.

Write your design in the following space. Your design should be a list of C++ comments without any code.

11b. Write a C++ program based on the design you created in Exercise 11a and name it **Realtor1.cpp**. Step through the code by hand.

Use the following memory table to show what occurs in memory when the C++ code is executed. (Include line numbers as documentation only. Do not use line numbers when entering your final program.) To fill out the memory table, use one or two lines for each variable. On one line, enter declaration information. Write the name of the declared variable, its data type, and the line number at declaration.

Variable Name	Data Type	Value in Memory	Line Number at Declaration	Line Number when Initialized

In the following space, show what is displayed on the screen after executing the output message.

11c.   Enter, compile, link, and execute **Realtor1.cpp**. Then copy the output and save it in a block comment at the end of your program. Save **Realtor1.cpp** in the Chap03 folder of your Student Disk.

The following is a copy of the screen results that might appear after running your program, depending on the data entered. The input entered by the user is shown in bold.

```
Please enter owner's last name: Garcia
Please enter the sales price of the home: 100000
    Home Owner    Price of Home    Seller's Cost    Agent's Commission
       Garcia    100000.00           6000.00                1500.00
```

11d.   The report output shows columns of values that could easily be altered. Change the **Realtor1.cpp** program to use the `fill` function or the manipulator `setfill` to put the '*' character in the blank spaces before all numbers so that the numbers cannot be altered. Save the program as **Realtor2.cpp** in the Chap03 folder of your Student Disk. Enter, compile, link, and execute **Realtor2.cpp**. Then copy the output and save it in a block comment at the end of your program.

The following is a copy of the screen results that might appear after running your program, depending on the data entered. The input entered by the user is shown in bold.

```
Please enter owner's last name: Garcia
Please enter the sales price of the home: 100000
    Home Owner    Price of Home         Seller's Cost  Agent's Commission
       Garcia*******100000.00***************6000.00************1500.00
```

11e. Although it is easier to read values when they are right-justified, it is difficult to read columns of strings that are right-justified. Rewrite **Realtor2.cpp** to left-justify the first field and right-justify all remaining fields using the `left` and `right` manipulators. Additionally, to test the `flush` function, remove one of your endl manipulators and call the `flush` function. Save the revised program as **Realtor3.cpp** in the Chap03 folder of your Student Disk. Enter, compile, link, and execute **Realtor3.cpp**. Then copy the output and save it in a block comment at the end of your program.

The following is a copy of the screen results that might appear after running your program, depending on the data entered. The input entered by the user is in bold.

```
Please enter owner's last name: Garcia
Please enter the sales price of the home: 100000
   Home Owner    Price of Home          Seller's Cost  Agent's Commission
     Garcia      *******100000.00***************6000.00************1500.00
```

LAB 3.3 USING THE GETLINE() FUNCTION WITH THE STRING TYPE

To read a string containing blanks, use the function `getline()`. This function reads until it reaches the end of the current line. The newline character is not stored in the string variable. To use the `getline()` function, you must correct the string library header file.

Note that if you are using Microsoft Visual C++ version 5 or version 6 and are having trouble compiling programs that use the `getline()` function, your version of the compiler might have a bug in the `getline()` function. This problem is caused by the Standard C++ Library template `getline` function reading an extra character after encountering the delimiter. See your instructor or technical support person for information on solving this problem.

Objectives

In this lab, you learn to use the `getline()` function, which allows you to read in strings containing blanks.

After completing this lab, you will be able to:

- Use the `getline()` function to read entire strings regardless of the characters contained in the string.

Estimated completion time: **15–20 minutes**

Using the getline() Function with the string Type

Design and write complete C++ programs that use the `getline()` function according to the instructions and output examples given.

1a.   Create the design for a program that prompts the user to enter their full name, street address, and city, state, and zip code, and reads them into three string variables. Display the strings as you would to address an envelope.

Write your design in the following space. Your design should be a list of C++ comments without any code.

1b. Write a C++ program based on the design you created in Lab 3.3, Exercise 1a and name it **Label.cpp**. Step through the code by hand.

Use the following memory table to show what occurs in memory when the C++ code is executed. (Include line numbers as documentation only. Do not use line numbers when entering your final program.) To fill out the memory table, use one or two lines for each variable. On one line, enter declaration information. Write the name of the declared variable, its data type, and the line number at declaration.

Variable Name	Data Type	Value in Memory	Line Number at Declaration	Line Number when Initialized

In the following space, show what is displayed on the screen after executing the output message.

1c. Enter, compile, link, and execute **Label.cpp**. Then copy the output and save it in a block comment at the end of your program. Save **Label.cpp** in the Chap03 folder of your Student Disk.

The following is a copy of the screen results that might appear after running your program, depending on the data entered. The input entered by the user is shown in bold.

```
Enter your name: Victor Martinez
Enter your street address: 506 Elm St.
Enter your city, state, and zip: Hollywood, CA 90210
Victor Martinez
506 Elm St.
Hollywood, CA 90210
```

2a. Create the design for a program that prompts the user to enter his or her name and e-mail address. Display the name and e-mail address in the format appropriate for an e-mail message. The name should be in double quotes followed by the e-mail address enclosed in angle brackets.

Write your design in the following space. Your design should be a list of C++ comments without any code.

2b. Write a C++ program based on the design you created in Exercise 2a and name it **Email.cpp**. Step through the code by hand.

Use the following memory table to show what occurs in memory when the C++ code is executed. (Include line numbers as documentation only. Do not use line numbers when entering your final program.) To fill out the memory table, use one or two lines for each variable. On one line, enter declaration information. Write the name of the declared variable, its data type, and the line number at declaration.

Variable Name	Data Type	Value in Memory	Line Number at Declaration	Line Number when Initialized

In the following space, show what is displayed on the screen after executing the output message.

2c.   Enter, compile, link, and execute **Email.cpp**. Then copy the output and save it in a block comment at the end of your program. Save **Email.cpp** in the Chap03 folder of your Student Disk.

The following is a copy of the screen results that might appear after running your program, depending on the data entered. The input entered by the user is shown in bold.

```
Enter your name: Abraham Pearl
Enter your email address: apearl@aol.com

Your e-mail should be addressed to: "Abraham Pearl" <apearl@aol.com>
```

LAB 3.4 USING FILES FOR INPUT AND OUTPUT

Inputting data from the keyboard and displaying the output on the screen is convenient when you are working with small amounts of data. For large amounts of data, however, that method is inefficient. Additionally, you might need to enter input where it can be prechecked for accuracy, and save output for later uses. In these cases, you can have the C++ program read data from and write it to a data file.

A file is an area in secondary storage used to hold information. The header file fstream is used for file I/O. The fstream header file defines the data type `ifstream` for input file stream and the data type `ofstream` for output file stream. The functions and manipulators used with `cin` in iostream are also defined for `ifstream` such as >>, `get`, `ignore`, `putback`, and `peek`, as well as `fill` and `setfill` for `cout` used in `ofstream`.

File stream variables that use functions and manipulators must be defined by the program. They are not predefined like `cin` and `cout`. The `fstream` variables must be associated with the I/O sources, including opening and closing the files.

File I/O is a five-step process:

1. Include the header file fstream in the program.

2. Declare file stream variables.

3. Associate the file stream variables with the input/output sources.

4. Use the file stream variables with >>, <<, or other input/output functions.

5. Close the files.

Objectives

In this lab, you use files for input and output. You also use files with iostream.

After completing this lab, you will be able to:

- Associate file variables with I/O sources.

- Open and close input and output files.

- Read data from input files.

- Write data to output files.

- Use file stream variables with `cin` and `cout`.

- Work with multiple data files.

Estimated completion time: **50–60 minutes**

Using Files for Input and Output

In the following exercises, you design and write programs that use files for input and output.

1a.   *Critical Thinking Exercise*: Suppose you are ordering merchandise for a small gift shop. The wholesaler requires that you send your order as a file over a modem. Create the design for a program that prompts the user to enter merchandise information consisting of the number of items, the wholesale cost, and the description of the item. Separate the number of items, cost, and description with a space. The description may contain spaces. Write the merchandise information to a file named **order.txt**, using an endl after entering each description. Your file will contain data only. Do not include column headings. After you have entered your data, display a message that states that the program is complete.

Write your design in the following space. Your design should be a list of C++ comments without any code.

1b.   Write a C++ program based on the design you created in Exercise 1a and name it **Gifts1.cpp**. Step through the code by hand.

Use the following memory table to show what occurs in memory when the C++ code is executed. (Include line numbers as documentation only. Do not use line numbers when entering your final program.) To fill out the memory table, use one or two lines for each variable. On one line, enter declaration information. Write the name of the declared variable, its data type, and the line number at declaration.

Variable Name	Data Type	Value in Memory	Line Number at Declaration	Line Number when Initialized

Use the following information to test your program:

Number of Items	Wholesale Cost	Description
4	5.35	Wine Stoppers
2	14.85	Silver Cheese Trays

In the following space, show what is displayed on the screen after executing the output message. Additionally, write what will be written to the **order.txt** file.

1c. Enter, compile, link, and execute **Gifts1.cpp**. Then copy the output and save it in a block comment at the end of your program. Save **Gifts1.cpp** in the Chap03 folder of your Student Disk.

Print the data files you read and write and submit them with your work. You can open your files within your SDK. (*Hint:* In the Open dialog box, remember to change the "Look in" box to the proper drive and the "Files of type" box to All files.)

2a. Create the design for a program using the order file that you created in Exercise 1. Now the order file created as output in Exercise 1 will be the input file for Exercise 2. Design a program to read **order.txt** and output a new file named **inventory.txt**, which will contain the number of items ordered, the retail cost (which is 2.4 times the wholesale cost), and the description of the item. After reading in all data, display a message that tells the user that the program is complete.

Write your design in the following space. Your design should be a list of C++ comments without any code.

2b.   Write a C++ program based on the design you created in Exercise 2a and name it **Gifts2.cpp**. Step through the code by hand.

Use the following memory table to show what occurs in memory when the C++ code is executed. (Include line numbers as documentation only. Do not use line numbers when entering your final program.) To fill out the memory table, use one or two lines for each variable. On one line, enter declaration information. Write the name of the declared variable, its data type, and the line number at declaration.

Variable Name	Data Type	Value in Memory	Line Number at Declaration	Line Number when Initialized

In the following space, show what is displayed on the screen after executing the output message.

2c.   Enter, compile, link, and execute **Gifts2.cpp**. Then copy the output and save it in a block comment at the end of your program. Save **Gifts2.cpp** in the Chap03 folder of your Student Disk.

4 Control Structures I (Selection)

In this chapter, you will:

O Learn about control structures

O Examine relational and logical operators

O Explore how to form and evaluate logical (Boolean) expressions

O Discover how to use the selection control structures `if`, `if...else`, and `switch` in a program

O Learn to use the `assert` function to terminate a program

CHAPTER 4: ASSIGNMENT COVER SHEET

Name _____   Date _____

Section _____

Lab Assignments	Assigned	Grade
Lab 4.1 Using Relational and Logical Operators to Evaluate Logical (Boolean) Expressions		
Lab 4.2 Using the Selection Control Structures `if` and `if...else`		
Lab 4.3 Using Nested `if` and `if...else` Statements		
Lab 4.4 Using the `if` Statement with Input Failure		
Lab 4.5 Using the Assignment Operator (=) for the Equality Operator (==)		
Lab 4.6 Using the Conditional Operator (?:)		
Lab 4.7 Using the `switch` Selection Control Structure (Critical Thinking Exercises)		
Lab 4.8 Using the `assert` Function to Terminate a Program		
Total Grade		

See your instructor or the introduction to this book for instructions on submitting your assignments.

LAB 4.1 USING RELATIONAL AND LOGICAL OPERATORS TO EVALUATE LOGICAL (BOOLEAN) EXPRESSIONS

A conditional statement is a control structure that allows a program to execute a selection of alternative statements depending on whether the condition is true or false. The program evaluates a condition by comparing two operands. In C++, this condition is called a logical (Boolean) expression. Additionally, `true` and `false` are logical (Boolean) values. A conditional statement uses relational operators to perform the relational comparison, which applies to all three simple data types and to strings of the string class. It also uses the ASCII collating sequence. When C++ evaluates a logical expression, it returns a non-zero integer value if the logical expression evaluates to `true`; it returns an integer value of 0 otherwise. In C++, any non-zero value is treated as `true`. Table 4-1 describes each operator.

Table 4-1 C++ Relational Operators

Operator	Description
==	Equal to
!=	Not equal to
<	Less than
<=	Less than or equal to
>	Greater than
>=	Greater than or equal to

Logical (Boolean) operators enable you to combine logical expressions. The three logical operators are and (`&&`), or (`||`), and not (`!`). The binary logical operators `&&` and `||` combine logical expressions. The unary logical operator `!` reverses the value of the logical expression. The `&&` operator evaluates to `false` unless both Boolean expressions are true. The `||` operator evaluates to `true` unless both Boolean expressions are false.

Like mathematical expressions, relational expressions have an order of precedence for evaluation. Parentheses can override the precedence of operators. The associativity of these operators is from left to right. After a program determines whether a compound expression is true or false, the rest of the expression is not evaluated. This is known as short-circuit evaluation. Table 4-2 lists the precedence of operators and the order of evaluation.

Table 4-2 Operator Precedence

Operators	Precedence
!, +, - (unary operators)	1
*, /, %	2
+, -	3
<, <=, >=, >	4
==, !=	5
&&	6
||	7
= (assignment operator)	Last

More recent versions of C++ contain a built-in data type, `bool`, that has the logical values `true` and `false`. The identifier `true` has the value 1 and the identifier `false` has the value 0.

Objectives

In this lab, you evaluate Boolean expressions using relational and Boolean operators. Additionally, you learn to evaluate these expressions by the order of precedence of their operators.

After completing this lab, you will be able to:

■ Evaluate logical expressions formed by the relationship of two operands.

■ Use relational operators to evaluate all three simple data types and strings.

■ Use logical (Boolean) operators to evaluate combined logical expressions.

■ Evaluate logical expressions by the correct order of precedence.

■ Recognize logical expressions that can be short–circuit evaluations.

Estimated completion time: **30–40 minutes**

Using Relational and Logical Operators to Evaluate Logical (Boolean) Expressions

Evaluate the logical (Boolean) expression in the Expression column, and circle all possible answers in the Result column. For `char` and `string` types, use the ASCII collating sequence.

Expression	Result (Circle all possible answers)
1. `int num1 = 3, num2 = 2;` `(num1 > num2)`	T F short-circuit
2. `double hours = 12.8;` `(hours > 40.2)`	T F short-circuit
3. `int funny = 7;` `(funny !=1)`	T F short-circuit
4. `char letter = 'A';` `('a' < letter)`	T F short-circuit
5. `short count = 1;` `count <=4;`	T F short-circuit
6. `double y = -2.3;` `y >=0.0;`	T F short-circuit

Expression	Result (Circle all possible answers)
1. `! (false  ||  false)  ||  true`	T F short-circuit
2. `false  &&  true  &&  false`	T F short-circuit
3. `! false  ||  (false  ||  ! true)`	T F short-circuit
4. `false  ||  (true  &&  (false  ||  false) )`	T F short-circuit
5. `1  ||  ! true &&  false`	T F short-circuit
6. `! (false  ||  false)  ||  false`	T F short-circuit
7. `true  &&  false  &&  false`	T F short-circuit
8. `! false  ||  (false  ||  ! true)`	T F short-circuit
9. `false  ||  (false  &&  (false  ||  true) )`	T F short-circuit
10. `0  ||  ! false &&  false`	T F short-circuit

Expression Use the following values:	Result (Circle all possible answers)

1. `string name1 = "Aaron";`
   `string name2 = "aaron";`
   `(name1 == name2)`
	T F short-circuit

2. `string name1 = "Aaron";`
   `string name2 = "Aardvark";`
   `(name1 <= name2)`
	T F short-circuit

3. `bool flag = true;`
   `int a = 2, b = 5, c = 10;`
   `(a * b <= c && ! flag)`
	T F short-circuit

4. `char letter = 'A';`
   `string word = "A";`
   `(letter == word)`
	T F short-circuit

LAB 4.2 USING THE SELECTION CONTROL STRUCTURES IF AND IF...ELSE

C++ uses logical expressions to implement the selection control structures. There are two selections, or branch control structures: if statements and the switch structure. A one-way selection uses the if statement, which uses the reserved word if followed by a logical (Boolean) expression. The two-way selection uses the if...else statement, which builds on the if statement by offering an alternative selection following the reserved word else.

Objectives

In this lab, you become acquainted with a one-way selection, the if statement. The statement or block of statements following the keyword if are executed when the expression evaluates to true. If you need to use more than one statement, a block is required. You also become acquainted with a two-way selection, the if...else statement.

After completing this lab, you will be able to:

■ Work with a one-way selection, which evaluates either to true or to false and is followed either by single statements or multiple statements.

■ Work with a two-way selection, which evaluates either to true or to false and is followed by either single or multiple statements.

Estimated completion time: **20–30 minutes**

Using the Selection Control Structure if

Write what the following statements display as output after the program executes. Use the following two assignment statements for Exercises 1 through 7.

```
int x = 6;
bool found = false;
```

1. if (x >10)
```
        cout << "x is greater than 10\n";
    cout << "Selection allows decision making.\n";
```

2. if (x == 6)
```
        cout << "A match is found.\n";
    cout << "Sequence continues after selection is complete\n";
```

```
3. if (x < 8)
       {
             cout << "x is within the range\n";
             cout << "This is a true statement\n";
       }
   cout << "And, after selection, the next statement is executed.\n";
```

```
4. if (x == 6 || found)
         cout << "Problem 4 is true\n";
   cout << "End of Problem 4\n";
```

```
5. if (x == 6 && found)
        cout << "Problem 5 is true\n";
   cout << "End of Problem 5\n";
```

```
6. if (x !=6 && !found)
        cout << "Problem 6 is true\n";
   cout << "End of Problem 6\n";
```

```
7. if (x > 0 && x < 10)
        cout << "x is in  range\n";
   cout << "The value of x is " + x;
```

Using the Selection Control Structure if...else

Use the following two assignment statement for Exercises 8 through 14 of this lab.

```
int x = 6;
bool found = false;
```

8.
```
int x = 6;
if (x > 10)
     cout << "x is greater than 10\n";
else
     cout << "x is less than or equal to 10\n";
cout << "Selection allows decision making.\n";
```

9.
```
if (x == 6)
     cout << "A match is found.\n";
else
     cout << "A match was not found.\n";
cout << "Sequence continues after selection is complete\n";
```

10.
```
if !(x < 8)
     {
         cout << "x is within the range\n";
         cout << "This is a true statement\n";
     }
else
     {
         cout << "x is out of range\n";
         cout << "This is a false statement\n";
     }
cout << "After selection, the next statement is executed.\n";
```

11.
```
if (x >= 5)
   {
   }
else
     cout << "Have a good day\n";
cout << "x is larger than 5\n";
```

```
12. if (x == 6 && found)
        cout << "Problem 12 is true\n";
    else
    {
        cout << "Problem 12 is false\n";
        cout << "Both conditions must be true\n";
    }
    cout << "End of Problem 12\n";
```

```
13. if (x !=6 && !found)
        cout << "Problem 13 is true\n";
    else
        cout << "Problem 13 is false\n";
    cout << "End of Problem 13\n";
```

```
14. if (x > 0 && x < 10)
        cout << "x is in range\n";
    else
        cout << "x is not in range\n";
```

LAB 4.3 USING NESTED IF AND IF...ELSE STATEMENTS

The statement(s) executed in a selection can be any valid C++ statement. This includes an `if` statement located within another `if` or `if...else` statement. These statements are called nested statements. When the selection requires more than one alternative, use the nested `if` statement.

An `else` statement is not required; however, when used, all `else` statements must be paired with an `if`. In a nested `if` statement, C++ associates an `else` with the most recent incomplete `if`—that is, the most recent `if` that has not been paired with an `else`. The `if` and `if...else` structures control only one statement at a time. To permit more complex statements, C++ provides a structure called a compound statement or a block of statements. Some problems require the implementation of more than two alternatives. When one control statement is located within another, it is said to be nested.

A sequence of `if...else` statements can accomplish the same task as a series of `if` statements. However, a sequence of `if...else` statements is more efficient because once a match has been found, the remainder of the tests are skipped. In a series of `if` statements, all statements are evaluated. An alternative to writing nested `if...else` statements is to write compound Boolean expressions.

One method of program development is an informal mixture of C++ and ordinary language, called pseudocode or pseudo. To find logical errors in your pseudo, you should always use a wide range of values in a walk-through to evaluate the code under as many different circumstances as possible. Once you have written your program, you should also test the program data values that test all program paths.

Objectives

In this lab, you evaluate Boolean expressions in nested if statements.

After completing this lab, you will be able to:

- Match the `else` statement with the appropriate `if` statement.

- Know when to nest and when not to nest `if` statements.

- Write code using nested `if`s.

- Write compound Boolean expressions using `if...else` statements.

- Test all paths of your program.

Estimated completion time: **60–75 minutes**

Using Nested if and if...else Statements

Write what the following statements display as output after the program executes. Then design and write a program that uses nested `if` and `if...else` statements.

1a.   Write what the following statements display as output after the program executes.

```cpp
int temperature = 78;
int month = 6;
string name = "Pat Boone";
if (temperature >= 70 && month >=6)
    cout << "Wear white shoes.\n";
else if (name == "Pat Boone")
    cout << "Wear white shoes.\n";
else
    cout << "Wear black shoes.\n";
```

1b.   What is the output of the program in Exercise 1a when temperature = 70, month = 5, and name = "Pat Boone"?

1c.   What is the output of the program in Exercise 1a when temperature = 60, month = 5, and name = "Pat Boone"?

1d.   What is the output of the program in Exercise 1a when temperature = 60, month = 5, and name = "Your name"?

2a.   Design a program that prompts the user to enter three names separated by spaces. Using compound and nested `if` statements, display the names in alphabetical order.

Write your design in the following space. Your design should be a list of C++ comments without any code.

2b.   Write a C++ program based on the design you created in Exercise 2a and name it **NameSort.cpp**. Step through the code by hand.

Use the following memory table to show what occurs in memory when the C++ code is exe-cuted. (Include line numbers as documentation only. Do not use line numbers when entering your final program.) To fill out the memory table, use two lines for each variable. On one line, enter declaration information. Write the name of the declared variable, its data type, and the line number at declaration.

Variable Name	Data Type	Value in Memory	Line Number at Declaration	Line Number when Initialized

In the following space, show what is displayed on the screen after executing the output message using following data: **George Joe Adam**

2c.   Enter, compile, link, and execute **NameSort.cpp**. Then copy the output and save it in a block comment at the end of your program. Save **NameSort.cpp** in the Chap04 folder of your Student Disk.

The following is a copy of the screen results that might appear after running your program, depending on the data entered. The input entered by the user is shown in bold.

```
Please enter 3 names: George Joe Adam
The alphabetical order of the names is:
Adam
George
Joe
```

2d.   Rerun **NameSort.cpp** with the names entered in this order: Joe Adam George

2e.   Rerun **NameSort.cpp** with the names entered in this order: Adam Joe George

2f.   Rerun **NameSort.cpp** with the names entered in this order: George Adam Joe

LAB 4.4 USING THE IF STATEMENT WITH INPUT FAILURE

Attempting to read invalid data causes the input stream to enter a fail state. Once an input stream enters a fail state, all subsequent input statements associated with that input stream are ignored, and the computer continues to execute the program, which produces erroneous results. Other than reading invalid data, two common causes of input failure are:

- Attempting to open an input file that does not exist.

- Attempting to read beyond the end of an input file.

You can use the `if` statement to check the status of an input stream variable. If the input stream enters the fail state, you also can include instructions that stop program execution.

When you use the input stream variable as an expression in an `if` statement, it evaluates to `true` if the last input succeeded and to `false` if the last input failed. For example, `if (cin)` or `if (infile)` evaluates to `true` if the last input from the input device succeeded.

If an input fails, a message can be displayed and a return statement included to terminate the program.

Objectives

In this lab, you evaluate the standard input device and an `ifstream` variable for input failure. If failure occurs, the programs terminate.

After completing this lab, you will be able to:

- Use the `if` statement to check for input failure.

- Evaluate the standard input variable for input failure.

- Evaluate the `ifstream` variable for input failure.

- Evaluate the `ofstream` variable for output failure.

Estimated completion time: **40–45 minutes**

Using the if Statement with Input Failure

Design and write a program that tests for input failure.

1a.   Design a program that prompts the user to enter his or her age and first initial. Include code that checks for input failure in case the user enters character data for numeric data. If input failure occurs, display a message and return the value 1 from your main function. If no input failure occurs, display a message that echoes the data entered.

Write your design in the following space. Your design should be a list of C++ comments without any code.

1b.   Write a C++ program based on the design you created in Exercise 1a and name it **Failure.cpp**. Step through the code by hand.

Use the following memory table to show what occurs in memory when the C++ code is executed. (Include line numbers as documentation only. Do not use line numbers when entering your final program.) To fill out the memory table, use two lines for each variable. On one line, enter declaration information. Write the name of the declared variable, its data type, and the line number at declaration.

Variable Name	Data Type	Value in Memory	Line Number at Declaration	Line Number when Initialized

In the following space, show what is displayed on the screen after executing the output message.

1c.   Enter, compile, link, and execute **Failure.cpp**. Then copy the output and save it in a block comment at the end of your program. Save **Failure.cpp** in the Chap04 folder of your Student Disk.

The following is a copy of the screen results that might appear after running your program, depending on the data entered. The input entered by the user is shown in bold.

```
Either
/*
Please enter your age and first initial: 19 J

Your age is 19 and your initial is J.
*/
or
/*
Please enter your age and first initial: J 19

You did not enter your age followed by your initial.
*/
```

2a.   Create the design for a program that prompts the user to create a name and address file from a name, street address, and city, state, and zip code entered. You should create the name and address file on drive A (or another drive with a removable disk). Check for input failure in case the user does not have access to the drive (for example, if the disk is not inserted in the drive). If input failure occurs, display a message indicating the problem, otherwise, display a message indicating that the program ended successfully.

Write your design in the following space. Your design should be a list of C++ comments without any code.

2b.   Write a C++ program based on the design you created in Exercise 2a and name it
NoDisk1.cpp. Step through the code by hand. Specify that the output file is named
address.txt.

Use the following memory table to show what occurs in memory when the C++ code is executed. (Include line numbers as documentation only. Do not use line numbers when entering your final program.) To fill out the memory table, use two lines for each variable. On one line, enter declaration information. Write the name of the declared variable, its data type, and the line number at declaration.

Variable Name	Data Type	Value in Memory	Line Number at Declaration	Line Number when Initialized

In the following space, show what is displayed on the screen after executing the output message.

2c.   Enter, compile, link, and execute **NoDisk1.cpp**. Execute the program twice, once with no disk in the drive and once with a disk in the drive. After your program is executed, copy the output and save it in a block comment at the end of your program. Save **NoDisk1.cpp** in the Chap04 folder of your Student Disk.

The following is a copy of the screen results that might appear after running your program, depending on the data entered. The input entered by the user is shown in bold.

```
/*
Cannot open output file. The program terminates.
*/


/*
Please enter a name: Judy Shaffer
Please enter a street address: 774 S. Main St.
Please enter a city, state, and zip code: Austin, Texas 78736

Your program ended successfully.
*/
```

3a.   Create the design for a program that reads the **address.txt** file that you created in Exercise 2 from drive A (or another drive with a removable disk). Read in the name, street address, and city, state, and zip code from **address.txt**, and display this information on the screen. Check for input failure in case the user does not have access to the drive (for example, if the disk is not inserted in the drive). If input failure occurs, display a message indicating the problem.

Write your design in the following space. Your design should be a list of C++ comments without any code.

3b.   Write a C++ program based on the design you created in Exercise 3a and name it **NoDisk2.cpp**. Step through the code by hand.

Use the following memory table to show what occurs in memory when the C++ code is executed. (Include line numbers as documentation only. Do not use line numbers when entering your final program.) To fill out the memory table, use two lines for each variable. On one line, enter declaration information. Write the name of the declared variable, its data type, and the line number at declaration.

Variable Name	Data Type	Value in Memory	Line Number at Declaration	Line Number when Initialized

In the following space, show what is displayed on the screen after executing the output message.

3c.   Enter, compile, link, and execute **NoDisk2.cpp**. Execute the program twice, once with no disk in the drive and once with a disk in the drive. After your program is executed, copy the output and save it in a block comment at the end of your program. Save **NoDisk2.cpp** in the Chap04 folder of your Student Disk.

The following is a copy of the screen results that might appear after running your program, depending on the data entered. The input comes from **address.txt**.

```
Either
/*
Judy Shaffer
774 S. Main St.
Austin, Texas 78736
*/
or
/*
Cannot open input file. The program terminates.
*/
```

LAB 4.5 USING THE ASSIGNMENT OPERATOR (=) FOR THE EQUALITY OPERATOR (==)

Any Boolean expression evaluates to `true` or `false`. An assignment expression used in a Boolean expression is evaluated after the assignment occurs. Any non-zero value evaluates to `true`. An `if` statement consisting of an assignment statement evaluates to `true` any time the value is not zero, when it evaluates to `false`; otherwise, it evaluates to `false`. C++ does not show this as a compile error.

Objectives

In this lab, you distinguish the assignment operator from an equality operator in a Boolean expression.

After completing this lab, you will be able to:

■ Recognize the problems related to confusing the assignment operator with the equality operator.

Estimated completion time: **5–10 minutes**

Using the Assignment Operator (=) for the Equality Operator (==)

1. Write what the following statements display as output after the program executes:

```
int x = 8;
if (x == 10)
     cout << "x is equal to 10\n";
else
     cout << "x is not equal to 10\n";
```

2. The following code is the same as the code in Exercise 1, but uses the assignment operator rather than the equality operator. Write what the following statements display as output after the program executes:

```
int x = 8;
if (x = 10)
    cout << "x is equal to 10\n";
else
    cout << "x is not equal to 10\n";
```

LAB 4.6 USING THE CONDITIONAL OPERATOR (?:)

You can write certain if...else statements concisely by using the conditional operator in C++. The conditional operator, written as ?:, is a ternary operator, which means that it takes three arguments. For example, examine the following code:

```
int x = 10, sum = 0;
if(x == 10)
    sum = x + 3;
else
    sum = x - 3;
Can be written as:
int x = 10, sum = 0;
(x==10) ? sum = x + 3 : sum = x - 3;
```

In the preceding examples, sum would be assigned 13 because x is equal to 10. Notice that this code does not use the reserved word if or a semi-colon (;) after the true statement.

The conditional expression is evaluated as follows: If expression1 evaluates to true, the result of the conditional expression is expression2. Otherwise, the result of the conditional expression is expression3.

Objectives

In this lab, you rewrite if...else statements using the conditional operators (?:)

After completing this lab, you will be able to:

■ Write if...else statements using the conditional operators (?:).

Estimated completion time: **10–15 minutes**

Using the Conditional Operator (?:)

Rewrite the following if...else statements using the conditional operator (?:). Assume these statements are part of a C++ program.

```
1. if (x  > 10)
       cout << "x is greater than 10\n";
   else
       cout << "x is less than or equal to 10\n";
```

```
2. if (x==6)
        cout << "A match is found.\n";
   else
        cout << "A match was not found.\n";
```

LAB 4.7 USING THE SWITCH SELECTION CONTROL STRUCTURE

Another control structure, called the `switch` statement, gives the computer the power to choose from many alternatives.

A `switch` structure evaluates an expression, then uses the value of the expression to perform the actions specified in the statements that follow the reserved word `case`. The value of the expression must be integral and is sometimes called the selector. An integral value is a value that evaluates to an integer value.

The syntax of the `switch` statement is as follows:

```
Switch (expression)
{
case value1:  statements1
        break;
case value2:  statements2
        break;
        …
case valuen:  statementsn
        break;
default: statements
}
```

The `switch` statement executes according to the following rules:

- When the value of the expression matches a case value, the statements execute until either a break statement is found or the end of the switch structure is reached.

- If the value of the expression does not match a case value, the statements following the default label execute. If there is no match and no default label, the entire switch statement is skipped.

The `switch` statement is an elegant way to implement multiple selections. If multiple selections involve a range of values, you should convert each range to a finite set of values. For instance, if the range of values includes 60-69, you could divide by 10, and then use the 6 as the finite value.

Objectives

In this lab, you write a `switch` statement using `break` statements, and a `switch` statement using the fall-through capability.

After completing this lab, you will be able to:

- Write `switch` control statements using the `break` statement.

- Write `switch` control statements using the fall-through capability.

Estimated completion time: **30–40 minutes**

Using the Selection Control Structure switch

Write and test programs that use a `switch` statement, and then test them with different values.

1a.   *Critical Thinking Exercise:* Design a program that prompts the user to select one of three television models, and provides a description of the models. Using the `switch` statement's fall-through capability, display the model the user chooses, the description, and the price. The user should make a selection by model number.

The user should be prompted with the following information:

- Model 100: Remote control, timer, and stereo for $1000

- Model 200: The same as Model 100, plus picture-in-picture, for $1200

- Model 300: The same as Model 200, plus HDTV, flat screen, and a 16 x 9 aspect ratio, for $2400

Display all features of the model selected.

Write your design in the following space. Your design should be a list of C++ comments without any code.

1b.   Write a C++ program based on the design you created in Exercise 1a and name it **TV.cpp**. Step through the code by hand.

Use the following memory table to show what occurs in memory when the C++ code is executed. (Include line numbers as documentation only. Do not use line numbers when entering your final program.) To fill out the memory table, use two lines for each variable. On one line, enter declaration information. Write the name of the declared variable, its data type, and the line number at declaration.

Variable Name	Data Type	Value in Memory	Line Number at Declaration	Line Number when Initialized

In the following space, show what is displayed on the screen after executing the output message.

1c.   Enter, compile, link, and execute **TV.cpp**. Execute the program three times, selecting a different model with each execution. Then copy the output and save it in a block comment at the end of your program. Save **TV.cpp** in the Chap04 folder of your Student Disk.

The following is a copy of the screen results that might appear after running your program, depending on the data entered. The input entered by the user is shown in bold.

```
Enter the model number of your choice:

Model 100: Remote control, timer, and stereo for $1000
Model 200: The same as Model 100, plus picture-in-picture, for $1200
Model 300: The same as Model 200, plus HDTV, flat screen,
           and a 16 x 9 aspect ratio, for $2400

100

You chose Model 100 TV with these features:
    remote control, timer, and stereo sound
```

```
Your price will be $1000

Enter the model number of your choice:

Model 100: Remote control, timer, and stereo for $1000
Model 200: The same as Model 100, plus picture-in-picture, for $1200
Model 300: The same as Model 200, plus HDTV, flat screen,
           and a 16 x 9 aspect ratio, for $2400

200

You chose Model 200 TV with these features:
    picture-in-picture
    remote control, timer, and stereo sound

Your price will be $1200

Enter the model number of your choice:

Model 100: Remote control, timer, and stereo for $1000
Model 200: The same as Model 100, plus picture-in-picture, for $1200
Model 300: The same as Model 200, plus HDTV, flat screen,
           and a 16 x 9 aspect ratio, for $2400

300

You chose Model 300 TV with these features:
    HDTV, flat screen, 16 x 9 aspect ratio
    picture-in-picture
    remote control, timer, and stereo sound

Your price will be $2400

Enter the model number of your choice:

Model 100: Remote control, timer, and stereo for $1000
Model 200: The same as Model 100, plus picture-in-picture, for $1200
Model 300: The same as Model 200, plus HDTV, flat screen,
           and a 16 x 9 aspect ratio, for $2400

400

Your choice is not available.
```

2a.   *Critical Thinking Exercise*: Create the design for a program that prompts the user to select one of three flooring options for a home to be built. The program also provides a description of the flooring options. Using the `switch` statement, display the option the user chooses, the description, and the price.

The user should be prompted with the following information:

■ Option 1: Scored concrete for $3000

■ Option 2: Carpeting for $5000

■ Option 3: Wood floors in the living areas, carpeting in the bedrooms, and tile in the bath areas for $10,000

Write your design in the following space. Your design should be a list of C++ comments without any code.

2b.   Write a C++ program based on the design you created in Exercise 2a and name it **Flooring.cpp**. Step through the code by hand.

Use the following memory table to show what occurs in memory when the C++ code is executed. (Include line numbers as documentation only. Do not use line numbers when entering your final program.) To fill out the memory table, use two lines for each variable. On one line, enter declaration information. Write the name of the declared variable, its data type, and the line number at declaration.

Variable Name	Data Type	Value in Memory	Line Number at Declaration	Line Number when Initialized

In the following space, show what is displayed on the screen after executing the output message.

2c.   Enter, compile, link, and execute **Flooring.cpp**. Then copy the output and save it in a block comment at the end of your program. Save **Flooring.cpp** in the Chap04 folder of your Student Disk.

The following are copies of the screen results that might appear after running your program, depending on the data entered. The input entered by the user is shown in bold.

```
Enter the number that matches your flooring choice:
Option 1: Scored concrete for $3000
Option 2: Carpeting for $5000
Option 3: Wood floors in the living areas, carpeting in the bedrooms,
          and tile in the bath areas for $10,000
1
```

```
You chose Option 1: Scored concrete for $3000
```

The following shows another set of possible input and output:

```
Enter the number that matches your flooring choice:
Option 1: Scored concrete for $3000
Option 2: Carpeting for $5000
Option 3: Wood floors in the living areas, carpeting in the bedrooms,
          and tile in the bath areas for $10,000
2
```

```
You chose option 2: Carpeting for $5000
```

The following shows another set of possible input and output:

```
Enter the number that matches your flooring choice:
Option 1: Scored concrete for $3000
Option 2: Carpeting for $5000
Option 3: Wood floors in the living areas, carpeting in the bedrooms,
          and tile in the bath areas for $10,000
3
```

```
You chose Option 3: Wood floors in the living areas, carpeting in the
bedrooms, and tile in the bath areas for $10,000
```

The following shows another set of possible input and output:

```
Enter the number that matches your flooring choice:
Option 1: Scored concrete for $3000
Option 2: Carpeting for $5000
Option 3: Wood floors in the living areas, carpeting in the bedrooms,
          and tile in the bath areas for $10,000
4
```

```
You chose Option 4
Your selection is not available.
```

LAB 4.8 USING THE ASSERT FUNCTION TO TERMINATE A PROGRAM

A predefined function, assert, stops program execution when certain elusive errors occur. Use the assert function to ensure that a program terminates with an appropriate error message indicating the type of error and the location in the program where the error occurred.

You can use the assert function with any logical expression. If the expression evaluates to true, the next statement executes. If the expression evaluates to false, the program terminates and indicates where the error occurred.

The assert function is included in the header file cassert. The assert function is useful during program development; however, a user would not understand what the error means. Therefore, you should remove assert statements when the program is ready for production. Rather than going through the code looking for the function, place the directive #define NDEBUG before the directive #include <cassert> to have the program ignore the assert function.

Objectives

In this lab, you use the assert function to test for division by 0. You then use the #define NDEBUG directive to ignore the assert function.

After completing this lab, you will be able to:

- User the assert function to ensure that a program terminates with an appropriate error message that indicates the type of error and the program location where the error occurred.

- Use the #define NDEBUG directive to ignore the assert function.

Estimated completion time: **50–60 minutes**

Using the assert Function to Terminate a Program

In the following exercises, design, write, and validate programs that use the assert function and the #define NDEBUG directive.

1a. Create the design for a program that evaluates a division problem and uses the assert function to determine whether an error occurs. Prompt the user for the numerator and denominator, but do not test to see if the denominator is equal to 0. Display a message with the values entered and the decimal representation of the fraction.

Write your design in the following space. Your design should be a list of C++ comments without any code.

1b.   Write a C++ program based on the design you created in Exercise 1a and name it
        divZero1.cpp. Step through the code by hand.

Use the following memory table to show what occurs in memory when the C++ code is executed. (Include line numbers as documentation only. Do not use line numbers when entering your final program.) To fill out the memory table, use two lines for each variable. On one line, enter declaration information. Write the name of the declared variable, its data type, and the line number at declaration.

Variable Name	Data Type	Value in Memory	Line Number at Declaration	Line Number when Initialized

In the following space, show what is displayed on the screen after executing the output message.

1c.   Enter, compile, link, and execute **divZero1.cpp**. Then copy the output and save it in a block comment at the end of your program. Save **divZero1.cpp** in the Chap04 folder of your Student Disk.

The following is a copy of the screen results that might appear after running your program, depending on the data entered. The input entered by the user is shown in bold.

```
Enter a numerator and a denominator: 2 0
Assertion failed: denominator, file C:\Chap04\divZero1.cpp, line 32

abnormal program termination
```

The following shows another set of possible input and output:

```
Enter a numerator and a denominator: 3 4

The decimal value of the numerator 3 divided by the denominator 4
is 0.75
```

1d.   Revise **divZero1.cpp** using the `#define NDEBUG` directive and save as **divZero2.cpp**. Remember to place `#define NDEBUG` before `#include <cassert>`. Use the same data as you did in Step 1c to run your program. The first output should be the same as for Lab 4.8, Exercise 1c. Other input and output may appear as follows:

```
Enter a numerator and a denominator: 2 0

The decimal value of the numerator 2 divided by the denominator 0 is
1.#INF
```

The following shows another set of possible input and output:

```
Enter a numerator and a denominator: 3 4

The decimal value of the numerator 3 divided by the denominator 4
is 0.75
```

Control Structures II
(Repetition)

In this chapter, you will:

O Learn about repetition (looping) control structures

O Explore how to construct and use count-controlled, sentinel-controlled, flag-controlled, and EOF-controlled repetition structures

O Examine `break` and `continue` statements

O Discover how to form and use nested control structures

CHAPTER 5: ASSIGNMENT COVER SHEET

Name _____   Date _____

Section _____

Lab Assignments	Assigned	Grade
Lab 5.1 Using the `while` Looping (Repetition) Structure		
Lab 5.2 Using the `for` Looping (Repetition) Structure		
Lab 5.3 Using the do...while Looping (Repetition) Structure (Critical Thinking Exercises)		
Lab 5.4 Using `break` and `continue` Statements		
Lab 5.5 Using Nested Control Structures (Critical Thinking Exercises)		
Lab 5.6 Debugging		
Total Grade		

See your instructor or the introduction to this book for instructions on submitting your assignments.

Lab 5.1 Using the while Looping (Repetition) Structure

The three looping (repetition) structures, while, for, and do...while, are reserved words in C++ and used when you want a program to repeat a set of statements. The three different types of looping structures offer flexibility in coding. This lab focuses on the while loop.

The reserved word while acts on a Boolean expression, which serves as a decision-maker. Rarely, the expression accomplishes the entire work of the loop. This lab does not cover that situation. Generally, the work of the loop is accomplished within the body of the loop, which can include one or more statements, and is executed when the expression evaluates to true. The expression is reevaluated after each iteration of the statements until the expression evaluates to false. An exit condition must exist within a loop; otherwise, an infinite loop will occur.

A looping expression contains the loop control variable. The variable must be initialized before it is evaluated and updated within the body of the loop to provide an exit condition. All loops with loop control variables require the following:

1. An initialization of the loop control variable.

2. Evaluation of the loop condition. If the loop condition is false, the body of the loop never executes. If true, the body of the loop is executed.

3. An update of the loop control variable.

4. Repetition of Steps 2 and 3 until the loop condition evaluates to false.

There are four types of while loops: counter-controlled, sentinel-controlled, flag-controlled, and end of file (EOF)-controlled.

Objectives

In this lab, you become acquainted with all four types of while loops.

After completing this lab, you will be able to:

- Write a counter-controlled while loop when you know exactly how many pieces of data need to be read.

- Write a sentinel-controlled while loop that uses a special sentinel value to end the loop.

- Write an EOF-controlled while loop that continues until the program reaches the end of the file.

Estimated completion time: **60–75 minutes**

Using the while Looping (Repetition) Structure

Design and write code for the following program that uses while loops.

1a.   Design a program that prompts the user to enter the number of students registered in a class. If the number is greater than 0, the program uses a counter-controlled while loop to prompt the user that number of times for the students' names. Write the students' names to an output file named **students.txt**. Display a message to the user when the program is complete.

Write your design in the following space. Your design should be a list of C++ comments without any code.

1b.   Write a C++ program based on the design you created in Exercise 1a and name it **Roster1.cpp**. Step through the code by hand.

Use the following memory table to show what occurs in memory when the C++ code is executed. (Include line numbers as documentation only. Do not use line numbers when entering your final program.) To fill out the memory table, use one or two lines for each variable. On one line, enter declaration information. Write the name of the declared variable, its data type, and the line number at declaration.

Variable Name	Data Type	Value in Memory	Line Number at Declaration	Line Number When Initialized

In the following space, show what is displayed on the screen after executing the output message.

1c.   Enter, compile, link, and execute **Roster1.cpp**. Then copy the output and save it in a block comment at the end of your program. Save **Roster1.cpp** in the Chap05 folder of your Student Disk.

The following is a copy of the screen results that might appear after running your program, depending on the data entered. The input entered by the user is shown in bold.

```
How many students may register for this class? 10
Enter the student's name: Yongrui Wuan
Enter the student's name: Marvella Garcia
Enter the student's name: Lola Zapata
Enter the student's name: Tony Pederzani
Enter the student's name: George Smith
Enter the student's name: John Patrick
Enter the student's name: Connor Bailey
Enter the student's name: Ryan Dennis
Enter the student's name: Susie Brown
Enter the student's name: Jack Cunningham

The program is complete.
```

2a.   Design a program that simulates an order room of a factory. To fill an order, workers place items on a conveyer belt to be grouped, billed, and shipped. Each item has a UPC code that designates the name of the item and its price. When an order is complete, a worker places a bar on the conveyor belt to separate the order from the next order. The bar has a UPC code of 999. In programming, a specific value to designate the end of a loop is called a sentinel value. The UPC code of 999 is a sentinel value.

After the computer system scans the UPC code of each item, it records the name and price in a file named **invoice1.txt**. This output file contains the product name and price on one line, separated by a pound sign (#). For example, if a hammer were purchased for the price of 9.95, the program writes this line as hammer#9.95. The program does not write the sentinel value to the output file. In your program, use a `while` repetition construct.

Because this is a program simulation, prompt the user to enter the name and price of each item. On a real order-scanning machine, no prompt would be used. When the system reads the value 999, display a thank you message, the name of the output file, and each item and price added to the output file.

Write your design in the following space. Your design should be a list of C++ comments without any code.

2b.   Write a C++ program based on the design you created in Exercise 2a and name it **Scan1.cpp**. Step through the code by hand.

Use the following memory table to show what occurs in memory when the C++ code is executed. (Include line numbers as documentation only. Do not use line numbers when entering your final program.) To fill out the memory table, use one or two lines for each variable. On one line, enter declaration information. Write the name of the declared variable, its data type, and the line number at declaration.

Variable Name	Data Type	Value in Memory	Line Number at Declaration	Line Number When Initialized

In the following space, show what is displayed on the screen after executing the output message.

2c.   Enter, compile, link, and execute **Scan1.cpp**. Then copy the output and save it in a block comment at the end of your program. Save **Scan1.cpp** in the Chap05 folder of your Student Disk.

The following is a copy of the screen results that might appear after running your program, depending on the data entered. The input entered by the user is shown in bold.

```
Please scan the name of the first item: hammer
Please scan the price of the hammer: 9.95

Please scan the name of the next item: saw
Please scan the price of the saw: 20.15

Please scan the name of the next item: shovel
Please scan the price of the shovel: 35.40

Please scan the name of the next item: 999

Thank you for your order.
invoice1.txt
hammer#9.95
saw#20.15
shovel#35.40
```

3a.   Design a program that prompts the user to enter the name of an item, searches the file **invoice1.txt** that was created in Exercise 2 for the item, and then displays the name and the price associated with that item. If the search item is not in the list, you reach the end of file. Use a compound flag-controlled `while` loop to search the list until either the item is found or the end of the file is reached. Display a message if the item is not found.

3b.   Write a C++ program based on the design you created in Exercise 3a and name it **Scan2.cpp**. Step through the code by hand.

Use the following memory table to show what occurs in memory when the C++ code is executed. (Include line numbers as documentation only. Do not use line numbers when entering your final program.) To fill out the memory table, use one or two lines for each variable. On one line, enter declaration information. Write the name of the declared variable, its data type, and the line number at declaration.

Variable Name	Data Type	Value in Memory	Line Number at Declaration	Line Number Where Value is Entered

In the following space, show what is displayed on the screen after executing the output message, depending on the data entered.

3c.   Enter, compile, link, and execute **Scan2.cpp**. Then copy the output and save it in a block comment at the end of your program. Save **Scan2.cpp** in the Chap05 folder of your Student Disk.

The following is a copy of the screen results that might appear after running your program, depending on the data entered. The input entered by the user is shown in bold.

```
Enter name of item for search: shovel

The item shovel costs 35.40
or
Enter name of item for search: hoe

The item hoe was not found
```

4a.   Design a program that reads names and prices, and then counts and accumulates all prices in the file **invoice1.txt**. Display each name and price, total count, and total of all prices in currency format.

Write your design in the following space. Your design should be a list of C++ comments without any code.

4b.   Write a C++ program based on the design you created in Exercise 4a and name it **Scan3.cpp**. Step through the code by hand.

Use the following memory table to show what occurs in memory when the C++ code is executed. (Include line numbers as documentation only. Do not use line numbers when entering your final program.) To fill out the memory table, use one or two lines for each variable. On one line, enter declaration information. Write the name of the declared variable, its data type, and the line number at declaration.

Variable Name	Data Type	Value in Memory	Line Number at Declaration	Line Number When Initialized

In the following space, show what is displayed on the screen after executing the output message.

4c.   Enter, compile, link, and execute **Scan3.cpp**. Then copy the output and save it in a block comment at the end of your program. Save **Scan3.cpp** in the Chap05 folder of your Student Disk.

The following is a copy of the screen results that might appear after running your program, depending on the data entered.

```
Invoice

        hammer    9.95
           saw   20.15
        shovel   35.40

Total   3 items   $   65.50
```

LAB 5.2 USING THE FOR LOOPING (REPETITION) STRUCTURE

The `for` looping structure, sometimes called a counted or indexed `for` loop, is a specialized form of the `while` loop that you use to simplify writing count-controlled loops.

To use the `for` looping structure, you write a `for` statement, where `for` is followed by the initial statement, loop condition, and update statement enclosed within parentheses. The program executes a `for` loop in the following sequence:

1. The initial statement executes.

2. The loop condition is evaluated. If the loop condition is false, the body of the loop never executes. If the loop condition is true, the body of the loop is executed.

3. The update statement executes after the body of the loop ends.

4. Steps 2 and 3 are repeated until the loop condition evaluates to false.

Objectives

In this lab, create programs that use the `for` loop.

After completing this lab, you will be able to:

- Write a `for` loop with an increment update condition.

- Write a `for` loop with a decrement update condition.

Estimated completion time: **40–50 minutes**

Using the for Looping (Repetition) Structure

In the following exercises, you design and write programs that use `for` loops.

1a.   Design a program that prompts the user to enter a positive integer number. Use a `for` loop to calculate and display the factorial value of that number. Increment the counter in your `for` loop. A factorial number is a number multiplied by every factor between 1 and the number, inclusive. For instance, 3 factorial is 3 * 2 * 1. If the user enters a negative number, display a message indicating that the program calculates only positive numbers. Otherwise, display the result of the calculation.

Write your design in the following space. Your design should be a list of C++ comments without any code.

1b.   Write a C++ program based on the design you created in Exercise 1a and name it **Factorial1.cpp**. Step through the code by hand.

146 Chapter 5   Control Structures II

Use the following memory table to show what occurs in memory when the C++ code is executed. (Include line numbers as documentation only. Do not use line numbers when entering your final program.) To fill out the memory table, use one or two lines for each variable. On one line, enter declaration information. Write the name of the declared variable, its data type, and the line number at declaration.

Variable Name	Data Type	Value in Memory	Line Number at Declaration	Line Number When Initialized

In the following space, show what is displayed on the screen after executing the output message.

1c.   Enter, compile, link, and execute **Factorial1.cpp**. Then copy the output and save it in a block comment at the end of your program. Save **Factorial1.cpp** in the Chap05 folder of your Student Disk.

The following is a copy of the screen results that might appear after running your program, depending on the data entered. The input entered by the user is shown in bold.

```
Enter a positive integer to find the factorial value: 5

The factorial of 5 is 120
```

2a.   Redesign the program you wrote in Exercise 1 to use a decrement counter in your **for** loop. Write your design in the following space. Your design should be a list of C++ comments without any code.

2b.   Write a C++ program based on the design you created in Exercise 2a and name it **Factorial2.cpp**. Step through the code by hand.

Use the following memory table to show what occurs in memory when the C++ code is executed. (Include line numbers as documentation only. Do not use line numbers when entering your final program.) To fill out the memory table, use one or two lines for each variable. On one line, enter declaration information. Write the name of the declared variable, its data type, and the line number at declaration.

Variable Name	Data Type	Value in Memory	Line Number at Declaration	Line Number When Initialized

In the following space, show what is displayed on the screen after executing the output message.

2c.   Enter, compile, link, and execute **Factorial2.cpp**. Then copy the output and save it in a block comment at the end of your program. Save **Factorial2.cpp** in the Chap05 folder of your Student Disk.

The following is a copy of the screen results that might appear after running your program, depending on the data entered. The input entered by the user is shown in bold.

```
Enter a positive integer to find the factorial value: 5

The factorial of 5 is 120
```

3a.   Redesign the program you wrote in Lab 5.1, Exercise 1 to use a `for` loop. Write your design in the following space. Your design should be a list of C++ comments without any code.

3b.   Write a C++ program based on the design you created in Exercise 3a and name it
        Roster2.cpp. Step through the code by hand.

3c.   Enter, compile, link, and execute **Roster2.cpp**. Then copy the output and save it in a block comment at the end of your program. Save **Roster2.cpp** in the Chap05 folder of your Student Disk.

Your screen results should be the same for Roster1.cpp and Roster2.cpp when running the same data.

LAB 5.3 USING THE DO...WHILE LOOPING (REPETITION) STRUCTURE

The third repetition structure is the do...while loop. The do...while loop differs from both the while loop and the for loop. The while loop is called a pre-test loop because the loop condition is evaluated before the loop begins. In both the while loop and for loop, the body of the loop may be skipped depending on the result of the condition.

The do...while loop is a post-test loop. This means that the loop condition is tested at the end of the loop body; therefore, the do...while loop is always executed at least once.

Objectives

In this lab, you create programs that use the do...while loop.

After completing this lab, you will be able to:

- Write a do...while counter-controlled loop when you know exactly how many pieces of data need to be read.

- Write a do...while sentinel-controlled loop that uses a special sentinel value to end the loop.

- Write a do...while flag-controlled loop that uses a Boolean variable as a decision-maker, and evaluates to false to end the loop.

- Write a do...while EOF-controlled loop that continues until the program reaches the end of the file.

Estimated completion time: **50–60 minutes**

Using the do...while Looping Repetition Structure

In the following exercises, you design and write programs that use do...while loops.

1a. *Critical Thinking Exercise:* Design a program that finds the smallest, largest, and average of three numbers entered. Use a do...while loop.

Write your design in the following space. Your design should be a list of C++ comments without any code.

1b.   Write a C++ program based on the design you created in Exercise 1a and name it **FindSLA.cpp**. Step through the code by hand.

Use the following memory table to show what occurs in memory when the C++ code is executed. (Include line numbers as documentation only. Do not use line numbers when entering your final program.) To fill out the memory table, use one or two lines for each variable. On one line, enter declaration information. Write the name of the declared variable, its data type, and the line number at declaration.

Variable Name	Data Type	Value in Memory	Line Number at Declaration	Line Number When Initialized

Variable Name	Data Type	Value in Memory	Line Number at Declaration	Line Number When Initialized

In the following space, show what is displayed on the screen after executing the output message.

1c.   Enter, compile, link, and execute **FindSLA.cpp**. Then copy the output and save it in a block comment at the end of your program. Save **FindSLA.cpp** in the Chap05 folder of your Student Disk.

The following is a copy of the screen results that might appear after running your program, depending on the data entered. The input entered by the user is shown in bold.

```
Enter the first number: 5
Enter a number: 16
Enter a number: 1

The smallest number entered:          1
The largest number entered:          16
The average of the numbers entered:  7.33
```

2a.   In this exercise, you modify the **Scan1.cpp** program you created in Lab 5.2, Exercise 2. Design the order-scanning program using a `do...while` repetition construct. Record the output in a file named **invoice2.txt**.

Write your design in the following space. Your design should be a list of C++ comments without any code.

2b.   Write a C++ program based on the design you created in Exercise 2a and name it **Scan1dw.cpp**. Step through the code by hand.

Use the following memory table to show what occurs in memory when the C++ code is executed. (Include line numbers as documentation only. Do not use line numbers when entering your final program.) To fill out the memory table, use one or two lines for each variable. On one line, enter declaration information. Write the name of the declared variable, its data type, and the line number at declaration.

Variable Name	Data Type	Value in Memory	Line Number at Declaration	Line Number When Initialized

In the following space, show what is displayed on the screen after executing the output message.

2c.   Enter, compile, link, and execute **Scan1dw.cpp**. Then copy the output and save it in a block comment at the end of your program. Save **Scan1dw.cpp** in the Chap05 folder of your Student Disk. If you also wrote **Scan1.cpp**, compare **invoice1.txt** and **invoice2.txt**. When using the same data, the files should be identical.

The following is a copy of the screen results that might appear after running your program, depending on the data entered. The input entered by the user is shown in bold.

```
Please scan the name of the first item: hammer
Please scan the price of the hammer: 9.95

Please scan the name of the next item: saw
Please scan the price of the saw: 20.15

Please scan the name of the next item: shovel
Please scan the price of the shovel: 35.40

Please scan the name of the next item: 999

Thank you for your order.
invoice2.txt
hammer#9.95
saw#20.15
shovel#35.40
```

3a.   In this exercise, you modify **Scan2.cpp**, the program you created in Lab 5.2, Exercise 2. Design a program that prompts the user to enter the name of an item, searches the file **invoice2.txt**, and displays the name and the price associated with that item as found in the file. If the search item is not in the list, you reach the end of file. Use a compound flag-controlled `while` loop to search the list until either the item is found or the end of the file is reached. Display a message if the item is not found.

3b.   Write a C++ program based on the design you created in Exercise 3a and name it **Scan2dw.cpp**. Step through the code by hand.

Use the following memory table to show what occurs in memory when the C++ code is executed. (Include line numbers as documentation only. Do not use line numbers when entering your final program.) To fill out the memory table, use one or two lines for each variable. On one line, enter declaration information. Write the name of the declared variable, its data type, and the line number at declaration.

Variable Name	Data Type	Value in Memory	Line Number at Declaration	Line Number Where Value is Entered

Variable Name	Data Type	Value in Memory	Line Number at Declaration	Line Number Where Value is Entered

In the following space, show what is displayed on the screen after executing the output message depending on the data entered.

3c. Enter, compile, link, and execute **Scan2dw.cpp**. Then copy the output and save it in a block comment at the end of your program. Save **Scan2dw.cpp** in the Chap05 folder of your Student Disk.

The following is a copy of the screen results that might appear after running your program, depending on the data entered. The input entered by the user is shown in bold.

```
Enter name of item for search: shovel

The item shovel costs 35.40
or
Enter name of item for search: hoe

The item hoe was not found
```

4a. Modify the design and rewrite the **Scan2dw.cpp** program you created in Exercise 3. Revise the design for the program that reads names and prices, and counts, and accumulates all prices in the file **invoice2.txt**. Display each name and price, total count, and total of all prices in currency format.

Write your design in the following space. Your design should be a list of C++ comments without any code.

4b.   Write a C++ program based on the design you created in Exercise 4a and name it **Scan3dw.cpp**. Step through the code by hand.

Use the following memory table to show what occurs in memory when the C++ code is executed. (Include line numbers as documentation only. Do not use line numbers when entering your final program.) To fill out the memory table, use one or two lines for each variable. On one line, enter declaration information. Write the name of the declared variable, its data type, and the line number at declaration.

Variable Name	Data Type	Value in Memory	Line Number at Declaration	Line Number When Initialized

In the following space, show what is displayed on the screen after executing the output message.

4c.   Enter, compile, link, and execute **Scan3dw.cpp**. Then copy the output and save it in a block comment at the end of your program. Save **Scan3dw.cpp** in the Chap05 folder of your Student Disk.

The following is a copy of the screen results that might appear after running your program, depending on the data entered.

```
Invoice

            hammer     9.95
               saw    20.15
            shovel    35.40

    Total   3 items   $   65.50
```

LAB 5.4 USING BREAK AND CONTINUE STATEMENTS

The `break` and `continue` statements alter the flow of control in a program. When you use a break in a `switch` statement or in a repetition structure, you provide an immediate exit from the structure. The program continues to execute with the first statement after the structure.

Use a `continue` statement in a repetition structure to end the current iteration only and proceed with the next iteration of the loop. In a `for` loop, the next statement is the update statement. Use a `break` statement in a repetition structure to end the entire repetition. Use these constructs sparingly. They are introduced for informational purposes, but are not suggested for general solutions.

Objectives

In this lab, you use `break` and `continue` statements to alter the control of a loop.

After completing this lab, you will be able to:

- Execute a loop until a `break` statement is encountered.

- Execute a loop and skip over the remaining loop statement when a `continue` statement is encountered and proceed in the loop until the loop terminates.

Estimated completion time: 20–30 minutes

Using break and continue Statements

In the following exercises, you evaluate the output in repetition control structures that use the `continue` or `break` statements. You also write programs from designs that use the `continue` or `break` statements.

1a. Design a program that prompts the user to enter 20 numbers. Add all positive numbers. Use a `for` loop with a `continue` statement to skip negative numbers. Output the total found.

Write your design in the following space. Your design should be a list of C++ comments without any code.

1b. Write a C++ program based on the design you created in Exercise 1a and name it **Continue.cpp**. Step through the code by hand.

Use the following memory table to show what occurs in memory when the C++ code is executed. (Include line numbers as documentation only. Do not use line numbers when entering your final program.) To fill out the memory table, use one or two lines for each variable. On one line, enter declaration information. Write the name of the declared variable, its data type, and the line number at declaration.

Variable Name	Data Type	Value in Memory	Line Number at Declaration	Line Number When Initialized

In the following space, show what is displayed on the screen after executing the output message.

1c.   Enter, compile, link, and execute **Continue.cpp**. Then copy the output and save it in a block comment at the end of your program.

The following is a copy of the screen results that might appear after running your program, depending on the data entered. The input entered by the user is shown in bold.

```
Enter a list of 20 numbers:
2 3 1 -6 10 2 6 5 9 -10 9 2 -4 3 1 2 -6 7 3 2

The sum of the positive numbers is: 67
```

2a.   Modify the design and rewrite the **Continue.cpp** program you created in Exercise 1. The program should prompt the user to enter 20 numbers. Add all numbers until the user enters a negative number. Use a **for** loop with a **break** statement to end the loop when a negative number is entered. Output the total found.

Write your design in the following space. Your design should be a list of C++ comments without any code.

2b.   Write a C++ program based on the design you created in Exercise 2a and name it **Break.cpp**. Step through the code by hand.

Use the following memory table to show what occurs in memory when the C++ code is executed. (Include line numbers as documentation only. Do not use line numbers when entering your final program.) To fill out the memory table, use one or two lines for each variable. On one line, enter declaration information. Write the name of the declared variable, its data type, and the line number at declaration.

Variable Name	Data Type	Value in Memory	Line Number at Declaration	Line Number When Initialized

In the following space, show what is displayed on the screen after executing the output message.

2c.   Enter, compile, link, and execute **Break.cpp**. Then copy the output and save it in a block comment at the end of your program. Save **Break.cpp** in the Chap05 folder of your Student Disk.

The following is a copy of the screen results that might appear after running your program, depending on the data entered. The input entered by the user is shown in bold.

```
Enter a list of 20 numbers:
2 3 1 -6 10 2 6 5 9 -10 9 2 -4 3 1 2 -6 7 3 2

The sum of the positive numbers is: 6
```

LAB 5.5 USING NESTED CONTROL STRUCTURES

One control structure can be nested (contained) within another control structure, and that structure can be nested within another control structure. The control structures do not have to be of the same type.

Inner control structures close before outer control structures.

Objectives

In this lab, you use a nested control structure within a control structure.

After completing this lab, you will be able to:

■ Recognize the beginning and end of control structures.

■ When an inner control structure is a `for` loop, recognize that the loop is reinitialized with each iteration of an outer loop.

Estimated completion time: **60–75 minutes**

Using Nested Control Structures

In the following exercises, you design and write programs that use nested control structures.

1a. *Critical Thinking Exercise:* Design a program that prompts the user to enter a character and a sentence. Count the number of times the character you entered appears in the sentence. (Remember that an uppercase and a lowercase version of a letter are different letters.) Display a message that tells how often the specified character appears in the sentence. Your program should allow the user to enter multiple sentences until the user chooses to quit the program.

Write your design in the following space. Your design should be a list of C++ comments without any code.

1b.   Write a C++ program based on the design you created in Exercise 1a and name it **CountChar.cpp**. Step through the code by hand.

Use the following memory table to show what occurs in memory when the C++ code is executed. (Include line numbers as documentation only. Do not use line numbers when entering your final program.) To fill out the memory table, use one or two lines for each variable. On one line, enter declaration information. Write the name of the declared variable, its data type, and the line number at declaration.

Variable Name	Data Type	Value in Memory	Line Number at Declaration	Line Number When Initialized

In the following space, show what is displayed on the screen after executing the output message.

1c.   Enter, compile, link, and execute **CountChar.cpp**. Then copy the output and save it in a block comment at the end of your program. Save **CountChar.cpp** in the Chap05 folder of your Student Disk.

The following is a copy of the screen results that might appear after running your program, depending on the data entered. The input entered by the user is shown in bold.

```
Enter a character to count the number of times it is in a sentence: c

Enter a sentence and to search for a specified character:
Learning to program in C++ is fun and challenging.

Your sentence had 1 c character(s)

Do you wish to enter another sentence (y/n)? y

Enter a sentence and to search for a specified character:
Working with nested loops requires using braces.

Your sentence had 1 c character(s)

Do you wish to enter another sentence (y/n)? n
```

2a.   *Critical Thinking Exercise*: Design a program that displays a table resembling a spreadsheet. The column headings should show the values A, B, C, D, and E, and the row headings should show 1, 2, 3, 4, 5. The row values should be multiples of the value of the row number. Use a **for** loop to output the column headings. Use nested **for** loops to output the row number and the values within the rows and columns. The output should look like the following:

```
     A      B      C      D      E
1    1      2      3      4      5
2    2      4      6      8      10
3    3      6      9      12     15
4    4      8      12     16     20
5    5      10     15     20     25
```

Write your design in the following space. Your design should be a list of C++ comments without any code.

2b.   Write a C++ program based on the design you created in Exercise 2a and name it **Table.cpp**. Step through the code by hand.

Use the following memory table to show what occurs in memory when the C++ code is executed. (Include line numbers as documentation only. Do not use line numbers when entering your final program.) To fill out the memory table, use one or two lines for each variable. On one line, enter declaration information. Write the name of the declared variable, its data type, and the line number at declaration.

Variable Name	Data Type	Value in Memory	Line Number at Declaration	Line Number When Changed

In the following space, show what is displayed on the screen after executing the output message.

2c.   Enter, compile, link, and execute **Table.cpp**. Then copy the output and save it in a block comment at the end of your program. Save **Table.cpp** in the Chap05 folder of your Student Disk.

The following is a copy of the screen results that might appear after running your program.

	A	B	C	D	E
1	1	2	3	4	5
2	2	4	6	8	10
3	3	6	9	12	15
4	4	8	12	16	20
5	5	10	15	20	25

Lab 5.6 Debugging

The following programs have logic errors, syntax errors, and may be inefficient. Mark the corrections, and then enter, compile, and execute your programs.

1. Convert Fahrenheit temperature to Centigrade temperature.

```cpp
/* The program FtoC.cpp is a program that converts
   Fahrenheit temperature to Centigrade temperature.
   to calculate Centigrade temperature, subtract 32
   from the Fahrenheit temperature and multiply the
   result by five ninths. */
/* Fahrenheit temperature is entered. */
/* Centigrade temperature is displayed


//header files
/* use the correct preprocessor directives for input/output */
# include <iostream>
using namespace std;


int main()


{
        //declare variables
        // a character variable again to control the loop
        char again = true;
        // double variables for Fahrenheit and Centigrade
        double fahrenheit, centigrade;

        // loop until the user chooses to end
        do
        {
                // prompt the user for a Fahrenheit temperature
                cout << "Enter a Fahrenheit temperature:";
                // enter the Fahrenheit temperature
                cin >> fahrenheit;
                // calculate the Centigrade temperature
                centigrade = 5/9 * fahrenheit - 32;
```

```
                    // display the Fahrenheit and Centigrade temperatures
                    cout << fahrenheit << " Fahrenheit is " << centigrade << " Centigrade\n";
            }while (again);


            return 0;
}
```

2. Count the number of iterations in a loop.

```
/* The program LoopCount.cpp loops 5 times and displays
   a message each time a loop is executed. */
/* A message is displayed each time a loop is executed */


//header files
/* use the correct preprocessor directives for input/output */
#include <iostream>
using namespace std;


// main function
int main()
{
        // declare variables
        // an integer variable to count the times through the loop
        int loop = 0;


        // loop 5 times and display a message each time through the loop
        while (loop < 5 || loop > 0)
                cout << ++loop << " times through the loop.\n";


        return 0;
}
```

3. Calculate the number of items purchased.

```
/* The program CalcBill.cpp ask the user for the number
   of items purchased, and the price of each item. A
   total of all purchases is calculated.
/* The number of items and the price of each item is entered. */
/* The total cost of all items is displayed. */
```

```cpp
//header files
/* use the correct preprocessor directives for input/output */
#include <iostream>
using namespace std;

// main function
int main()
{
        // declare variables
        // an integer variable to count the times through the loop
        /* double variable price to enter the price, total to
           total the values entered */
        int numItems;
        double price, total = 0;

        // prompt the user for the number of items purchased
        cout << "How many items were purchased? ";
        // enter the number of items purchased
        cin >> numItems;

        // loop to enter the price of each item
        for (int loop = 1; loop < numItems; loop++)
        {
                // prompt the user for the price of an item
                cout << "Enter the price of item " << loop << ":";
                // enter the price
                cin >> price;
                // add the price to the total
                total += price;
        }

        // display the total of the items entered
        cout << "The total of all items is " << total << endl;
        return 0;

}
```

6

User-Defined Functions I

In this chapter, you will:

O Learn about standard (predefined) functions and discover how to use them in a program

O Learn about user-defined functions

O Examine value-returning functions, including actual and formal parameters

O Explore how to construct and use a value-returning, user-defined function in a program

CHAPTER 6: ASSIGNMENT COVER SHEET

Name _____   Date _____

Section _____

Lab Assignments	Assigned	Grade
Lab 6.1 Using Standard (Predefined) Functions		
Lab 6.2 Adding User-Defined Value-Returning Functions (Critical Thinking Exercises)		
Lab 6.3 Using User-Defined Value-Returning Functions (Critical Thinking Exercises)		
Lab 6.4 Testing and Debugging a Program with Value-Returning User-Defined Functions		
Total Grade		

See your instructor or the introduction to this book for instructions on submitting your assignments.

Lab 6.1 Using Standard (Predefined) Functions

Functions, also called modules, divide complicated programs into manageable pieces. Functions also offer the following advantages:

- You can concentrate on the part of the program that contains a function to construct, and then debug and perfect it.

- Different people can work on different functions at the same time.

- You can write a function once and use it many times.

- Using functions reduces the complexity of the function main.

C++ includes predefined functions, also called standard functions that perform algebraic calculations. For example, `sqrt(x)` calculates the square root of a value. Predefined functions are already written for you, and are stored in C++ header files. For instance, the header file `cmath` contains predefined C++ math functions and the header file `cctype` contains character functions. To use predefined functions in a program, you must:

- Know the name of the header file that contains the function's specification.

- Use an include statement to reference each of the appropriate header files in your program.

- Know the name and type of the function, and the number and type of its arguments, or parameters.

Predefined functions such as `pow`, `sqrt`, `tolower`, and `abs` are value-returning functions because their calculations produce, or return, a value. Any value-returning function has a data type, which is the same as the data type of the return value. For instance, the `pow` function returns a double value, so `pow` is of the data type `double`.

The values a function uses in a calculation are called its arguments, or parameters. For example, the square root function calculates the square root of one value, x, meaning it has one parameter. This function name is written as `sqrt(x)`. Other predefined functions also include parameters in their names, as in `pow(x, y)` and `tolower(x)`.

When using standard (predefined) functions, you only need to represent that function in the design with an explanation of the formal parameters required by the function and the return type. A formal parameter is a variable declared in the function heading. For example, the following heading is for the `pow` function:

```
double pow (double base, double exponent)
```

This function heading contains two variables—base and exponent—which are the formal parameters of `pow`.

Objectives

In this lab, you include the correct library files for standard functions, write function calls to standard functions, provide the missing code, and test the code. To complete this lab you need to use the `tolower()`, `ceil()`, `floor()`, and `fabs()` standard functions.

After completing this lab, you will be able to:

- Use standard (predefined) value-returning functions with parameters.

- Write function calls to standard (predefined) functions.

- Use values from value-returning standard (predefined) functions.

Estimated completion time: **60–75 minutes**

Using Standard (Predefined) Functions

In the following exercises, you modify existing programs, and design and create new ones using standard functions.

1a.   In Lab 5.5, Exercise 1, you designed and implemented a character count program named **CountChar.cpp**. However, this program treats uppercase and lowercase letters differently. Modify your design to create a program that prompts the user to enter a character and a sentence. Treat uppercase and lowercase letters as the same letters. Count the number of times the character you entered appears in the sentence. (Use the `tolower` standard function so that your program will not be case sensitive.) Display a message that tells how often the specified character appears in the sentence. Your program should allow the user to enter multiple sentences until the user chooses to quit the program.

Write your design in the following space. Your design should be a list of C++ comments without any code.

Chapter 6   User-Defined Functions I   187

1b. Write a C++ program based on the design you created in Exercise 1a and name it **CountChar2.cpp**. Step through the code by hand.

Use the following memory table to show what occurs in memory when the C++ code is executed. (Include line numbers as documentation only. Do not use line numbers when entering your final program.) To fill out the memory table, use one or two lines for each variable. On one line, enter declaration information. Write the name of the declared variable, its data type, and the line number at declaration.

Variable Name	Data Type	Value in Memory	Line Number at Declaration	Line Number When Initialized

In the following space, show what is displayed on the screen after executing the output message.

1c.   Enter, compile, link, and execute **CountChar2.cpp**. Then copy the output and save it in a block comment at the end of your program. Save **CountChar2.cpp** in the Chap06 folder of your Student Disk.

The following is a copy of the screen results that might appear after running your program, depending on the data entered. The input entered by the user is shown in bold.

```
Enter a character to count the number of times it appears in a
sentence: c

Enter a sentence to search for a specified character:
Learning to program in C++ is fun and challenging.

Your sentence had 2 c character(s)

Do you want to enter another sentence? (y/n) y

Enter a sentence to search for a specified character:
Working with nested loops requires using braces.

Your sentence had 1 c character(s)

Do you want to enter another sentence? (y/n) n
```

2a.   Create the design for a program that prompts the user to enter a `double` value. Using the standard (predefined) math functions `ceil`, `floor`, and `fabs` in the `cmath` header file to find and display the following values:

- The smallest whole number greater than or equal to the number

- The greatest whole number less than or equal to the number

- The absolute value of the number

Your program should allow the user to enter multiple values until the user chooses to quit the program.

Write your design in the following space. Your design should be a list of C++ comments without any code.

2b.	Write a C++ program based on the design you created in Exercise 2a and name it **MathFunc.cpp**. Step through the code by hand.

Use the following memory table to show what occurs in memory when the C++ code is executed. (Include line numbers as documentation only. Do not use line numbers when entering your final program.) To fill out the memory table, use one or two lines for each variable. On one line, enter declaration information. Write the name of the declared variable, its data type, and the line number at declaration.

Variable Name	Data Type	Value in Memory	Line Number at Declaration	Line Number When Initialized

In the following space, show what is displayed on the screen after executing the output message.

2c.   Enter, compile, link, and execute **MathFunc.cpp**. Then copy the output and save it in a block comment at the end of your program. Save **MathFunc.cpp** in the Chap06 folder of your Student Disk.

The following is a copy of the screen results that might appear after running your program, depending on the data entered. The input entered by the user is shown in bold.

```
Enter a float number and I will tell you:
the smallest whole number >= to the number
the largest whole number <= to the number
and the absolute value of the number: 5.82

The smallest whole number greater than 5.82 is 6
The largest whole number less than 5.82 is 5
The absolute value of 5.82 is 5.82

Enter a float number and I will tell you:
the smallest whole number >= to the number
the largest whole number <= to the number
and the absolute value of the number: -14.23

The smallest whole number greater than -14.23 is -14
The largest whole number less than -14.23 is -15
The absolute value of -14.23 is 14.23

Enter a float number and I will tell you:
the smallest whole number >= to the number
the largest whole number <= to the number
and the absolute value of the number: 0
```

Suppose a user wants to calculate either the square of a number or the square root of a number and display the results. To create a program to solve this problem, answer the following questions to help you determine the design for the program.

3. What do you need to know about the standard functions involving squares and square roots?

4. In the program, users will enter a character value to designate whether they want to calculate the square or square root of a number. Should you make any assumptions about the case of the character entered? Explain why or why not. Does your decision about case require the use of any other standard functions? If so, which one?

5. What variables are needed for user input and calculations? Of what types are these variables?

6. Users should be allowed to enter numbers for the calculation until they enter a specified value to quit. What kind of loop works best in this situation? Explain why.

7. When users enter a numeric value for the calculation, should the program validate the number? Explain why or why not. If you choose to validate, what validation method would you use? Does the validation depend on which math function the program calls?

8. What values will be used as arguments to the `math` function?

9. The `sqrt` and `pow` functions are value returning. How will the program handle those returned values?

10. Should your output be formatted? If so, how will you format it and what header file do you need?

11a. Create the design for a program that prompts the user to indicate whether to find the square or the square root of a number, and to enter the number. Then the program calculates the answer.

Write your design in the following space. Your design should be a list of C++ comments without any code.

11b.   Write a C++ program based on the design you created in Exercise 11a and name it **SqrSqrt.cpp**. Step through the code by hand.

Use the following memory table to show what occurs in memory when the C++ code is executed. (Include line numbers as documentation only. Do not use line numbers when entering your final program.) To fill out the memory table, use one or two lines for each variable. On one line, enter declaration information. Write the name of the declared variable, its data type, and the line number at declaration.

Variable Name	Data Type	Value in Memory	Line Number at Declaration	Line Number When Initialized

In the following space, show what is displayed on the screen after executing the output message.

11c.   Enter, compile, link, and execute **SqrSqrt.cpp**. Then copy the output and save it in a block comment at the end of your program. Save **SqrSqrt.cpp** in the Chap06 folder of your Student Disk.

The following is a copy of the screen results that might appear after running your program, depending on the data entered. The input entered by the user is shown in bold.

```
Enter (s)quare or square (r)oot or (q): s
Enter the value to be squared: 14
The value 14.00 squared is 196.00

Enter (s)quare or square (r)oot or (q): r
Enter a positive value for the square root: -5
You must enter a positive number for a square root

Enter (s)quare or square (r)oot or (q): r
Enter a positive value for the square root: 24
The square root of  24.00 is 4.90

Enter (s)quare or square (r)oot or (q): q
```

Lab 6.2 Adding User-Defined Value-Returning Functions

Because C++ does not provide every function you might ever need, you can write your own functions, called user-defined functions. User-defined functions can be value-returning functions (those that have a data type) or void functions (those that do not have a data type).

You use, or call, a value-returning function in an expression. The expression can be part of an assignment statement or an output statement. A function call in a program causes the body of the called function to execute.

A value-returning function returns a value via the return statement. The data type of the value must match the function type.

Functions in a C++ program can appear in any order. When determining the best sequence for including user-defined functions in a program, remember the rule that you must declare an identifier before you can use it. The compiler compiles the program sequentially from beginning to end.

When using some functions, such as main, which you customarily place before other user-defined functions, you can place a function prototype before the function definition to work around the problem of undeclared identifiers. When you use a function prototype, you do not have to specify the variable name in the parameter list, though you must specify the data type of each parameter. Because function prototypes appear before any function definition, the compiler translates the prototypes first so it can correctly translate a function call.

Objectives

In this lab, you include the prototype, call, and the function header of user-defined void functions, implement the missing code, and then run and test the code.

After completing this lab, you will be able to:

- Use user-defined void functions with and without parameters.

Estimated completion time: **50–60 minutes**

Adding User-Defined Value-Returning Functions

In the following exercises, you complete and test a C++ program that includes value-returning user-defined functions.

1a. Examine the following C++ program that calls two value user-defined functions. Provide the missing code by replacing the bold text with C++ statements, including the correct prototypes and calls to the functions. The program asks the user for today's year and month, and his or her year and month of birth. The program calculates and displays the user's age.

```
// Enter your name as a comment for program identification
// Program assignment Age.cpp
// Enter your class section, and time

/* The program Age.cpp prompts the user to input today's
date and his/her birth date, then calculates and displays
the user's age. The program utilizes user-defined functions.*/
/* Dates are entered in integer format for month and year. */
/* An age, described in months and years is displayed. */

//header files
/* use the correct preprocessor directives for input/output */
```

```
#include <iostream>
#include <string>

using namespace std;

// user-defined function prototypes
/* the function getValue returns an integer value
entered by the user in response to the prompt
in the string message */
 /* the function getLetter returns a character value
    entered by the user in response to the prompt
    in the string message */


int main()
{
// declare variables
/* declare integer variables thisYear, thisMonth,
year, month, and ageMonth and ageYear. declare a character
variable again to indicate if the process is
to continue. */
int thisYear, thisMonth, year, month, ageYear, ageMonth;
char again = 'y';

// display program instructions
cout << "This program asks you to enter today's year in 4 digits,\n"
<< "and today's month number in 2 digits.\n\n"
<< "Then it asks you to enter your birth year in 4 digits,\n"
<< "and your birth month in 2 digits.\n\n"
<< "The program will calculate and display your age in years and
months.\n";

// assign to thisYear the value returned from a call to getValue


// assign to thisMonth the value returned from a call to getValue



// loop until the user indicates to end
while (again == 'y')
{
// assign to year the value returned from a call to getValue

// assign to month the value returned from a call to getValue


// assign age the value of thisYear - year
ageYear = thisYear - year;
ageMonth = thisMonth - month;

/* test to see if thisMonth is less than month
if true
subtract 1 from age and add 12 to month
*/
```

```
if (thisMonth < month)
{
        ageYear--;
        ageMonth += 12;
}

// display the age in years and months
cout << "\nYou are " << ageYear << " years and " << ageMonth
        << "months old.\n";

// assign to again the value returned from getLetter

// convert the value of again to lowercase
again = tolower(again);


}

return 0;
}

/* the function getValue returns an integer value
   entered by the user in response to the prompt
   in the string message */
int getValue(string message)
{
// declare variables
// declare an integer value to enter a value
int value;

// prompt the user with the message passed to the function
cout << message;
// read in the value entered
cin >> value;
// return the value
return value;
}

/* the function getLetter returns a character value
   entered by the user in response to the prompt
   in the string message */
char getLetter(string message)
{
// declare variables
// declare a character value to enter a value
char letter;

// prompt the user with the message passed to the function
cout << message;
// read in the value entered
cin >> letter;
// return the value
return letter;
}
```

1b.   Step through the code by hand. Then use the following memory tables (one for each function) to show what occurs in memory when the C++ code is executed. (Include line numbers as documentation only. Do not use line numbers when entering your final program.) To fill out the memory table, use one or two lines for each variable. On one line, enter declaration information. Write the name of the declared variable, its data type, and the line number at declaration.

main function

Variable Name	Data Type	Value in Memory	Line Number at Declaration	Line Number When Initialized

getValue function

Variable Name	Data Type	Value in Memory	Line Number at Declaration	Line Number When Initialized

getLetter function

Variable Name	Data Type	Value in Memory	Line Number at Declaration	Line Number When Initialized

In the following space, show what is displayed on the screen after executing the output message.

1c.   Enter, compile, link, and execute **Age.cpp**. Then copy the output and save it in a block comment at the end of your program. Save **Age.cpp** in the Chap06 folder of your Student Disk.

The following is a copy of the screen results that might appear after running your program, depending on the data entered. The input entered by the user is shown in bold.

```
This program asks you to enter today's year in 4 digits
and today's month number in 2 digits.

Then it asks you to enter your birth year in 4 digits,
and your birth month in 2 digits.

The program will calculate and display your age in years and months.

Enter today's 4-digit year: 2003
Enter today's month number: 07

Enter the 4-digit year of your birth: 1981
Enter the month number of your birth: 02

You are 22 years and 5 months old.

Do you want to enter more data? y/n y

Enter the 4-digit year of your birth: 1984
Enter the month number of your birth: 12

You are 18 years and 7 months old.

Do you want to enter more data? y/n y

Enter the 4-digit year of your birth: 1986
Enter the month number of your birth: 12

You are 16 years and 7 months old.

Do you want to enter more data? y/n n
```

LAB 6.3 USING USER-DEFINED VALUE-RETURNING FUNCTIONS

One method of designing a C++ program is to separate the design into design modules. Each module designates a different step of the program. This allows you to focus on one part of the program at a time. The process of constructing, debugging, and perfecting part of a program one module at a time is called stepwise refinement.

Objectives

In this lab, you design and write a program using design modules.

After completing this lab, you will be able to:

- Design and write a program with user-defined value-returning functions with and without formal parameters.

Estimated completion time: **40–50 minutes**

Using User-Defined Value-Returning Functions

In the following exercises, you design and write a program that includes user-defined value-returning functions for calculating leap years.

1a.   *Critical Thinking Exercise*: Create the design for a program that prompts the user to enter a year and then determines whether it is a leap year. Your program should have a loop and continue while the user enters the character 'y'.

Write three methods according to the following descriptions:

- getYear has no formal parameters, asks the user to enter a year, and returns an integer value that is assigned to the integer variable year.

- isLeap has an integer formal parameter, year, determines whether the year is a leap year, and returns the Boolean value true if the year is a leap year and false if it is not. A year is a leap year if it is divisible by 4, but is not divisible by 100 except when divisible by 400. (The year 2000 was a leap year.)

- moreData has no formal parameters and returns a char value.

Write your design in the following space. Your design should be a list of C++ comments without any code.

1b. Write a C++ program based on the design you created in Exercise 1a and name it **LeapYear.cpp**. Step through the code by hand.

Use the following memory table to show what occurs in memory when the C++ code is executed. (Include line numbers as documentation only. Do not use line numbers when entering your final program.) To fill out the memory table, use one or two lines for each variable.

On one line, enter declaration information. Write the name of the declared variable, its data type, and the line number at declaration.

main function

Variable Name	Data Type	Value in Memory	Line Number at Declaration	Line Number When Initialized

getYear function

Variable Name	Data Type	Value in Memory	Line Number at Declaration	Line Number When Initialized

isLeap function

Variable Name	Data Type	Value in Memory	Line Number at Declaration	Line Number When Initialized

moreData function

Variable Name	Data Type	Value in Memory	Line Number at Declaration	Line Number When Initialized

In the following space, show what is displayed on the screen after executing the output message.

1c. Enter, compile, link, and execute **LeapYear.cpp**. Then copy the output and save it in a block comment at the end of your program. Save **LeapYear.cpp** in the Chap06 folder of your Student Disk.

The following is a copy of the screen results that might appear after running your program, depending on the data entered. The input entered by the user is shown in bold.

```
This program asks you to enter a year in 4 digits.
The output shows if the year is a leap year

Enter a year: 1492
1492 is a leap year.

Do you want to enter more data? y/n y

Enter a year: 2000
2000 is a leap year.

Do you want to enter more data? y/n y

Enter a year: 2005
2005 is not a leap year.

Do you want to enter more data? y/n y

Enter a year: 1800
1800 is not a leap year.

Do you want to enter more data? y/n n
```

LAB 6.4 TESTING AND DEBUGGING A PROGRAM WITH VALUE-RETURNING USER-DEFINED FUNCTIONS

An advantage to modular programming is the ability to test functions and reuse them with confidence that the coding is correct. By adding `cout` statements to display values before a function call, inside of a function, and after returning from a function, you can test the reliability of the function.

To debug a modular program, you should first correct any syntax errors found when compiling. One way to debug logic errors is to test the functions using `cout` statements before, inside functions, and after function calls.

Objectives

In this lab, you test and debug a program with both syntax and logic errors.

After completing this lab, you will be able to:

- Write output statements to trace values in a logically incorrect program.

Estimated completion time: **40–50 minutes**

Testing and Debugging a Program with Value-Returning User-Defined Functions

In the following exercises, you correct logic and syntax errors in a program.

1a. Examine the following program, which contains logic and syntax errors.

The purpose of the program is to calculate the cost to a company for a proposed raise. The program prompts for the number of employees and each employee's salary, and then calculates the individual raise and the total cost of raises. Employees earning $25,000 or less will receive a 5% raise. Employees earning between $25,001 and $35,000 will receive a 4% raise. Employees earning $35,001 or greater will receive a 3% raise. Display each employee's raise and the total raises.

First mark your changes in the following copy of **Buggy.cpp**.

```
// Enter your name as a comment for program identification
// Program assignment Buggy.cpp
// Enter your class section and time

/* The program Buggy.cpp calculates the cost to a
   company for a proposed raise. The program prompts
   for the number of employees and each employee's salary
   then calculates the individual raise and the total cost
   of raises. Employees earning $25,000 or less
   will receive a 5% raise. Employees earning
   between $25,001 and $35,000 will receive a 4%
   raise. Employees earning $35,001 or greater will receive
   a 3% raise. Display each employee's raise and
   the total raises. */
/* Input the number of employees and each employee's salary. */
/* Display each employee's raise and the total cost of raises. */

//header files
/* use the correct preprocessor directives for input/output */
#include <iostream>
#include <iomanip>
```

```cpp
// user-defined function prototypes
/* the function getNumber returns an integer value
   entered by the user giving the number of employees */
int getNumber();
/* the function getSalary returns a float value
   entered by the user giving the employee's salary */
double getSalary(int empNumber);
/* the function calcRaise returns the raise
   calculated for the salary passed */
double calcRaise(double salary);
/* the function totalRaises returns the new
   total of raises using the current total and
   current raise being processed */
double totalRaises(double raise, double total);


int main()
{
        // declare variables
        /* declare an integer variable number to enter the
           number of employees, a float variable salary to
           enter the current employee's salary, a float variable
           raise to calculate raise amount, a float variable
            total to accumulate the total of employee raises */
        int number;
        double salary, raise, total;

        // set the formatting for output
        cout << fixed << showpoint << setprecision(2);

        // instruct the user regarding use of the program
        cout >> "This program asks the user to enter the number "
             >> "of employees and\nthe individual salary for each "
             >> "employee. \nThe individual employee's raise and "
             >> "the total raises are displayed.\n";

        // assign to number the value returned from getNumber
        number = getNumber();

        // loop until all employees are processed
        for (int count = 1; count < number; count++)
        {
            // assign to raise the value returned from getSalary
            salary = getSalary(count);
            // assign to raise the value returned from calcRaise
            raise = calcRaise(salary);
            // assign to total the accumulated raises
            total = totalRaises(total, raise);

            // display current employee raise
            cout << "Employee " << count << " receives a raise of $"
               << salary << endl;
        }

        // display total raises
        cout << "\n\nThe total cost of raises: $" << raise << endl;


    return 0;
}
```

```
/* the function getNumber returns an integer value
   entered by the user giving the number of employees */
int getNumber()
{
        // declare variables
        /* declare an integer variable number to enter the
           number of employees */
        int number;
        // prompt the user for the number of employees
        cout << "\nEnter the number of employees: ";
        // read in the number of employees
        cin >> number;
        // return the number of employees
        return number;

}

/* the function getSalary returns a float value
   entered by the user giving the employee's salary */
double getSalary(int empNumber)
{
        // declare variables
        /* declare an double variable salary to enter the
           individual employee's raise */
        double salary;
        // prompt the user for the employee salary
        cout << "\nEnter the salary for an employee "
             << empNumber << ": ";
        // read in the employee salary
        cin >> salary;
        // return the employee salary
        return salary;

}

/* the function calcRaise returns the raise
   calculated for the salary passed */
int calcRaise(double salary)
{
        /* test salary value to calculate raise and
           return salary times percentage applicable */
        if (salary <= 25000)
            return salary * .05;
        else if (salary <= 35000)
            return salary * .04;
        else
            return salary * .03;

}

/* the function totalRaises returns the new
   total of raises using the current total and
   current raise being processed */
double totalRaises(double raise, double total);
{
        return total + raise;
}
```

After marking your changes, open the program named **Buggy.cpp** stored in the Chap06 folder of your Student Disk. Correct the syntax errors, and save your program as **TestRaises.cpp** in the Chap06 folder of your Student Disk. Compile, link, and execute **TestRaises.cpp**. Then copy the output and save it in a block comment at the end of your program.

1b.   As written, the output of **TestRaises.cpp** has no syntax errors, but contains logic errors, as follows:

Output with logic errors, no syntax errors

```
This program asks the user to enter the number of employees and
the individual salary for each employee.
The individual employee's raise and the total raises are displayed.

Enter the number of employees: 2

Enter the salary for employee 1: 100000
Employee 1 receives a raise of $100000.00


The total cost of raises: $-
92559631349317831000000000000000000000000000000000000000
0000000000.00
```

To help find logic errors, insert the following types of error-checking output statements in **TestRaises.cpp**:

- Output statements of arguments to functions

- Output statements of variables that are assigned values returning from functions

Save **TestRaises.cpp**, and then compile, link, and execute it. Copy the output and save it in a block comment at the end of your program.

The following is a copy of the screen results that might appear after running your program, depending on the data entered. The input entered by the user is shown in bold.

```
/* output with test messages and no logic errors
This program asks the user to enter the number of employees and
the individual salary for each employee.
The individual employee's raise and the total raises are displayed.

Before getNumber, the number of employees entered is: -858993460
Enter the number of employees: 3
Inside getNumber, the number of employees entered is: 3
After getNumber, the number of employees entered is: 3

Before getSalary, the salary entered is: -
9255963134931783100000000000000000000000
00000000000000000000000.00
Enter the salary for employee 1: 18600
Inside getSalary, salary is: 18600.00
After getSalary, the salary entered is: 18600.00

Before calcRaise, raise is: -
92559631349317831000000000000000000000000000000000000000
00000000000.00
Inside calcRaise, raise is not defined.
After calcRaise, raise is: 930.00

Before totalRaises, total is: 0.00
```

```
Before totalRaises, raise is: 930.00
Inside totalRaises, total is: 930.00

Inside totalRaises, raise is: 0.00

After totalRaises, total is: 930.00

After totalRaises, raise is: 930.00
Employee 1 receives a raise of $930.00

Before getSalary, the salary entered is: 18600.00
Enter the salary for employee 2: 48000
Inside getSalary, salary is: 48000.00
After getSalary, the salary entered is: 48000.00

Before calcRaise, raise is: 930.00
Inside calcRaise, raise is not defined.
After calcRaise, raise is: 1440.00

Before totalRaises, total is: 930.00

Before totalRaises, raise is: 1440.00
Inside totalRaises, total is: 1440.00

Inside totalRaises, raise is: 930.00

After totalRaises, total is: 2370.00

After totalRaises, raise is: 1440.00
Employee 2 receives a raise of $1440.00

Before getSalary, the salary entered is: 48000.00
Enter the salary for employee 3: 31500
Inside getSalary, salary is: 31500.00
After getSalary, the salary entered is: 31500.00

Before calcRaise, raise is: 1440.00
Inside calcRaise, raise is not defined.
After calcRaise, raise is: 1260.00

Before totalRaises, total is: 2370.00

Before totalRaises, raise is: 1260.00
Inside totalRaises, total is: 1260.00

Inside totalRaises, raise is: 2370.00

After totalRaises, total is: 3630.00

After totalRaises, raise is: 1260.00
Employee 3 receives a raise of $1260.00


The total cost of raises: $3630.00
*/
```

1c.   Remove your error-checking output statements and save your program as **Raises.cpp** in the Chap06 folder of your Student Disk. Compile, link, and execute **Raises.cpp**. Then copy the output and save it in a block comment at the end of your program.

The following is a copy of the screen results that might appear after running your program, depending on the data entered. The input entered by the user is shown in bold.

```
This program asks the user to enter the number of employees and
the individual salary for each employee.
The individual employee's raise and the total raises are displayed.

Enter the number of employees: 7

Enter the salary for employee 1: 18600
Employee 1 receives a raise of $930.00

Enter the salary for employee 2: 24685
Employee 2 receives a raise of $1234.25

Enter the salary for employee 3: 32000
Employee 3 receives a raise of $1280.00

Enter the salary for employee 4: 48000
Employee 4 receives a raise of $1440.00

Enter the salary for employee 5: 21700
Employee 5 receives a raise of $1085.00

Enter the salary for employee 6: 19800
Employee 6 receives a raise of $990.00

Enter the salary for employee 7: 31500
Employee 7 receives a raise of $1260.00


The total cost of raises: $8219.25
```

7 User-Defined Functions II

In this chapter, you will:

○ Learn how to construct and use void functions in a program

○ Discover the difference between value and reference parameters

○ Explore reference parameters and value-returning functions

○ Learn about the scope of an identifier

○ Examine the difference between local and global identifiers

○ Discover static variables

○ Learn function overloading

○ Explore functions with default parameters

CHAPTER 7: ASSIGNMENT COVER SHEET

Name _____   Date _____

Section _____

Lab Assignments	Assigned	Grade
Lab 7.1 Calling Void Functions without Parameters		
Lab 7.2 Calling Void Functions with Value Parameters		
Lab 7.3 Calling Void Functions with Value and Reference Parameters		
Lab 7.4 Accessing an Identifier by Its Scope		
Lab 7.5 Using Static and Automatic Variables		
Lab 7.6 Using Function Overloading (Critical Thinking Exercises)		
Lab 7.7 Using Default Parameters (Critical Thinking Exercises)		
Group Project: The payroll program written and refined in Labs 7.1, Ex. 8, 7.2, Ex. 7, 7.3, Ex. 6, and 7.5, Ex. 3 can be used for a Group Project. The group should work together to establish the use and purpose of each function, and then individual group members can be assigned different functions.		
Total Grade		

See your instructor or the introduction to this book for instructions on submitting your assignments.

LAB 7.1 CALLING VOID FUNCTIONS WITHOUT PARAMETERS

The order in which functions appear in a program does not matter if you use prototypes because the `main` function is always executed first. A void function does not have a data type and does not need a return statement. You can use the keyword `return` with no value to exit the program; otherwise the program exits at the end of the function definition.

Void functions are not called as part of an expression; the call is a stand-alone statement. You can write a void function definition without parameters if you use the keyword `void` in place of the parameter list or if you leave the parameter list empty.

Void functions are useful for displaying information about the program or printing statements.

Objectives

In this lab, you write two void functions with no parameters and include the function prototypes and the driver function (`main`) that calls the functions.

After completing this lab, you will be able to:

- Call a void function with no parameters from the `main` function.

- Write a prototype for a void function with no parameters.

- Write a void function definition that has no parameters.

Estimated completion time: **20–30 minutes**

Calling Void Functions Without Parameters

In the following exercises, you determine whether statements are true or false. You also begin to design and create a payroll program that you will refine throughout other labs in this chapter.

Question	Answer (Circle the correct answer)
1. Given the following prototype: `void pageHeading ();` The following statement is valid in the main function: `pageHeading ();`	T F
2. Using the same prototype given in Question 1, the following statement is valid in the `main` function: `cout << pageHeading() << endl;`	T F
3. Although void functions without parameters are legal in C++, they are not very useful because they do not communicate data between functions.	T F
4. In C++, void is a reserved word.	T F
5. Void functions with no parameters are very useful for writing reports.	T F
6. Because void functions without parameters do not communicate data between functions, they are limited to containing only output statements.	T F
7. Functions without parameters still require parenthesis signifying a parameter list.	T F

8a.   When users run a program, they often need information concerning the purpose of the program and how they should use it. Additionally, after users run a program, they often want to view a report with the results. In this exercise, create the design for a program that has in addition to the main function, two void functions with no parameters. Name one function instruction—it should provide information about the program to the user. Name the other function reportTitle—it should display the headings for a future report.

You will develop the program through several lab exercises so that it eventually processes a payroll by calculating paychecks for each employee. In this exercise, you work with a text file, **payroll.txt**, which is available in the Chap07 folder of your Student Disk. It contains the following information:

- Employee name
- Hourly rate of pay
- Number of hours worked
- Tax percentage to be deducted

The program will create a report in columnar format showing the following:

- Employee name
- Hourly rate of pay
- Number of hours worked
- Tax rate
- Gross pay
- Net pay

Manipulators are often included in the report title function because this function is used to set up a report. In this case, because it is a payroll program, use the manipulators fixed, showpoint, and left, and show values to two decimal points.

After all employees are processed, the program displays the total gross pay and the total net pay.

Write your design in the following space. Your design should be a list of C++ comments without any code. Use the report layout grid provided or graph paper to plan your report columns.

Report Layout Grid

8b.   Write a C++ program based on the design you created in Exercise 8a and name it
Payroll1.cpp. Step through the code by hand.

In the following space, show what is displayed on the screen after executing the output message.

8c.   Enter, compile, link, and execute **Payroll1.cpp**. Then copy the output and save it in a block
comment at the end of your program. Save **Payroll1.cpp** in the Chap07 folder of your
Student Disk.

The following is a copy of the screen results that might appear after running your program:

```
This payroll program calculates an individual employee pay and
company totals using data from a data file payroll.txt.


A payroll report showing payroll information is displayed.

Employee            Hourly   Hours    Tax      Gross    Net
Name                Rate     Worked   Rate     Amount   Amount
```

LAB 7.2 CALLING VOID FUNCTIONS WITH VALUE PARAMETERS

Information is communicated between calling functions and called functions through a communication link called a parameter list. There are two types of parameters: value parameters and reference parameters. This lab focuses on functions with value parameters.

Parameters enable functions to manipulate different data each time they are called. A formal parameter that is a value parameter receives a copy of the content of the corresponding actual parameter. The formal parameter list found in the function definition lists the data type and the variable name. A void function definition with value parameters has the following syntax:

```
void functionName(formal parameter list)
```

The formal parameter list has the following syntax:

```
dataType variable, dataType variable, …
```

A function call to a void function with value parameters has the following syntax:

```
functionName(actual parameter list)
```

The actual parameter list has the following syntax:

```
expression or variable, expression or variable, …
```

The parameter lists must be in the same order to create a one-to-one correspondence.

If a formal parameter is a value parameter, after copying the value of the actual parameter, there is no connection between the formal parameter and actual parameter. Therefore, during program execution, the formal parameter manipulates the data stored in its own memory space.

Objectives

In this lab, you continue using stepwise refinement to build a program step by step. You build on the program you designed and wrote in the previous lab. You write a void function with value parameters, use the function prototype, and declare the variables needed to call a function with values.

After completing this lab, you will be able to:

- Use stepwise refinement as a program design technique.
- Call a void function with value parameters from the **main** function.
- Write a prototype for a void function with value parameters.
- Write a void function definition that has value parameters.
- Align a report in columnar format.

Estimated completion time: **30–45 minutes**

Calling Void Functions with Value Parameters

In the following exercises, you answer a series of multiple-choice questions. You also continue to design and create the payroll program that you began in Lab 7.1.

Question	**Answer** **(Circle the correct answer)**

1. Given the following function:

```
void increment (int x)
{
      x++;
}
```

and the following code in the **main** function:

```
int x = 5;
increment (x);
cout << x << endl;
```

The output is:

a. 5

b. 6

c. 7

d. a compiler error occurs

2. Using the increment function given in Question 1 and the following code in the **main** function:

```
const int x = 5;
increment(x);
cout << x << endl;
```

The output is:

a. 5

b. 6

c. 7

d. a compiler error occurs

3. Using the increment function given in Question 1 and the following code in the **main** function:

```
int x = 5;
increment(x + 1);
cout << x << endl;
```

The output is:

a. 5

b. 6

c. 7

d. a compiler error occurs

4. Given the following function:

```
void displayData (int x, char l)
{
      cout << "The number is " << x << endl
<< "The letter is " << l << endl;
}
```

and the following code in the **main** function:

```
int number = 80;
char letter = 'A';
displayData (letter, number);
```

The output is:

a. the number is 80
   the letter is A

b. the number is 65
   the letter is P

c. a compiler error occurs

5. Using the **displayData** function given in Question 4 and the following code in the **main** function:

```
int number = 80;
char letter = 'A';
displayData (static_cast<int>(letter),
static_cast<char>(number));
```

The output is:

a. the number is 80

   the letter is A

b. the number is 65

   the letter is P

c. a compiler error occurs

6. When a function parameter list contains value parameters, legal actual parameters are:

a. variables

b. expressions

c. constants

d. all of the above

7a.   This lab exercise expands on the one you completed for Lab 7.1, Exercise 8 that gives instructions to use a payroll processing program and provides report titles for a report. Expand your design to read in data values from a data file for the following employee data:

- Employee name

- Hourly rate of pay

- Number of hours worked

- Tax percentage to be deducted

Using this data, calculate the gross pay and net pay for the employee, and call a function to display the information to a report. You can use the data in **payroll.txt** in the Chap07 folder of your Student Disk.

Write your design in the following space. Your design should be a list of C++ comments without any code. Use the report layout grid provided or graph paper to plan your report columns.

Report Layout Grid

7b.   Write a C++ program based on the design you created in Exercise 7a and name it **Payroll2.cpp**. Step through the code by hand.

Use the following memory table to show what occurs in memory when the C++ code is executed. (Include line numbers as documentation only. Do not use line numbers when entering your final program.) To fill out the memory table, use one or two lines for each variable. On one line, enter declaration information. Write the name of the declared variable, its data type, and the line number at declaration.

main function

Variable Name	Data Type	Value in Memory	Line Number at Declaration	Line Number When Initialized

displayEmployeeInfo function

Variable Name	Data Type	Value in Memory	Line Number at Declaration	Line Number When Initialized

totalAmounts function

Variable Name	Data Type	Value in Memory	Line Number at Declaration	Line Number When Initialized

In the following space, show what is displayed on the screen after executing the output message.

7c.   Enter, compile, link, and execute **Payroll2.cpp**. Then copy the output and save it in a block comment at the end of your program. Save **Payroll2.cpp** in the Chap07 folder of your Student Disk.

The following is a copy of the screen results that might appear after running your program, depending on the data entered.

```
This payroll program calculates an individual employee pay and
company totals using data from a data file payroll.txt.


A payroll report showing payroll information is displayed.
```

Employee Name	Hourly Rate	Hours Worked	Tax Rate	Gross Amount	Net Amount
John Smith	10.45	40.00	15.00	418.00	355.30
Jane Doe	12.50	45.00	15.00	843.75	717.19
Harry Morgan	20.00	40.00	20.00	800.00	640.00
Carmen Martinez	25.00	35.00	25.00	875.00	656.25
Jacintha Washington	50.85	60.00	35.00	4576.50	2974.72
Totals				7513.25	5343.46

LAB 7.3 CALLING VOID FUNCTIONS WITH VALUE AND REFERENCE PARAMETERS

Local variables are variables declared within a function. Variables in the formal parameter list are also considered to be local variables to the function. When using value parameters, new local variables are allocated in memory and the value is copied into the new memory location. Reference parameters are parameters declared in the parameter list but they do not use new memory locations. When using reference parameters, the address of the actual parameter passes to the called function and the memory location from the calling function is used. When a function changes a reference parameter, the change is in the memory location passed through the parameter list.

You use the ampersand symbol (&) after the dataType to designate a reference parameter; it stands for the address of operator. A formal value parameter receives a copy of the actual parameter. A reference parameter receives the location (memory address) of the corresponding actual parameter. You use reference parameters to share results with the calling function. Think of a reference parameter name as a synonym for the actual parameter name. The reference parameter name represents the same memory location. Stream variables must always be passed by reference.

It is not recommended that you use reference parameters in value returning functions. If more than one value needs to be returned, use a void function with reference parameters. By combining all types of functions, you can create a modular program where the work of the `main` function is done by calling multiple functions. You may have selection and repetition control structures in `main` that determine which functions are called, but little other work is done in `main`.

Objectives

In this lab, you continue use all function types to modularize your program. You modify the program you designed and wrote in the previous labs. You add the use of void function with reference parameters and the function prototype.

After completing this lab, you will be able to:

- Call a void function with reference parameters from the `main` function.

- Write a prototype for a void function with reference parameters.

- Write a void function definition with reference parameters.

Estimated completion time: **20–30 minutes**

Calling Void Functions with Value and Reference Parameters

In the following exercises, you answer a series of multiple-choice questions. You also continue to design and create the payroll program that you began in Lab 7.1.

Question	**Answer** (Circle the correct answer)

1. Given the following function:

```
void increment (int &x)
{
    x++;
}
```

and the following code in the `main` function:

```
int x = 5;
increment (x);
cout << x << endl;
```

The output is:

a. 5

b. 6

c. 7

d. a compiler error occurs

2. Using the increment function given in Question 1 and the following code in the **main** function:

```
const int x = 5;
increment(x);
cout << x << endl;
```

The output is:

a. 5

b. 6

c. 7

d. a compiler error occurs

3. Using the increment function given in Question 1 and the following code in the **main** function:

```
int x = 5;
increment(x + 1);
cout << x << endl;
```

The output is:

a. 5

b. 6

c. 7

d. a compiler error occurs

4. When a function parameter list contains reference parameters, legal actual parameters are:

a. variables

b. expressions

c. constants

d. all of the above

5. A function parameter list may contain either reference parameters or value parameters but not both in the same parameter list.

T   F

6a.   In **Payroll2.cpp** payroll you wrote that input of data and payroll computations were carried out in your **main** function. Your **main** function should be a series of function calls with any control structures necessary to make those function calls. Using void functions with reference parameters, modify your program design to include a function to read in your data. Create another function with both value and reference parameters to perform your payroll calculations. Do not use reference parameters when value parameters will work.

Write your design in the following space. Your design should be a list of C++ comments without any code.

6b.   Write a C++ program based on the design you created in Exercise 6a and name it **Payroll3.cpp**. Step through the code by hand.

Use the following memory table to show what occurs in memory when the C++ code is executed. (Include line numbers as documentation only. Do not use line numbers when entering your final program.) To fill out the memory table, use one or two lines for each variable. On one line, enter declaration information. Write the name of the declared variable, its data type, and the line number at declaration.

main function

Variable Name	Data Type	Value in Memory	Line Number at Declaration	Line Number When Initialized

main function (continued)

Variable Name	Data Type	Value in Memory	Line Number at Declaration	Line Number When Initialized

displayEmployeeInfo function

Variable Name	Data Type	Value in Memory	Line Number at Declaration	Line Number When Initialized

totalAmounts function

Variable Name	Data Type	Value in Memory	Line Number at Declaration	Line Number When Initialized

readData function

Variable Name	Data Type	Value in Memory	Line Number at Declaration	Line Number When Initialized

calculate function

Variable Name	Data Type	Value in Memory	Line Number at Declaration	Line Number When Initialized

In the following space, show what is displayed on the screen after executing the output message.

6c.   Enter, compile, link, and execute **Payroll3.cpp**. Then copy the output and save it in a block comment at the end of your program. Save **Payroll3.cpp** in the Chap07 folder of your Student Disk. Compare the output from your Payroll3 to your output from your Payroll2 program. With the same data, the output should be the same.

The following is a copy of the screen results that might appear after running your program, depending on the data entered.

```
This payroll program calculates an individual employee pay and
company totals using data from a data file payroll.txt.


A payroll report showing payroll information  is displayed.

Employee               Hourly      Hours       Tax       Gross        Net
Name                     Rate      Worked      Rate      Amount      Amount

John Smith              10.45       40.00      15.00      418.00      355.30
Jane Doe                12.50       45.00      15.00      843.75      717.19
Harry Morgan            20.00       40.00      20.00      800.00      640.00
Carmen Martinez         25.00       35.00      25.00      875.00      656.25
Jacintha Washington     50.85       60.00      35.00     4576.50     2974.72

Totals                                                   7513.25     5343.46
```

LAB 7.4 ACCESSING AN IDENTIFIER BY ITS SCOPE

The scope of an identifier refers to where an identifier is accessible in the program. Local identifiers are not accessible outside of the function (or block). An identifier declared within a block is accessible only within the block from the point at which it is declared until the end of the block. When a block is nested within another block, an identifier from the outer block is recognized in the inner block. The exception to this occurs if the inner block has an identifier of the same name.

The scope rule for variables declared in a `for` statement differ between standard C++ and ANSI C++. This book uses the ANSI C++ standard.

A global variable can be declared inside a function if it is declared as an external variable and there is no other identifier with the same name.

If you use global variables, then the function is not independent and typically cannot be used in more than one program. It is recommended that you do not use global variables.

Objectives

The objectives of this lab are to demonstrate the difference between local and global variables and the scope of their identifiers.

After completing this lab, you will be able to:

- Differentiate between the scope of local and global variables.

- Use local and global variables in the same program.

Estimated completion time: **40–50 minutes**

Accessing an Identifier by Its Scope

In the following exercises, you answer a series of multiple-choice questions. You also continue to design and create the payroll program that you began in Lab 7.1.

Question	**Answer** (Circle the correct answer)

1. Given the following statements:

```
{      // block 1
   int x = 2;
   int y = 3;
   int z = 4;
   .
   .
   .
   {      // block 2
      int x = 3;
      cout << x << ' ' << y << ' '
           << z << endl;
   }

}
```

The output is:

    a. 2 3 4

    b. 3 3 4

    c. a compiler error occurs

2. Using the coding example in Question 1, which variables are global variables?

    a. x

    b. y

    c. z

    d. none are global variables

3. To avoid the confusion that might occur between value and reference variables, you should code with global variables.   **T**   **F**

4. The terms global variable and reference variable mean the same thing.   **T**   **F**

5. Given the following function definition:

   a. 5 10

   ```
   void swap (int &x, int &y)
   {
       return;
   }
   ```

   b. 10 5

   c. a compiler error occurs

   and the following code in the main function:

   ```
   int x = 5;
   int y = 10;
   swap (y, x)
   cout << x << ' ' << y << endl;
   ```

   The output is:

6a. Create the design for a program that shows the scope of global and local variables. Your design should have three functions—main, parameters, and useGlobals. You should have two global integer variables named num1 initialized to 10 and num2 initialized to -5.

   Your **main** function should have the following characteristics:

   - Begin the program block

   - Declare two local variables—num1 initialized to 20 and num2 initialized to 13

   - Call the function parameters with the actual arguments num1 and num2

   - Call the function parameters with the actual arguments num2 and num1

   - Call the function useGlobals with no actual arguments

   - Begin another program block

   - Declare two local variables—num1 initialized to 94 and num2 initialized to 50

   - Call the function parameters with the actual arguments num1 and num2

   - Call the function parameters with the actual arguments num2 and num1

   - Call the function useGlobals with no actual arguments

   - End the second block

   - Call the function parameters with the actual arguments num1 and num2

   - Call the function parameters with the actual arguments num2 and num1

   - Call the function useGlobals with no actual arguments

   - Before each function call, display a message showing the value of num1 and num2

   - After calling each function, display a message showing the value of num1 and num2

   Your parameters function should have the following characteristics:

   - Have the data type void

   - Have two formal integer parameters num1 and num2

   - Display a message showing the value of num1 and num2; in **main**, create two local integer variables named num1 and num2

Your useGlobals function should have the following characteristics:

- Have the data type void

- Have no formal parameters

- Display a message showing the value of num1 and num2; in `main`, create two local integer variables named num1 and num2

Write your design in the following space. Your design should be a list of C++ comments without any code.

6b.   Write a C++ program based on the design you created in Exercise 6a and name it **Scope.cpp**. Step through the code by hand.

Use the following memory table to show what occurs in memory when the C++ code is executed. (Include line numbers as documentation only. Do not use line numbers when entering your final program.) To fill out the memory table, use one line for each variable. Write the name of the declared variable, its data type, the line number at declaration, and the line number at initialization.

global variables

Variable Name	Data Type	Value in Memory	Line Number at Declaration	Line Number When Initialized

main function

Variable Name	Data Type	Value in Memory	Line Number at Declaration	Line Number When Initialized

parameters function

Variable Name	Data Type	Value in Memory	Line Number at Declaration	Line Number When Initialized

useGlobals function

Variable Name	Data Type	Value in Memory	Line Number at Declaration	Line Number When Initialized

6c. Enter, compile, link, and execute **Scope.cpp**. Then copy the output and save it in a block comment at the end of your program. Save **Scope.cpp** in the Chap07 folder of your Student Disk.

The following is a copy of the screen results that might appear after running your program.

```
The following values refer to block 1 of main.


Calling parameters with num1 as the first argument
and num2 as the second argument block 1:
     Before calling function parameters block 1      num1: 20, num2: 13
     Inside function parameters                      num1: 20, num2: 13
     After  calling function parameters block 1      num1: 20, num2: 13

Calling parameters with num2 as the first argument
and num1 as the second argument block 1:
     Before calling function parameters block 1      num1: 20, num2: 13
     Inside function parameters                      num1: 13, num2: 20
     After  calling function parameters block 1      num1: 20, num2: 13

Calling useGlobals with no arguments block 1:
     Before calling function useGlobals block 1      num1: 20, num2: 13
     Inside function useGlobals                      num1: 10, num2: -5
     After  calling function useGlobals block 1      num1: 20, num2: 13


The following values refer to block 2 of main.


Calling parameters with num1 as the first argument
and num2 as the second argument block 2:
     Before calling function parameters block 2      num1: 94, num2: 50
     Inside function parameters                      num1: 94, num2: 50
     After  calling function parameters block 2      num1: 94, num2: 50
```

```
Calling parameters with num2 as the first argument
and num1 as the second argument block 2:
     Before calling function parameters block 2        num1: 94, num2: 50
     Inside function parameters                        num1: 50, num2: 94
     After  calling function parameters block 2        num1: 94, num2: 50

Calling useGlobals with no arguments block 2:
     Before calling function useGlobals block 2        num1: 94, num2: 50
     Inside function useGlobals                        num1: 10, num2: -5
     After  calling function useGlobals block 2        num1: 94, num2: 50
End of block 2

The following values refer to block 1 of main.


Calling parameters with num1 as the first argument
and num2 as the second argument block 1:
     Before calling function parameters block 1        num1: 20, num2: 13
     Inside function parameters                        num1: 20, num2: 13
     After  calling function parameters block 1        num1: 20, num2: 13

Calling parameters with num2 as the first argument
and num1 as the second argument block 1:
     Before calling function parameters block 1        num1: 20, num2: 13
     Inside function parameters                        num1: 13, num2: 20
     After  calling function parameters block 1        num1: 20, num2: 13

Calling useGlobals with no arguments block 1:
     Before calling function useGlobals block 1        num1: 20, num2: 13
     Inside function useGlobals                        num1: 10, num2: -5
     After  calling function useGlobals block 1        num1: 20, num2: 13
```

LAB 7.5 USING STATIC AND AUTOMATIC VARIABLES

A variable for which memory is allocated at block entry and deallocated at block exit is called an automatic variable. A variable for which memory remains allocated as long as the program executes is called a static variable.

Static variables are declared within a block and are local to that block. Their scope is the same as that of any other local identifier of that block. However, because memory is allocated only once for static variables and not de-allocated at the end of the function like automatic variables, the value of static variables remains with each function call, which prevents other functions from manipulating their values. Static variables are deallocated at the end of `main`.

Objectives

In this lab, you continue using stepwise refinement, and you recognize when to use static variables.

After completing this lab, you will be able to:

- Use static variables.

Estimated completion time: **15–25 minutes**

Using Static and Automatic Variables

In the following exercises, you answer a series of multiple-choice questions. You also continue to design and create the payroll program that you began in Lab 7.1.

Question	Answer (Circle the correct answer)

1. Suppose function changeX has the statements

   ```
   static int x = 2;
    x = x * 2;
   cout << x << endl;
   ```

   If changeX is called three times from **main**, what is displayed?

   a. 4
      8
      16

   b. 4
      4
      4

   c. 16

2. Memory for static variables is allocated for all functions before execution of the **main** function.   **T**   **F**

3a.   In this lab, you continue to use stepwise refinement to revise your payroll program. You will add a counter that is a static variable in your function and displays the employee information to count the number of employees receiving a paycheck. Add column headings to allow for an employee number, add the number of the employee being processed in each employee information data line, and adjust your total line to align correctly.

   Write your design in the following space. Your design should be a list of C++ comments without any code.

3b.   Write a C++ program based on the design you created in Exercise 3a and name it **Payroll4.cpp**. Step through the code by hand.

Use the following memory table to show the change to your displayEmployeeInfo function when the C++ code is executed. (Include line numbers as documentation only. Do not use line numbers when entering your final program.) To fill out the memory table, use one or two lines for each variable. On one line, enter declaration information. Write the name of the declared variable, its data type, and the line number at declaration. On the next line in the memory table, enter test data for that variable. The variable name is entered as an example but may use different line numbers in your design.

displayEmployeeInfo function

Variable Name	Data Type	Value in Memory	Line Number at Declaration	Line Number When Initialized

In the following space, show what is displayed on the screen after executing the output message.

3c.   Enter, compile, link, and execute **Payroll4.cpp**. Then copy the output and save it in a block comment at the end of your program. Save **Payroll4.cpp** in the Chap07 folder of your Student Disk.

The following is a copy of the screen results that might appear after running your program, depending on the data entered.

```
This payroll program calculates an individual employee pay and
company totals using data from a data file payroll.txt.


A payroll report showing payroll information is displayed.

Emp. Employee             Hourly     Hours      Tax       Gross      Net
No.  Name                 Rate       Worked     Rate      Amount     Amount

1    John Smith           10.45      40.00      15.00     418.00     355.30
2    Jane Doe             12.50      45.00      15.00     843.75     717.19
3    Harry Morgan         20.00      40.00      20.00     800.00     640.00
4    Carmen Martinez      25.00      35.00      25.00     875.00     656.25
5    Jacintha Washington  50.85      60.00      35.00     4576.50    2974.72

Totals                                                    7513.25    5343.46
```

LAB 7.6 USING FUNCTION OVERLOADING

In a C++ program, functions can have the same name, but they must have a different set of parameters. The types of parameters determine which function to execute. This is called function overloading. The return type or void is not considered a part of function overloading.

Objectives

In this lab, you use function overloading according to the type of data being processed.

After completing this lab, you will be able to:

- Use function overloading.

Estimated completion time: **15–20 minutes**

Using Function Overloading

In the following exercises, you determine whether statements are true or false. You also design and write a program that uses function overloading.

Question	Answer (Circle the correct answer)
1. C++ function names, like other identifiers, must be unique.	T F
2. In C++, if multiple functions have the same name, then the return type must be different.	T F
3. Function overloading occurs when multiple functions have the same name but different parameter lists.	T F

4a.   Design a program that asks the user to enter a character, a string, an integer, and a float value. The user should be prompted for each data item in a separate function with the name getData and a reference parameter of the type of data item being read. Display the data entered twice, using a different function each time named displayData that have different parameter lists.

Write your design in the following space. Your design should be a list of C++ comments without any code.

4b. Write a C++ program based on the design you created in Exercise 4a and name it **Overload.cpp**. Step through the code by hand.

Use the following memory table to show what occurs in memory when the C++ code is executed. (Include line numbers as documentation only. Do not use line numbers when entering your final program.) To fill out the memory table, use one or two lines for each variable. On one line, enter declaration information. Write the name of the declared variable, its data type, and the line number at declaration. On the next line in the memory table, enter test data for that variable. The variable name is entered as an example but may use different line numbers in your design.

main function

Variable Name	Data Type	Value in Memory	Line Number at Declaration	Line number When Initialized or Changed

getData function

Variable Name	Data Type	Value in Memory	Line Number at Declaration	Line Number When Initialized or Changed

getData function

Variable Name	Data Type	Value in Memory	Line Number at Declaration	Line Number When Initialized or Changed

getData function

Variable Name	Data Type	Value in Memory	Line Number at Declaration	Line Number When Initialized or Changed

getData function

Variable Name	Data Type	Value in Memory	Line Number at Declaration	Line Number When Initialized or Changed

displayData function

Variable Name	Data Type	Value in Memory	Line Number at Declaration	Line number When Initialized or Changed

displayData function

Variable Name	Data Type	Value in Memory	Line Number at Declaration	Line number When Initialized or Changed

In the following space, show what is displayed on the screen after executing the output message.

4c.   Enter, compile, link, and execute **Overload.cpp**. Then copy the output and save it in a block comment at the end of your program. Save **Overload.cpp** in the Chap07 folder of your Student Disk.

The following is a copy of the screen results that might appear after running your program, depending on the data entered. The input entered by the user is shown in bold.

```
Enter a character: x
Enter a word: hello
Enter a whole number: 5
Enter a number with a decimal point: 4.2

You entered the following data:
letter:   x
string:   hello
integer:  5
float:    4.2

Your data displayed again:
integer:  5
float:    4.2
letter:   x
string:   hello
```

LAB 7.7 USING DEFAULT PARAMETERS

When a function is called, the number of actual and formal parameters must be the same except in the case of default parameters. The value of a default parameter is specified when the function name appears for the first time, such as in the prototype.

If a default parameter is not specified, the default value is used for that parameter. The caller has the option of specifying a value other than the default for any default parameter. In the case of multiple parameters, the default parameters must be rightmost.

Objectives

In this lab, you call functions with default parameters.

After completing this lab, you will be able to:

- Call a function with arguments that have default values.

- Call the same function without arguments that have default values.

- Call the same function with some arguments and some missing arguments that use default values.

Estimated completion time: **20–30 minutes**

Using Default Parameters

In the following exercises, you match definitions with C++ terms. You also design and write a program that uses default parameters.

Definition	Vocabulary word	Enter number for match
1. A global variable declared after the definition of a function.	global identifiers	
2. Identifiers that are declared within a function (or block) and are not accessible outside of the function (block).	default parameter	
3. Where in the program an identifier is accessible (visible).	reference parameter	
4. A formal parameter that receives a copy of the content of the corresponding actual parameter.	local identifiers	
5. A formal parameter that receives the location (memory address) of the corresponding actual parameter.	value parameter	
6. Identifiers that are declared outside of every function definition.	external variable	
7. The value defaulted to a parameter when the caller has no matching argument.	scope of an identifier	

8a.   *Critical Thinking Exercise*: A carpet cleaning company estimates cleaning prices assuming a room size of 10 feet by 12 feet at a cost of $39. Rooms smaller than 10 feet by 12 feet are charged at the standard room size. Rooms larger than 10 by 12 feet are charged the standard rate plus $.25 per square foot for each foot greater than the standard room size. Design a program that asks the user for the number of rooms to be cleaned and the size of each room. Calculate the cost of cleaning the rooms. Your function that calculates room areas should use the default values of 10 and 12.

Write your design in the following space. Your design should be a list of C++ comments without any code.

8b.   Write a C++ program based on the design you created in Exercise 8a and name it **Cleaning.cpp**. Step through the code by hand.

Use the following memory table to show what occurs in memory when the C++ code is executed. (Include line numbers as documentation only. Do not use line numbers when entering your final program.) To fill out the memory table, use one or two lines for each variable. On one line, enter declaration information. Write the name of the declared variable, its data type, and the line number at declaration. On the next line in the memory table, enter test data for that variable. The variable name is entered as an example but may use different line numbers in your design.

main function

Variable Name	Data Type	Value in Memory	Line Number at Declaration	Line Number When Initialized or Changed

getNumber function

Variable Name	Data Type	Value in Memory	Line Number at Declaration	Line Number When Initialized or Changed

getSize function

Variable Name	Data Type	Value in Memory	Line Number at Declaration	Line Number When Initialized or Changed

calcCost function

Variable Name	Data Type	Value in Memory	Line Number at Declaration	Line Number When Initialized or Changed

displayCost function

Variable Name	Data Type	Value in Memory	Line Number at Declaration	Line Number When Initialized or Changed

In the following space, show what is displayed on the screen after executing the output message.

8c.   Enter, compile, link, and execute **Cleaning.cpp**. Then copy the output and save it in a block comment at the end of your program. Save **Cleaning.cpp** in the Chap07 folder of your Student Disk.

The following is a copy of the screen results that might appear after running your program, depending on the data entered. The input entered by the user is shown in bold.

```
Enter the number of rooms to be cleaned: 3

Enter the width and length of room 1: 8 10
The cost to clean room 1: $39

Enter the width and length of room 2: 10 12
The cost to clean room 2: $39

Enter the width and length of room 3: 14 16
The cost to clean room 3: $65

The total cost of cleaning 3 room(s): $143
```

User-Defined Simple Data Types, Namespaces, and the `string` Type

CHAPTER 8: ASSIGNMENT COVER SHEET

Name _____   Date _____

Section _____

Lab Assignments	Assigned	Grade
Lab 8.1 Creating and Manipulating Enumerated Data Types (Critical Thinking Exercises)		
Lab 8.2 Using the `typedef` Statement		
Lab 8.3 Using the `namespace` Mechanism		
Lab 8.4 Using the `string` Data Type and Various `string` Functions to Manipulate Strings		
Lab 8.5 Challenge Programming Using `string` Manipulations (Critical Thinking Exercises)		
Total Grade		

See your instructor or the introduction to this book for instructions on submitting your assignments.

LAB 8.1 CREATING AND MANIPULATING ENUMERATED DATA TYPES

The enumeration data type is an ordered set of distinct values defined by the user. Specifying your own data type allows you to determine what values of that type are allowed. In C++, the values specified must be identifiers, or enumerators, and are constants, not variables.

Values can be assigned to the constants at definition, but they must be ordered. The default value of enumerators starts with the assigned value of the first identifier as 0 (zero) and the second value is 1, etc. Within the same block, the same value (identifier) cannot be assigned to more than one enumerated type.

Although C++ does not allow arithmetic operations directly on the enumeration type, you can use type casting to perform arithmetic operations. Because enumerators are ordered, relational operators are allowed. However, the enumeration type cannot be input or output directly. Output of the enumeration type results in the value assigned to the enumerator being displayed.

The enumeration type can be value and reference parameters to functions as well as return types. When used as value or reference parameters, the formal parameter must be an integer data type. The enumeration type that is defined without a type name, called anonymous, cannot be a function parameter.

Objectives

In this lab, you define your own enumeration type and write a program using that type.

After completing this lab, you will be able to:

- Define your own enumeration type.
- Use the `static_cast` operator to increment and decrement an enumeration type.
- Use the enumeration type in a `for` loop.
- Use the enumeration type in a `switch` statement.

Estimated completion time: **60–75 minutes**

Creating and Manipulating Enumerated Data Types

In the following exercises, you determine whether statements are true or false. You also design and create a baseball scoring program.

Question	Answer (Circle the correct answer)
1. When using the enumerated type, you can directly enter the value as input.	T F
2. When using the enumerated type as output, the name of the enumerated value is displayed.	T F
3. You use the same syntax to declare variables of an enumerated type as you do to declare variables of standard data types.	T F
4. You can assign integer values to enumerated data types.	T F
5. You can assign enumerated data values to integer data types.	T F
6. You may use the increment and decrement operations on enumeration types.	T F
7. You can use the cast operator to perform arithmetic operations on enumeration types.	T F

8a. In this exercise, you design a baseball scoreboard program. In your program, prompt the user to enter whether a batter makes a hit, an out, or a walk when the batter is up to bat. Display the batter's name and the at bat result. Allowing for nine batters, use the enumeration type for the batting order with the last names of the batters as the constant enumerated types and begin initialization of their values with the value 1. Your looping control structure must use the enumeration type for initialization, comparison, and incrementation.

After all data has been entered, the program displays the complete selection. Include comments to identify the program author, to describe the program, and to describe program statements. Additionally, remember to include all preprocessor directives that you need.

Write your design in the following space. Your design should be a list of C++ comments without any code.

8b.   Write a C++ program based on the design you created in Exercise 8a, and name it **BaseBall.cpp**. Step through the code by hand.

In the following space, show what is displayed on the screen after executing the output message.

8c.   Enter, compile, link, and execute **BaseBall.cpp**. Then copy the output and save it in a block comment at the end of your program. Save **BaseBall.cpp** in the Chap08 folder of your Student Disk.

The following is a copy of the screen results that might appear after running your program, depending on the data entered. The input entered by the user is shown in bold.

```
This program is a baseball scoreboard program.
When prompted, enter a (h)it, (o)ut, or (w)alk next to the batter number.
Then the batter's name and the at bat result are displayed.

Enter (h)it, (o)ut, or (w)alk for batter 1: w
Scholl had a walk
Enter (h)it, (o)ut, or (w)alk for batter 2: o
Garza had a out
Enter (h)it, (o)ut, or (w)alk for batter 3: g
Invalid entry, please re-enter
Enter (h)it, (o)ut, or (w)alk for batter 3: h
Soso had a hit
```

```
Enter (h)it, (o)ut, or (w)alk for batter 4: h
Malik had a hit
Enter (h)it, (o)ut, or (w)alk for batter 5: h
Smith had a hit
Enter (h)it, (o)ut, or (w)alk for batter 6: w
Anderson had a walk
Enter (h)it, (o)ut, or (w)alk for batter 7: o
Ryan had a out
Enter (h)it, (o)ut, or (w)alk for batter 8: h
Ruiz had a hit
Enter (h)it, (o)ut, or (w)alk for batter 9: o
Clyde had a out
```

9a.   *Critical Thinking Exercise:* Expand your design for your baseball scoring program to keep score. After three outs, the program should stop. You must restart the batting order if all players come to bat without three outs occurring.

Write your design in the following space. Your design should be a list of C++ comments without any code.

9b. Write a C++ program based on the design you created in Exercise 9a and name it **BaseBall2.cpp**. Step through the code by hand.

In the following space, show what is displayed on the screen after executing the output message.

9c.   Enter, compile, link, and execute **BaseBall2.cpp**. Then copy the output and save it in a block comment at the end of your program. Save **BaseBall2.cpp** in the Chap08 folder of your Student Disk.

The following is a copy of the screen results that might appear after running your program, depending on the data entered. The input entered by the user is shown in bold.

```
This program is a baseball scoreboard program.
When prompted, enter a (h)it, (o)ut, or (w)alk next to the batter number.
Then the batter's name and the at bat result are displayed.

Enter (h)it, (o)ut, or (w)alk for batter 1: h
Scholl had a hit
```

```
Enter (h)it, (o)ut, or (w)alk for batter 2: h
Garza had a hit
Enter (h)it, (o)ut, or (w)alk for batter 3: h
Soso had a hit
Enter (h)it, (o)ut, or (w)alk for batter 4: w
Malik had a walk
Enter (h)it, (o)ut, or (w)alk for batter 5: w
Smith had a walk
Enter (h)it, (o)ut, or (w)alk for batter 6: w
Anderson had a walk
Enter (h)it, (o)ut, or (w)alk for batter 7: h
Ryan had a hit
Enter (h)it, (o)ut, or (w)alk for batter 8: o
Ruiz had a out
Enter (h)it, (o)ut, or (w)alk for batter 9: o
Clyde had a out
Enter (h)it, (o)ut, or (w)alk for batter 1: h
Scholl had a hit
Enter (h)it, (o)ut, or (w)alk for batter 2: w
Garza had a walk
Enter (h)it, (o)ut, or (w)alk for batter 3: o
Soso had a out

There have been 3 outs, 5 hits, and 4 walks
```

LAB 8.2 USING THE TYPEDEF STATEMENT

In C++, the `typedef` creates an alias to an existing data type. It does not create a new data type. When you change your program from one computer to another, the data types can have different sizes. If you are writing code for different machines, it can be difficult to use the default sizes. You can write directives at the beginning of the code to define the `typedef`. It is easier to change only the beginning `typedef` to use the data type than to change the entire program.

Objectives

In this lab, you use `typedef` statements to redefine data types of a particular size.

After completing this lab, you will be able to:

■ Write `typedef` statements for integer declarations for byte sizes 1, 2, and 4.

Estimated completion time: **30–40 minutes**

Using the `typedef` Statement

In the following exercises, you determine whether statements are true or false. You also design and create a program that finds the size of data types on your computer. Recall that `typedef` statements are statements that redefine existing data types. Therefore, you might need to find out the size of different data types before writing a program using `typedef` statements to define integer types with the byte sizes of 1, 2, and 4.

Question	Answer (Circle the correct answer)
1. The `typedef` statement does not create any new data type; it creates only an alias to an existing data type.	T F
2. The following statement creates an alias, Boolean, for the data type int: `typedef int Boolean;`	T F
3. The `typedef` statement allows you to create new data types.	T F

4a.   Design a program that uses the sizeof operator to find the size of `char`, `short`, `int`, and `long` on your computer. Display your results.

Write your design in the following space. Your design should be a list of C++ comments without any code.

4b.   Write a C++ program based on the design you created in Lab 8.2, Exercise 4a and name it **sizeOf.cpp**. Step through the code by hand.

In the following space, show what is displayed on the screen after executing the output message.

4c.   Enter, compile, link, and execute **sizeOf.cpp**. Then copy the output and save it in a block comment at the end of your program. Save **sizeOf.cpp** in the Chap08 folder of your Student Disk.

The following is a copy of the screen results that might appear after running your program, depending on your computer.

```
The size of char on this computer is 1
The size of short on this computer is 2
The size of int on this computer is 4
The size of long on this computer is 4
```

5a.   After you run **sizeOf.cpp** and determine the number of bytes used on your computer for the data types `char`, `short`, `int`, and `long`, design a program that uses `typedef` statements to define the following identifiers:

- shortInt with a size of 1 byte

- integer with a size of 2 bytes

- longInt with a size of 4 bytes

Then use the sizeof operator to find the size of shortInt, integer, and longInt. Display your results.

5b.   Write a C++ program based on the design you created in Exercise 5a and name it **sizeOf2.cpp**. Step through the code by hand.

In the following space, show what is displayed on the screen after executing the output message.

5c.   Enter, compile, link, and execute **sizeOf2.cpp**. Then copy the output and save it in a block comment at the end of your program. Save **sizeOf2.cpp** in the Chap08 folder of your Student Disk.

The following is a copy of the screen results that might appear after running your program.

```
The size of shortint on this computer is 1
The size of integer on this computer is 2
The size of longint on this computer is 4
```

LAB 8.3 USING THE NAMESPACE MECHANISM

Some additional features of C++ are available for ANSI/ISO Standard C++ that are not available for Standard C++. When including header files with global identifiers, those global identifiers are recognized in your C++ program. If you define your own global identifiers with the same name as global identifiers in the header files, you receive a syntax error such as "identifier redefined." To avoid this problem, global identifiers from libraries generally start with the underline (_) character, as in _xxx.

ANSI/ISO Standard C++ uses the `namespace` mechanism to solve the problem of overlapping global identifier names.

Objectives

In this lab, you use ANSI/ISO Standard C++ header files. Additionally, you use the predefined `namespace std`, use the scope resolution operator for global identifiers that are part of the header files, and write your own namespace definition.

After completing this lab, you will be able to:

- Use ANSI/ISO Standard C++ header files with the scope resolution operator.

- Define a namespace.

Estimated completion time: **20–30 minutes**

Using the namespace Mechanism

In the following exercises, you determine whether statements are true or false. You also design and create a program that displays a message.

Question	Answer (Circle the correct answer)
1. When a header file is included in a program, the global identifiers for the header file become global identifiers in the program.	T F
2. To avoid overlapping global identifiers, you should make it a practice to name your global identifiers beginning with an underline (_) character.	T F
3. The scope of a namespace member is local to the namespace.	T F
4. You access a namespace member by using the dot operator, for example: `namespace_name.identifier`	T F
5. To simplify the accessing of identifiers in iostream, cmath, and iomanip, use the following statement: `using namespace std;`	T F

6a.   Create the design for a program that displays the message "Hello World" and do not define it using **namespace std**.

Write your design in the following space. Your design should be a list of C++ comments without any code.

6b.   Write a C++ program based on the design you created in Exercise 6a and name it **Hello.cpp**. Step through the code by hand.

In the following space, show what is displayed on the screen after executing the output message.

6c.   Enter, compile, link, and execute **Hello.cpp**. Then copy the output and save it in a block comment at the end of your program. Save **Hello.cpp** in the Chap08 folder of your Student Disk.

The following is a copy of the screen results that might appear after running your program.

```
Hello World
```

7a.   Design a program that declares a namespace named message. The namespace should declare a **string** variable greeting. In your main function, assign "Hello World" to the **string** greeting. Then display the **string** greeting.

7b.   Write a C++ program based on the design you created in Exercise 7a and name it **Hello2.cpp**. Step through the code by hand.

In the following space, show what is displayed on the screen after executing the output message.

7c.   Enter, compile, link, and execute **Hello2.cpp**. Then copy the output and save it in a block comment at the end of your program. Save **Hello2.cpp** in the Chap08 folder of your Student Disk.

The following is a copy of the screen results that might appear after running your program.

```
Hello World
```

LAB 8.4 USING THE STRING DATA TYPE AND THE VARIOUS STRING FUNCTIONS TO MANIPULATE STRINGS

The data type string is a programmer-defined type and it is not part of the C++ language; the C++ standard library supplies it in the header file string. The positions in a string are counted from the beginning of the string starting with zero. With the positions in the string, you can use the array subscript operator [] to access individual characters in the string.

The operator plus (+) is used for concatenation. For example, if str1, str2, and str3 are strings, the statement str3 = str1 + str2; appends str2 to the end of str1 and assigns the new string to str3.

The data type string contains several functions for string manipulation. The following are five string functions:

1. length—returns the number of characters currently in the string

2. size—the same as length, returns the number of characters currently in the string

3. find—searches a string to find the first occurrence of a particular substring and returns the starting position in the string of the substring or it returns the value npos (not a position within the string)

4. substr—returns a particular substring of a string from the position and length specified in the parameter list

5. swap—exchanges the contents of two string variables

Objectives

In this lab, you use ANSI/ISO Standard C++ string header file functions for string manipulations.

After completing this lab, you will be able to:

■ Use the binary operator + to allow the string concatenation operation.

■ Use the length function to find the number of characters currently in the string (same as size).

■ Use the size function to find the number of characters currently in the string (same as length).

■ Use the find function to search a string to find the first occurrence of a particular substring and return the position in the string where the match begins.

■ Use the substr function to search a string, beginning at a specified starting position and returning a substring of a specified length.

■ Use the swap function to interchange the contents of two string variables.

Estimated completion time: **30–40 minutes**

Using the string Data Type and the Various string Functions to Manipulate Strings

In the following exercises, you provide short answers to a series of questions or indicate whether a statement is true or false. You also design and create a program that prompts the user to enter a first name, middle initial, and last name.

Question	**Answer**
	(Circle the correct answer)

1. Write the code needed to concatenate two strings "abc" and "xyz".

2. What do the following C++ statements display?
```
string message = "Hello World";
cout << message[3] << endl;
```

3. What do the following C++ statements display?
```
string message = "Hello World";
cout << message.length() << endl;
```

4. What do the following C++ statements display?
```
string message = "Hello World";
cout << message.substr(6,5);
```

5. What occurs when the following C++ statements are executed?
```
string message = "Hello World";
cout << size() << endl;
```

6. In ANSI standard C++, the data type string requires the   **T**   **F**
iostream header file.

7. The function length returns a value one less than the function   **T**   **F**
size returns because length begins counting with position 0
and size begins counting with position 1.

8a.   Design a program that prompts the user to enter a first name, middle initial, and last name.
With the string, perform and display the results of the following manipulations:

- Concatenate the name so that a new string is created with the full name in the order last
  name, a comma, a space, the first name, a blank, and middle initial. Display the full name.

- Display the length of the full name.

- Display the size of the full name.

- Display the location of the comma in the full name.

- Display the substring within the full name that stops with the comma.

- Swap the first name and the last name and display the result.

Write your design in the following space. Your design should be a list of C++ comments
without any code.

8b. Write a C++ program based on the design you created in Exercise 8a. Step through the code by hand.

In the following space, show what is displayed on the screen after executing the output message.

8c. Enter, compile, link, and execute **Strings.cpp**. Then copy the output and save it in a block comment at the end of your program. Save **Strings.cpp** in the Chap08 folder of your Student Disk.

The following is a copy of the screen results that might appear after running your program, depending on the data entered. The input entered by the user is shown in bold.

```
Enter your first name, middle initial, and last name: Samantha L Jones
The full name is: Jones, Samantha L
The length of the name is: 17
The size of the name is: 17
The comma is in location 5
The last name is: Jones
Now your first name is Jones and your last name is Samantha
```

LAB 8.5 CHALLENGE PROGRAMMING USING STRING MANIPULATIONS

The data type `string` is associated with a data type (`string::size_type`), and a named constant (`string::npos`), which are defined in Table 8-1.

Table 8-1   Data type and named constant for the strings

Data type	Description
`string:: size_type`	An unsigned integer (data) type related to the characters in the `string`
`string::npos`	The maximum value of the (data) type `string::size_type`, a number such as 4294967295 on many machines

Objectives

In this lab, you combine the use of various `string` manipulations, testing when a search is not successful.

After completing this lab, you will be able to:

- Combine various `string` manipulations to solve a problem.

- Test for a successful search of a `string`.

Estimated completion time: **50–60 minutes**

1a.   *Critical Thinking Exercise:* Design a program that prompts the user to enter a sentence. Count the number of vowels in the sentence. Display the length of the sentence and the number of each vowel in the sentence.

Write your design in the following space. Your design should be a list of C++ comments without any code.

1b.   Write a C++ program based on the design you created in Exercise 1a and name it **Vowel.cpp**. Step through the code by hand.

In the following space, show what is displayed on the screen after executing the output message.

1c.   Enter, compile, link, and execute **Vowel.cpp**. Then copy the output and save it in a block comment at the end of your program. Save **Vowel.cpp** in the Chap08 folder of your Student Disk.

The following is a copy of the screen results that might appear after running your program, depending on the data entered. The input entered by the user is shown in bold.

```
Please enter a sentence
The name of the game is to make an A in C++.

The sentence has 44 characters

There are 5 a's, 5 e's, 2 i's, 2 o's, and 0 u's
```

Arrays and Strings

In this chapter, you will:

O Learn about arrays

O Explore how to declare and manipulate data into arrays

O Understand the meaning of "array index out of bounds"

O Become familiar with the restrictions on array processing

O Discover how to pass an array as a parameter to a function

O Learn about C-strings

O Examine the use of string functions to process C-strings

O Discover how to input data into—and output data from—a C-string

O Learn about parallel arrays

O Discover how to manipulate data in a two-dimensional array

O Learn about multidimensional arrays

CHAPTER 9: ASSIGNMENT COVER SHEET

Name _____   Date _____

Section _____

Lab Assignments	Assigned	Grade
Lab 9.1 Declaring and Manipulating Data into Arrays		
Lab 9.2 Checking Index Bounds and Initializing Arrays (Critical Thinking Exercises)		
Lab 9.3 Passing Arrays as Parameters to Functions (Critical Thinking Exercises)		
Lab 9.4 Coding with C-strings		
Lab 9.5 Inputting and Outputting Data Using C-strings		
Lab 9.6 Coding with Parallel Arrays		
Lab 9.7 Manipulating Data in a Two-Dimensional Array (Critical Thinking Exercise)		
Lab 9.8 Using a Multidimensional Array (Critical Thinking Exercises)		
Total Grade		

See your instructor or the introduction to this book for instructions on submitting your assignments.

LAB 9.1 DECLARING AND MANIPULATING DATA INTO ARRAYS

Structured data types are collections of other data types. Simple data types are the building blocks of structured data types. An array is a structured data type that is a collection of a fixed number of components wherein all of the components are arranged in a list. Arrays are declared using square brackets with the number of components shown inside the brackets, as in `int num[5]`. To access a component of the array, you also use the square bracket with an integer inside the brackets indicating the position from the beginning of the array. The size at declaration should not be confused with the position from the beginning of the array.

To access a component of the array, you also use an expression that evaluates to a non-negative integer that appears inside the brackets and indicates the position from the beginning of the array. Do not confuse the size at declaration with the position from the beginning of the array. Additionally, the size of the array does not need to be specified at compile time.

Working with arrays almost always requires iteration. Like all variables, an array and its size must be declared when the program is compiled. An individual array component is treated the same as any individual variable. Operations are the same for individual components as an operation on any variable.

For example, the following code would assign the fourth variable of an array to the variable `num`:

```cpp
int array[5] = {5, 8, 9, 6, 4};
int num;
num = array[3];
```

Objectives

In this lab, you process individual array components. Given the program design, write the code for the design given.

After completing this lab, you will be able to:

- Declare arrays and process each array element individually.

> Estimated completion time: **40–50 minutes**

Declaring and Manipulating Data into Arrays

In the following exercises, enter or select the correct answer for each question. Then provide the array-processing code missing from a C++ program.

Question	Answer (Enter or circle the correct answer)
1. How many components are contained in the following array declarations? `double values [14];`	a. 14 b. 15
2. Write a `for` loop that sums the numbers in an array with five components.	
3. An array _____.	a. is a simple data type b. is a structured data type
4. Simple data types are building blocks for arrays.	T F
5. An array index starts at 1.	T F
6. In C++, array is a reserved word.	T F

7. The following code allows the size of an array to be   T   F
determined at execution:

```
int n;
cout << "Enter the size of the array: ";
cin >> n;
int array[n];
```

8a.   The following C++ program is missing the code, which is designed for array processing. In this exercise, you write a program from a design that prompts a user to enter 10 numbers. This program reads the numbers into an array, finds the smallest number in the list, the largest number in the list, the sum of the 10 numbers, and the average of the 10 numbers. Using the comments, add the missing code.

// Enter your name as a comment for program identification

// Program assignment List.cpp

// Enter your class section, and time

/* The program List.cpp prompts the user for 10 numbers. */

/* The numbers are input into an array. Then the

smallest, largest, and average of the numbers in the

list are found. */

// The user inputs 10 values.

/* The largest, smallest, and average of the number is

displayed. */

//header files

// use the correct preprocessor directives for input/output

// function prototypes

/* The function instruct describes the use

and purpose of the program. */

/* The function getNumber reads in a value

one at a time. */

/* The function findLargest returns the

largest of two numbers. */

/* The function findSmallest returns the

smallest of two numbers. */

/* The function display reports the

largest, smallest, and average of the

numbers in the list. */

// main function

    // declare variables

    /* an integer variable smallest initialized
       to INT_MAX to hold the smallest number in
       the list, an integer variable largest
       initialized to INT_MIN to hold the largest
       number in the list, an integer array number
       to hold the 10 values in a list, an integer
       variable sum to sum all the numbers, an
       integer variable count initialized to 0 to
       count the values in the list, a double variable
       average to hold the average of the numbers */

    // call the function instruct

    // loop for all values in the list

       /* assign to an array element the value
          returned from getNumber */

       /* assign to largest the value returned
          from findLargest that has arguments largest
          and the current array element */

       /* assign to smallest the value returned
          from findSmallest that has arguments
          smallest and the current array element */

       /* increment sum by the current array element */

    // display a message identifying the values
    // write a for loop to display the array of numbers

    // calculate the average
    // call the display function to display the results

/* The function instruct describes the use
and purpose of the program. */

/* The function getNumber reads in a value
one at a time. */
  /* declare an integer variable value
   to read in each array component */
  // read in data value
  // return data value

/* The function findLargest returns the
largest of two numbers. */
  // test for largest value
  // return largest value

/* The function findSmallest returns the
smallest of two numbers. */
  // test for smallest value
  // return smallest value

/* The function display reports the
smallest, largest, sum, and average of the
numbers in the list. */
// display the smallest, largest, sum, and average

8b. In the following space, show what is displayed on the screen after executing the output message.

8c. Enter, compile, link, and execute **List.cpp**. Then copy the output and save it in a block comment at the end of your program. Save **List.cpp** in the Chap09 folder of your Student Disk.

The following is a copy of the screen results that might appear after running your program, depending on the data entered. The input entered by the user is shown in bold.

```
This program asks the user to enter 10 numbers, each separated by a space.
The program will find the smallest, largest, sum, and average of the numbers.

Enter your list of numbers: 10 5 3 -5 9 14 -8 0 2 -6

Your array has these values:
10 5 3 -5 9 14 -8 0 2 -6

From your list of 10 numbers:
        smallest: -8
        largest:  14
        sum:      24
        average:  2.4
```

LAB 9.2 CHECKING INDEX BOUNDS AND INITIALIZING ARRAYS

An array can be initialized at declaration by placing the values between braces separated by commas. If the size of the array is not indicated at declaration, it defaults to the number of values in the initialization block. If partial initialization of an array occurs at declaration, the size of the array must be indicated and all remaining values are initialized to 0.

For example, an array with no initialization is defined as follows:

```
dataType[size] arrayName;
```

An array with initialization can be defined as follows:

```
dataType[] arrayName = {value1, value2, value3, …, valuen};
dataType[5] arrayName = { value1, value2, value3, value4, value5};
dataType[5] arrayName = {0};
```

The C++ compiler does not check whether an array index is out of bounds. The programmer must do this. Because the index position starts counting with the number 0, there is no array position that is the same number as the size of the array.

Arrays do not accept aggregate operations. Operations must be done one component at a time, called component wise in programming. To copy the values of one array into another, you would need to copy each value.

```
for (int index = 0; index < 5; index++)
            arrayA[index] = arrayB[index];
```

Objectives

In this lab, you check to see that an index value is in bounds, and initialize an array at declaration.

After completing this lab, you will be able to:

- Check for an array index that is out of bounds.

- Initialize arrays at declaration.

- Process data in an array.

Estimated completion time: **60–75 minutes**

Checking Index Bounds and Initializing Arrays

In the following exercises, select the correct answer for each question. Then design and write a program that checks index bounds and initializes arrays.

Question	Answer (Circle the correct answer)
1. How many components are contained in the following array declarations? `double values [14];`	a. 14 b. 15

2. The following statements assign 5 to the last value in the array.
 	
`int array [10];`
`array [10] = 5;`
	T F

3. Given:

```
int array[5] =  { 1, 2, 3};
```

What are the values of each array component?

4. The following code initializes each component to 0:   **T**   **F**

```
int array[3];
array[3] = {0};
```

5. The following code initializes each component to 0:   **T**   **F**

```
int array[3] = {0};
```

6. The following code correctly initializes each component to 0:   **T**   **F**

```
int array[3];
for (int count = 0; count <= 3; count++)
    array[count] = 0;
```

7. The following code initializes each component to 0:   **T**   **F**

```
int array[3];
for (int count = 1; count <= 3; count++)
    array[count] = 0;
```

8a.   *Critical Thinking Exercise:* Design a program for a trucking company that has seven trucks in its fleet. Each truck is identified by a number from one to seven and has a maximum weight allowance, which has already been determined. Assign the maximum weight limit to each truck at initialization. Before a truck can begin its route, it must be weighed to see if it falls within its weight allowance. Ask the user for the truck number and the loaded weight. Display a message indicating whether the truck falls in the allowable weight limit. Use the following values as maximum weight limits and enter the weigh-in values for each truck:

Truck Number	Maximum Weight Limit (in lbs)	Truck Weigh-In (in lbs)
1	50,000	45,000
2	25,000	30,000
3	20,000	20,000
4	35,000	30,000
5	40,000	35,000
6	25,000	27,000
7	30,000	20,000

Write your design in the following space. Your design should be a list of C++ comments without any code.

8b.   Write a C++ program based on the design you created in Exercise 8a and name it **Trucks.cpp**. Step through the code by hand.

In the following space, show what is displayed on the screen after executing the output message.

8c.   Enter, compile, link, and execute **Trucks.cpp**. Then copy the output and save it in a block comment at the end of your program. Save **Trucks.cpp** in the Chap09 folder of your Student Disk.

The following is a copy of the screen results that might appear after running your program, depending on the data entered. The input entered by the user is shown in bold.

```
This program asks the user for the truck number
and the weigh-in value for each truck in a fleet.

The weigh-in value is compared to the established maximum weight limit.
A message is displayed to tell the user whether the truck is within weight
limits.


Please enter the truck number and weight: 1 45000
Your truck is ready to roll.

Please enter the truck number and weight: 2 30000
You have exceeded your allowable weight allowance.

Please enter the truck number and weight: 3 20000
Your truck is ready to roll.

Please enter the truck number and weight: 0 40000
Your entered an invalid truck number or weight.

Please enter the truck number and weight: 4 33000
Your truck is ready to roll.

Please enter the truck number and weight: 5 41000
You have exceeded your allowable weight allowance.
```

```
Please enter the truck number and weight: 6 18000
Your truck is ready to roll.

Please enter the truck number and weight: 7 28000
Your truck is ready to roll.

All trucks have weighed-in.
```

9a.   Design a program for a shoe distribution company that has five salespersons. Each salesperson has an ID number of one to five. An array is used to accumulate total sales for each salesperson. Sales can be entered multiple times for multiple sales by each salesperson. The user enters −1 to complete the input step. After all the input has been entered, a table is printed with each salesperson's ID in the first row and the total sales in the second row.

Write your design in the following space. Your design should be a list of C++ comments without any code.

9b. Write a C++ program based on the design you created in Exercise 9a and name it **Sales.cpp**. Step through the code by hand.

In the following space, show what is displayed on the screen after executing the output message.

9c. Enter, compile, link, and execute **Sales.cpp**. Then copy the output and save it in a block comment at the end of your program. Save **Sales.cpp** in the Chap09 folder of your Student Disk.

The following is a copy of the screen results that might appear after running your program, depending on the data entered. The input entered by the user is shown in bold.

```
Five salespersons work for the Comfort Shoe Company.
The sales for each salesperson are called in to the company to be entered.
```

The salesperson's ID (a number one through five) is entered first.

```
If a valid ID is entered, the amount of sale is then entered.
Multiple sales for the same salesperson can be entered,
but each time the ID must also be entered.
Enter -1 to end the program.

Enter sales ID number: 1
Enter sales amount: 1000
Enter sales ID number: 2
Enter sales amount: 2000
Enter sales ID number: 3
Enter sales amount: 3000
Enter sales ID number: 9
Invalid ID entered.
Enter sales ID number: 4
Enter sales amount: 350
Enter sales ID number: 5
Enter sales amount: -700
```

```
Invalid amount entered.
Enter sales amount: 120
Enter sales ID number: 1
Enter sales amount: 300
Enter sales ID number: 2
Enter sales amount: 800
Enter sales ID number: -1

The sales total for each of the salespersons is:
        1         2         3         4         5
   1300.00   2800.00   3000.00    350.00    120.00
```

LAB 9.3 PASSING ARRAYS AS PARAMETERS TO FUNCTIONS

Function parameters and arguments are not limited to individual array components; they can also be entire arrays. When an entire array is passed, it is passed by reference. You do not use the address of "&" operator. Because arrays are passed by reference, use the reserved word const in the declaration of the formal parameter to prevent the function from changing the actual parameters.

The name used to identify the array is a reference to the array. Used by itself, it is the memory address of the first component of the array. In other words, the value contained in the reference of the array is the memory address of the first component of the array. When you pass an array as a parameter, the base address of the actual array is passed to the formal parameter. Although you may pass an entire array, functions cannot return a value of the type array. You can use any integral type as an array index. The size of an array must be defined with a constant or constant expression. The size must be declared before the array is declared and cannot be initialized interactively.

Objectives

In this lab, you initialize an array at declaration, use an array as arguments to a function, and use a constant array as a formal parameter.

After completing this lab, you will be able to:

- Partially initialize an array at declaration.

- Use arrays as actual arguments to functions.

- Use constant arrays as formal parameters.

> Estimated completion time: **50–60 minutes**

Passing Arrays as Parameters to Functions

In the following exercises, select the correct answer for each question. Then design and write a program that passes arrays as parameters to functions.

Question	Answer (Circle the correct answer)
1. Given the prototype: `void function(int array[5]);` The formal parameter is an array of five elements.	T F
2. When passing an array to a function, the size of the array is automatically passed.	T F

3. Given the declaration:
`int array[5];`
and the prototype:
`void function(int []);`
Which code calls a function with array as the argument?
	a. `function (array);`
	b. `function (array[]);`
	c. `function (array[5]);`

4. Which prototype for a function reads in an integer array and returns the array to the calling function?

   a. `int function();`

   b. `int[] function();`

   c. `void function(int array[]);`

   d. `void function(int &array[]);`

5a.   *Critical Thinking Exercise:* Design a program that prompts the user for a word, and then prompts the user for a letter. Your program should count the number of times the letters entered appear in the word, and then continue prompting for new letters. The program should list the letters found. *Hint*: Declare a Boolean array of size 26 to track whether a letter has been found.

Write your design in the following space. Your design should be a list of C++ comments without any code.

5b.   Write a C++ program based on the design you created in Exercise 5a and name it **HangMan.cpp**. Step through the code by hand.

In the following space, show what is displayed on the screen after executing the output message.

5c.   Enter, compile, link, and execute **HangMan.cpp**. Then copy the output and save it in a block comment at the end of your program. Save **HangMan.cpp** in the Chap09 folder of your Student Disk.

The following is a copy of the screen results that might appear after running your program, depending on the data entered. The input entered by the user is shown in bold.

```
Please enter a word: howdy
The word contains 5 characters.

What letter would you like to guess? (Enter zero to quit.) a
There are 0 a's.
What letter would you like to guess? (Enter zero to quit.) e
There are 0 e's.
What letter would you like to guess? (Enter zero to quit.) d
There are 1 d's.
```

```
What letter would you like to guess? (Enter zero to quit.) o
There are 1 o's.
What letter would you like to guess? (Enter zero to quit.) y
There are 1 y's.
What letter would you like to guess? (Enter zero to quit.) b
There are 0 b's.
What letter would you like to guess? (Enter zero to quit.) 0
You found these letters
d       o       y
```

LAB 9.4 CODING WITH C-STRINGS

A character array is an array whose components are of the type char. A string is a sequence of zero or more characters enclosed in double quotation marks. In C++, C-strings (or strings) are always terminated with the null character. A character array may or may not end with a null character.

Most rules that apply to other arrays also apply to character arrays. C++ provides a set of functions that can be used for string manipulation. The header file cstring describes these functions. The function `strcpy(s1, s2)` copies string s2 into string variable s1. The function `strcmp(s1,s2)` returns a value < 0 if s1 is less than s2, 0 if s1 and s2 are the same, and a value >0 if s1 is greater than s2. The function `strlen(s)` returns the length of the string s, excluding the null character.

Objectives

In this lab, you use char arrays that end with the null terminator. You also use the string function `strlen` to determine the length of the string contained in the char array.

After completing this lab, you will be able to:

- Use char arrays that end with the null terminator.

- Use the string function `strlen`.

Estimated completion time: **40–50 minutes**

Coding with C-strings

In the following exercises, enter the correct answer for each question. Then redesign a program you already wrote to use the cstring class instead of the string class.

Question

Answer
(Enter the correct answer)

1. The null character is represented as:

2. How many bytes does it take to represent the character 'A'?

3. How many bytes does it take to represent the cstring "A"?

4. How many characters are in the string

   "Hello World"?

5. How many characters are in the array str1?
   ```
   char str1[] = "Hello";
   ```

6. Given the following:
   ```
   char str1[] = "Hello";
   char str2[] = "Hello";
   cout << strcmp(str1, str2) << endl/
   ```
   What is displayed?

7. Given the following:
   ```
   char greeting[15];
   ```
   What occurs with the following code?
   ```
   greeting = "Hello World";
   ```

8a.   Redesign your **HangMan.cpp** program to omit the use of the string class. Instead, use the cstring class.

Write your design in the following space. Your design should be a list of C++ comments without any code.

8b. Write a C++ program based on the design you created in Exercise 8a and name it **HangMan2.cpp**. Step through the code by hand.

In the following space, show what is displayed on the screen after executing the output message.

8c. Enter, compile, link, and execute **HangMan2.cpp**. Then copy the output and save it in a block comment at the end of your program. Save **HangMan2.cpp** in the Chap09 folder of your Student Disk. Compare the output of HangMan2 to the output of HangMan.

The following is a copy of the screen results that might appear after running your program, depending on the data entered. The input entered by the user is shown in bold.

```
Please enter a word: howdy
The word contains 5 characters.

What letter would you like to guess? (Enter zero to quit.) a
There are 0 a's.
What letter would you like to guess? (Enter zero to quit.) e
There are 0 e's.
What letter would you like to guess? (Enter zero to quit.) d
There are 1 d's.
What letter would you like to guess? (Enter zero to quit.) o
There are 1 o's.
What letter would you like to guess? (Enter zero to quit.) y
There are 1 y's.
What letter would you like to guess? (Enter zero to quit.) b
There are 0 b's.
What letter would you like to guess? (Enter zero to quit.) 0
You found these letters
d        o        y
```

LAB 9.5 INPUTTING AND OUTPUTTING DATA USING C-STRINGS

Aggregate operations such as assignment and comparison are not allowed on arrays. However, the one place where C++ allows aggregate operations on arrays is the input and output of strings (that is, character arrays). However, because there is no check on array index bounds, strings longer than the declared array size store the entire string, extending into and corrupting adjacent memory cells if necessary.

Strings containing blanks cannot be read in using the extraction operator (>>). To read in a string with blanks, and to limit the number of characters read into the string, use the function `cin.get`(str,m+1) where str is the name of the character array or string and m+1 is the length of the string. Input stops either at the indicated length or when the newline character is found. If the string is shorter than the length specified, the newline character needs to be discarded. However, if the length is longer than the length specified, the remainder of the string remains in the buffer.

C++ allows an aggregate operation for output until the null character is found. Additionally, C++ allows the name of a file to be entered at execution. However, the string type does not contain the null terminator. In the string header file in ANSI/ISO Standard C++, the function `c_str()` converts the type string to a null-terminated character array.

Objectives

In this lab, you use the `cin.get` function to input strings of a specified length, specify file names at execution time, and use the string type as the data type for a variable file name.

After completing this lab, you will be able to:

- Use the `cin.get()` function to input strings of a specified length.

- Specify the name of a file at execution time.

- Use the string type as the data type for a variable file name.

Estimated completion time: **40–50 minutes**

Inputting and Outputting Data Using C-strings

In the following exercises, enter or select the correct answer for each question. Then design and write a program that prompts the user to enter names and output the names to a file.

Question	Answer (Enter or circle the correct answer)

1. Given:
   ```
   char name[20];
   cin >> name;
   ```
   What does name contain if the user enters "George Washington"?

2. Using the code in Question 1, what value is returned from the following?
   ```
   cout << strlen(name) << endl;
   ```
       a. 6

       b. 20

       c. 17

       d. 18

3. Aggregate operations are allowed on strings for input and output.　　　**T**　　　**F**

4. Given:

```
char name[5] = {'H', 'e', 'l', 'l', 'o'};
cout << name << endl;
```

What is output?

    a. Hello

    b. Hello???????...???

5. Given:

```
int name[5];
cout << "Enter a name: ";
cin >> name;
```

If the user enters "Washington", what occurs?

6. To avoid corrupting adjacent memory cells when reading in a string, use the `cin.get` function with a maximum length to be read.　　　　**T**　　**F**

7. The `cin.get` function reads in input and clears the buffer after the read.　　　　**T**　　**F**

8a.   Design a program that prompts the user to enter names and output the names to a file. The lengths of the strings to be output are limited to 20 characters. When the name is greater than 20 characters, the output file will be multiple lines. The user should enter the string "stop" to quit. The filename should be declared as a string and entered by the user.

    Write your design in the following space. Your design should be a list of C++ comments without any code.

8b. Write a C++ program based on the design you created in Exercise 8a and name it
     Names.cpp. Step through the code by hand.

     In the following space, show what is written to the output file.

8c. Enter, compile, link, and execute **Names.cpp**. Save **Names.cpp** in the Chap09 folder of your
     Student Disk. Print your output file and submit it with your program.

The following is a copy of the screen results that might appear after running your program, depending on the data entered. The input entered by the user is shown in bold.

```
Enter the name of the output file to be created: (Do not use spaces.)
names.txt

Enter a list of names to create a file. Enter stop to end the list.
George Washington Carver
Thomas Alva Edison
Dwight David Eisenhower
John Quincy Adams
stop
```

Following is the output of names.txt. Because the character arrays are limited to 20 characters, some names require more than one line.

```
George Washington C
arver
Thomas Alva Edison
Dwight David Eisenh
ower
John Quincy Adams
```

LAB 9.6 CODING WITH PARALLEL ARRAYS

Parallel arrays are two or more arrays whose corresponding components hold related information. If you need to keep track of multiple items that are related, you can create more than one array where the information is related by the placement within the arrays.

Objectives

In this lab, you process parallel arrays.

After completing this lab, you will be able to:

■ Process parallel arrays.

Estimated completion time: **50–60 minutes**

Coding with Parallel Arrays

In the following exercises, select the correct answer for each question. Then design and write a program that uses parallel arrays.

Question	Answer (Circle the correct answer)	
1. Parallel arrays can be different data types.	T	F
2. Parallel arrays can be different sizes.	T	F

3a.   Create the design for a program that keeps track of the hits, walks, and outs of a baseball team. Use parallel arrays to keep track of each player's statistics. The player number is the index of the array. Read the **PlayBall.txt** file, which contains data that includes the player number, hits, walks, and outs. The data file will contain multiple games. Not every player will have stats in each game. The arrays should be initialized to zero (0) and should be accumulators to allow for stats for each game of the season.

Write your design in the following space. Your design should be a list of C++ comments without any code.

3b.   Write a C++ program based on the design you created in Exercise 3a and name it **PlayBall.cpp**. Step through the code by hand.

In the following space, show what is displayed on the screen after executing the output message.

3c.   Enter, compile, link, and execute **PlayBall.cpp**. Then copy the output and save it in a block comment at the end of your program. Save **PlayBall.cpp** in the Chap09 folder of your Student Disk.

The following is a copy of the screen results that might appear after running your program, depending on the data entered.

```
This program keeps track of the hits, walks, and outs of a baseball team.

Player  Hits    Walks   Outs

1       4       4       4
2       3       12      15
3       6       8       10
4       5       5       8
5       2       2       2
6       6       0       0
7       0       0       6
8       6       10      2
9       6       4       2
10      6       6       6
11      14      2       2
12      0       0       0
13      8       1       3
14      2       4       6
15      0       0       0
16      0       0       0
17      4       2       6
18      9       8       1
19      3       2       1
20      0       10      14
```

Lab 9.7 Manipulating Data in a Two-Dimensional Array

Sometimes data is provided in a table form called a two-dimensional array, a collection of a fixed number of components arranged in rows and columns, in which all components are of the same type. To access the components of a two-dimensional array, you need a pair of indices—one for the row position and one for the column position. However, two-dimensional arrays are stored in row order in memory.

You can initialize two-dimensional arrays at declaration. Use braces for the initialization values. You can use additional braces separated by commas to subdivide each row for initialization.

You also can use enumeration types to enhance readability. However, be sure to use the default starting value of zero (0) for the enumerated value.

Objectives

In this lab, you become acquainted with the two-dimensional array, including processing by row and column, initializing at declaration, printing, inputting, summing by column, and finding the largest element in a column.

After completing this lab, you will be able to:

- Search the first column of a two-dimensional array for a particular value.

- Use the second column of a two-dimensional array to hold data that is related to the first column.

- Initialize a two-dimensional array to zero (0) at declaration.

- Process a two-dimensional array by row.

- Process column elements of a two-dimensional array.

- Print all elements of a two-dimensional array.

- Pass a two-dimensional array to a function.

- Input values into a column of a two-dimensional array.

- Sum the values of a column of a two-dimensional array.

- Find the largest element in a column of a two-dimensional array.

Estimated completion time: **50–60 minutes**

Manipulating Data in a Two-Dimensional Array

In the following exercises, select the correct answer for each question. Then redesign a program to use two-dimensional arrays.

Question	Answer (Enter or circle the correct answer)	
1. In a two-dimensional array, the actual parameter and the formal parameter must have the same number of columns.	T	F
2. Two-dimensional arrays are stored in column order in memory.	T	F

3. Given:

```
int stats[25][3];
```

How many components are in the array stats?

4. Given:

```
int stats[2][3] = {4, 4, 4, 3, 12, 15};
int totalHits = 0;
for (int row = 0; row < 2; row++)
     totalHits += stats[row][0];
```

What is the value of totalHits?

5. Given:

```
int stats[2][3] = {4, 4, 4, 3, 12, 15};
int atBats[2] = {0};
for (int row = 0; row < 2; row++)
{
     for (int column = 0; column < 3; column++)
         atBats[row] += stats[row][column];
cout << "Player " << row + 1
       << " was up to bat " << atBats[row]
       << " times.\n";
}
```

What is output?

6a.   Redesign your **PlayBall.cpp** program to use a two-dimensional array instead of parallel arrays. Add an additional column that keeps track of the number of times a player was up to bat. When printing the report, add a totals line that totals the number of hits, walks, and outs for the team. Find the player(s) with the greatest number of hits, the player(s) with the greatest number walks, and the player(s) with the greatest number of outs.

Write your design in the following space. Your design should be a list of C++ comments without any code.

6b.   Write a C++ program based on the design you created in Lab 9.7, Exercise 6a and name it **PlayBall2**. Step through the code by hand.

In the following space, show what is displayed on the screen after executing the output message.

6c.   Enter, compile, link, and execute **PlayBall2.cpp**. Then copy the output and save it in a block comment at the end of your program. Save **PlayBall2.cpp** in the Chap09 folder of your Student Disk.

The following is a copy of the screen results that might appear after running your program, depending on the data entered.

```
This program keeps track of the hits, walks, outs, at bats, and team totals
of a baseball team.

        Player   Hits    Walks   Outs    At Bats

        1        4       4       4       12
        2        3       12      15      30
        3        6       8       10      24
        4        5       5       8       18
        5        2       2       2       6
        6        6       0       0       6
        7        0       0       6       6
        8        6       10      2       18
        9        6       4       2       12
        10       6       6       6       18
        11       14      2       2       18
        12       0       0       0       0
        13       8       1       3       12
        14       2       4       6       12
        15       0       0       0       0
        16       0       0       0       0
        17       4       2       6       12
        18       9       8       1       18
        19       3       2       1       6
        20       0       10      14      24
        ----------------------------------------
Totals:          84      80      88      252

Player 11 had the most hits
Player 2 had the most walks
Player 2 had the most outs
Player 2 had the most at bats
Press any key to continue
```

Lab 9.8 Using a Multidimensional Array

In C++, there is no limit on the dimension of arrays. An array is a collection of a fixed number of elements arranged in *n* dimensions (n >=1), called an n-dimensional array. The base address of an array is the address of the first array component. The first dimension of an array does not need to be declared as a formal parameter, but you must declare all other dimensions.

Objectives

In this lab, you become acquainted with processing three-dimensional arrays. You will initialize the array to zero (0) at declaration, sum components from each dimension, and sum all components. Then you display the sums computed. Additionally, you will find the component of the array with the largest value.

After completing this lab, you will be able to:

- Initialize a three-dimensional array to zero (0) at declaration.

- Process individual components of a three-dimensional array.

- Print all elements of a three-dimensional array.

- Pass a three-dimensional array to a function.

- Sum the values of a three-dimensional array by the first dimension, second dimension, third dimension, and by all components.

- Find the largest element in a three-dimensional array.

Estimated completion time: **60–75 minutes**

Using a Multidimensional Array

In the following exercise, you design and write a program using a three-dimensional array.

1a.   *Critical Thinking Exercise:* Design a program that keeps track of ticket sales for an auditorium. A concert will be performed over three days in an auditorium with three levels of seating—floor, balcony, and upper balcony. There are 20 seats for each type of seating. Write a program that initializes all seats to the '*' character. Allow a user to request a seat for a particular seat assignment area on a specific day. Use a three-dimensional array to keep track of the ticket sales. The first dimension indicates the performance day: T for Thursday, F for Friday, and S for Saturday. The second dimension indicates the type of seating: F for floor, B for balcony, and U for upper balcony. The third dimension indicates if a seat is sold, using S for sold.

The floor seats sell for $30, the balcony seats sell for $20, and the upper balcony seats sell for $10 each. The program must allow input of ticket requests until an X is entered to indicate that no more sales will be made. After the close of sales, calculate the amount of ticket sales for each performance for each day. Calculate the number of each type of seat sold for each day. Calculate the sales amount for each performance for each day. Calculate the total number of seats sold for all performances.

Write your design in the following space. Your design should be a list of C++ comments without any code.

1b.   Write a C++ program based on the design you created in Exercise 1a and name it **Concert.cpp**. Step through the code by hand.

In the following space, show what is displayed on the screen after executing the output message.

1c.   Enter, compile, link, and execute **Concert.cpp**. Then copy the output and save it in a block comment at the end of your program. Save **Concert.cpp** in the Chap09 folder of your Student Disk.

The following is a copy of the screen results that might appear after running your program, depending on the data entered. The input entered by the user is shown in bold.

```
This program keeps track of ticket sales for an auditorium. Tickets are
available for three days--Thursday, Friday, and Saturday--for 20 seats in
each of three levels: the floor, balcony, and upper balcony.

Enter day, (T)hursday, (F)riday, (S)aturday for concert, (X)closed
Enter level, (F)loor, (B)alcony, (U)pper Balcony
TF
Enter day, (T)hursday, (F)riday, (S)aturday for concert, (X)closed
Enter level, (F)loor, (B)alcony, (U)pper Balcony
TF
Enter day, (T)hursday, (F)riday, (S)aturday for concert, (X)closed
Enter level, (F)loor, (B)alcony, (U)pper Balcony
FU
Enter day, (T)hursday, (F)riday, (S)aturday for concert, (X)closed
Enter level, (F)loor, (B)alcony, (U)pper Balcony
FU
Enter day, (T)hursday, (F)riday, (S)aturday for concert, (X)closed
Enter level, (F)loor, (B)alcony, (U)pper Balcony
FU
Enter day, (T)hursday, (F)riday, (S)aturday for concert, (X)closed
Enter level, (F)loor, (B)alcony, (U)pper Balcony
SB
Enter day, (T)hursday, (F)riday, (S)aturday for concert, (X)closed
Enter level, (F)loor, (B)alcony, (U)pper Balcony
SB
Enter day, (T)hursday, (F)riday, (S)aturday for concert, (X)closed
Enter level, (F)loor, (B)alcony, (U)pper Balcony
SB
Enter day, (T)hursday, (F)riday, (S)aturday for concert, (X)closed
Enter level, (F)loor, (B)alcony, (U)pper Balcony
FB
Enter day, (T)hursday, (F)riday, (S)aturday for concert, (X)closed
Enter level, (F)loor, (B)alcony, (U)pper Balcony
FB
Enter day, (T)hursday, (F)riday, (S)aturday for concert, (X)closed
Enter level, (F)loor, (B)alcony, (U)pper Balcony
TB
Enter day, (T)hursday, (F)riday, (S)aturday for concert, (X)closed
Enter level, (F)loor, (B)alcony, (U)pper Balcony
TB
Enter day, (T)hursday, (F)riday, (S)aturday for concert, (X)closed
Enter level, (F)loor, (B)alcony, (U)pper Balcony
x
Thursday Floor           Tickets sold: 2 $60
         Balcony         Tickets sold: 2 $40
         Upper Balcony   Tickets sold: 0 $0
Friday   Floor           Tickets sold: 0 $0
         Balcony         Tickets sold: 2 $40
         Upper Balcony   Tickets sold: 3 $30
Saturday Floor           Tickets sold: 0 $0
         Balcony         Tickets sold: 3 $60
         Upper Balcony   Tickets sold: 0 $0

Total tickets sold for all concerts: 12 $ 230
```

```
Total Floor             tickets sold for all concerts: 2 $60

Total  Balcony          tickets sold for all concerts: 7 $140

Total  Upper Balcony  tickets sold for all concerts: 3 $30

Total tickets sold for Thursday  concerts: 4 $100
Total tickets sold for Friday    concerts: 5 $70
Total tickets sold for Saturday  concerts: 3 $60
```

10

Applications of Arrays and the vector Type

In this chapter, you will:

O Learn how to implement the sequential search algorithm

O Explore how to sort an array using the bubble sort and selection sort algorithms

O Learn how to implement the binary search algorithm

O Become familiar with the vector type

CHAPTER 10: ASSIGNMENT COVER SHEET

Name _____   Date _____

Section _____

Lab Assignments	Assigned	Grade
Lab 10.1 Implementing the Sequential Search Algorithm		
Lab 10.2 Sorting an Array Using Selection Sort		
Lab 10.3 Implementing the Binary Search Algorithm		
Lab 10.4 Using Arrays of Strings (Critical Thinking Exercises)		
Lab 10.5 Using the vector Type (Critical Thinking Exercises)		

See your instructor or the introduction to this book for instructions on submitting your assignments.

LAB 10.1 IMPLEMENTING THE SEQUENTIAL SEARCH ALGORITHM

A list is a set of values of the same type. Because all values are of the same type, lists can be stored in arrays. Because lists may be of varying sizes, the size of the array should be declared as the maximum size of the list. You can perform the following basic operations on a list:

- Input a list.
- Output a list.
- Search the list for a given item.
- Sort the list.
- Insert an item in the list.
- Delete an item from the list.

To search a list, you need to know the length of the list and the item for which you are searching. After searching a list, you need to know whether the item was found. If the item was found, you need to know where it was found.

Searching each location of a list until an item is found is called a sequential search or a binary search.

Objectives

In this lab, you search a list of a particular size for a value and then indicate whether the item is found. If it is, indicate the location where the item was found.

After completing this lab, you will be able to:

- Search a list of a given size for a particular value.
- Report whether an item is found in the list.
- Report where an item is found in the list.

Estimated completion time: **60–90 minutes**

Implementing the Sequential Search Algorithm

Question	Answer (Circle the correct answer)
1. The average number of comparisons in an unordered sequential search is one-half the number of items in the list.	T F
2. To search a list sequentially, you only need to know the array name and the search item.	T F
3. Given: `int list[6] = {93, 14, 3, 52, 44, 39};` In a sequential search, how many comparisons are needed to find the number 44?	a. 6 b. 3 c. 5 d. 4

4. Given:

   ```
   int list[6] = {93, 14, 3, 52, 44, 39};
   ```

   In a sequential search, how many comparisons are needed to find that the number 66 is not in the list?

   a. 6

   b. 3

   c. 5

   d. 4

5. Given:

   ```
   int list[6] = {3, 14, 39, 44, 52, 93 };
   ```

   In a sequential search, how many comparisons are needed to find the number 44?

   a. 6

   b. 3

   c. 5

   d. 4

6. Given:

   ```
   int list[6] = {3, 14, 39, 44, 52, 93 };
   ```

   In a sequential search, how many comparisons are needed to find that the number 66 is not in the list?

   a. 6

   b. 3

   c. 5

   d. 4

7. A sequential search requires an ordered list.   **T   F**

8a. Design a program that simulates a contest for a radio station that awards a $10,000 prize to the first caller who correctly guesses a number in a list of randomly generated numbers. A caller can make one guess per call. The contest is held until a number has been matched or the user enters a value of −1. The code used to generate a random list between 1 and 500 is in **CreateList.cpp** in the Chap10 folder of your Student Disk. The list generated from running CreateList is **PrizeList.txt** in the Chap10 folder of your Student Disk.

   The following list is the file **PrizeList.txt**

   ```
   42
   468
   335
   1
   170
   225
   479
   359
   463
   465
   206
   146
   282
   329
   462
   492
   496
   443
   328
   437
   ```

Write your design in the following space. Your design should be a list of C++ comments without any code.

8b.   Write a C++ program based on the design you created in Exercise 8a. Step through the code by hand.

In the following space, show what is displayed on the screen after executing the output message.

8c.   Enter, compile, link, and execute **Prize.cpp**. Then copy the output and save it in a block comment at the end of your program. Save **Prize.cpp** in the Chap10 folder of your Student Disk.

The following is a copy of the screen results that might appear after running your program, depending on the data entered. The input entered by the user is in bold.

```
This program simulates a radio station that asks the caller to guess a
number.
The number is compared against a list of 20 numbers between 1 and 500
inclusive.

The contest is held until a number has been matched or a value of -1 is
entered.

A message is displayed containing the winning number, the location
in the list of numbers, the number of calls made, and the amount of
the prize.
```

Hello Caller. What number between 1 and 500 are you guessing? **250**
250 is not in the list. Call again.

Hello Caller. What number between 1 and 500 are you guessing? **625**
Your guess must be between 1 and 500 inclusively.

Hello Caller. What number between 1 and 500 are you guessing? **423**
423 is not in the list. Call again.

Hello Caller. What number between 1 and 500 are you guessing? **122**
122 is not in the list. Call again.

Hello Caller. What number between 1 and 500 are you guessing? **42**
Caller. Your number 42 was found at location 1 of the list
Counting you, there were 4 callers. Your winnings are $10,000.

Lab 10.2 Sorting an Array Using Selection Sort

The selection sort algorithm rearranges a list by selecting an element in the list and moving it to its proper position. For example, first the smallest item in the list is moved to the first location. Starting with the second item in the list, the next smallest item is moved to the second location. You can also sort by placing the largest value in the first position, the second largest value in the second position, and so on.

Once a list has been sorted—also called ordered—the list can be sequentially searched. In a sequential search on an ordered list, once a value in the list is greater than the value being searched for, the search is complete and the item is not found. (In a descending list, once a value in the list is smaller than the value being searched for, the search is complete and the item is not found.)

Objectives

In this lab, you become acquainted with the selection sort. You also search an ordered list of a particular size for a value. Indicate whether the item is found; if it is, indicate the location where the item was found. If the number is not in the search list, discontinue the search once a list value exceeds the search value.

After completing this lab, you will be able to:

- Sort an unordered list using the selection sort.

- Search an ordered list of a given size for a particular value.

- Report whether an item is found in the list.

- If the item was found, report the location in the list where it was found.

- If the item was not found, stop the search once a list value exceeds the search value and then indicate that the value was not found.

Estimated completion time: **60–90 minutes**

Sorting an Array Using Selection Sort

1a.   Design for a program that reads the file **PrizeList.txt** in the Chap10 folder of your Student Disk that you used in Lab 10.1. Sort the array using the selection sort algorithm.

1b.   Write a C++ program based on the design you created in Exercise 1a. Step through the code by hand.

In the following space, show what is displayed on the screen after executing the output message.

1c.   Enter, compile, link, and execute **SortList.cpp**. Then copy the output and save it in a block comment at the end of your program. Save **SortList.cpp** in the Chap10 folder of your Student Disk.

The following is a copy of the screen results that might appear after running your program.

```
The program SortList.cpp reads the file PrizeList.txt into an array and
sorts the array using the selection sort algorithm.
The sorted array is written to a file named PrizeList.srt.

Your list has been sorted.
```

The following is the file PrizeList.txt:

```
1
42
146
170
206
225
282
328
329
335
359
437
443
462
463
465
468
479
492
496
```

2a.   Redesign your program **Prize.cpp** to sequentially search the ordered list **PrizeList.srt** created in Exercise 1. Because the list is ordered, you can make your search a "smart search" by first checking to see if the value is less than the first element in the list or greater than the first element in the list. If the value falls in the range of the list, then the list should be searched. You may start searching the list at the beginning of the list or at the end of the list. Include an output line that shows how many comparisons it takes to search for each guess.

Write your design in the following space. Your design should be a list of C++ comments without any code.

2b.   Write a C++ program based on the design you created in Exercise 2a. Step through the code by hand.

In the following space, show what is displayed on the screen after executing the output message.

2c.   Enter, compile, link, and execute **Prize2.cpp**. Then copy the output and save it in a block comment at the end of your program. Save **Prize2.cpp** in the Chap10 folder of your Student Disk.

The following is a copy of the screen results that might appear after running your program, depending on the data entered. The input entered by the user is in bold.

```
This program simulates a radio station
that asks the caller to guess a number.
The number is compared against an ordered
list of 20 numbers between 1 and 500 inclusive.
The contest is held until a number has been
matched or a value of -1 is entered.
```

A message is displayed containing the winning
number, the location in the list of numbers,
the number of calls made, the number of
comparisons, and the amount of the prize.

Hello Caller. What number between 1 and 500 are you guessing? **500**
It took 0 comparisons to check the list.
Your number is not in the list.

Hello Caller. What number between 1 and 500 are you guessing? **25**
It took 20 comparisons to check the list.
Your number is not in the list.

Hello Caller. What number between 1 and 500 are you guessing? **1**
Caller. Your number 1 was found at location 1 of the list.
Counting you, there were 3 callers.
Your winnings are $10,000.
It took 20 comparisons to check the list.

LAB 10.3 IMPLEMENTING THE BINARY SEARCH ALGORITHM

A sequential search on an ordered list usually requires searching about half the list. For long lists, the binary search is much faster than the sequential search. The first search item is compared with the middle element of the list. Then, the search item is compared either with the middle of the first half of the list or the middle of the second half of the list. This process is repeated until the search item is found or there are no more list items.

Each time the item is searched, the list is cut in half. Because every iteration of the loop makes two item comparisons, the binary search will make at most $2*\log_2 n + 2$ item comparisons. In non-mathematical turns, the number of comparisons can be calculated by the size of the list. This example has a list size of 20. The number 2 raised to the power of 4 is 16. The number 2 raised to the power of 5 is 32. The list size of 20 is greater than 2 to the power of 4 and less than 2 to the power of 5. It should take four or five comparisons to search the list since the list is cut in half each time.

Objectives

In this lab, you use a binary search on an ordered list of a given size to find a particular value. Indicate whether the item is found. If it is, indicate the location where the item was found.

After completing this lab, you will be able to:

- Use a binary search on an ordered list of a given size for a particular value.
- Report whether an item is found in the ordered list.
- If the item was found, report the location in the list where it was found.

Estimated completion time: **40–50 minutes**

Implementing the Binary Search Algorithm

Question

	Answer (Enter or circle the correct answer)

1. A binary search is usually a faster alternative to search an unordered list.

   T   F

2. Suppose a list has 32 components. What is the most number of comparisons needed in a binary search to determine if a particular value is in the list?

   a. 5

   b. 32

   c. it depends on the location of the value in the list

   d. 31

3. Suppose you have a list
   ```
   int list[8] = {1, 2, 3, 4, 5, 6, 7, 8};
   ```
   Using a binary search, what is the most number of comparisons needed to find the number 5?

   a. 3

   b. 4

   c. 5

   d. 8

4. Suppose you have a list
   ```
   int list[8] = {1, 2, 3, 4, 5, 6, 7, 8};
   ```
   Using a sequential search, what is the most number of comparisons needed to find the number 5?

   a. 3

   b. 4

   c. 5

   d. 8

5. Suppose you have a list

   ```
   int list[8] = {1, 3, 5, 7, 9, 11, 13, 15};
   ```

   Using a binary search, what is the most number of comparisons
   needed to see if the number 14 is in the list?

6. Suppose you have a list

   ```
   int list[8] = {1, 3, 5, 7, 9, 11, 13, 15};
   ```

   Using a sequential search, what is the most number of comparisons
   needed to see if the number 14 is in the list?

7. A binary search is always preferable to a sequential search.   **T   F**

8a.   Redesign your program **Prize2.cpp** to use a binary search the ordered list **PrizeList.srt**
      created in Exercise 1.

      Write your design in the following space. Your design should be a list of C++ comments
      without any code.

8b.   Write a C++ program based on the design you created in Exercise 8a. Step through the code by hand.

In the following space, show what is displayed on the screen after executing the output message.

8c.   Enter, compile, link, and execute **Prize3.cpp**. Then copy the output and save it in a block comment at the end of your program. Save **Prize3.cpp** in the Chap10 folder of your Student Disk.

The following is a copy of the screen results that might appear after running your program, depending on the data entered. Compare you output with the output for your program **Prize2.cpp**.

```
This program simulates a radio station
that asks the caller to guess a number.
The number is compared against an ordered
list of 20 numbers between 1 and 500 inclusive.
The contest is held until a number has been
matched or a value of -1 is entered.

A message is displayed containing the winning
number, the location in the list of numbers,
the number of calls made, the number of
comparisons, and the amount of the prize.

Hello Caller. What number between 1 and 500 are you guessing? 500
It took 0 comparisons to check the list.
Your number is not in the list.

Hello Caller. What number between 1 and 500 are you guessing? 25
It took 4 comparisons to check the list.
Your number is not in the list.

Hello Caller. What number between 1 and 500 are you guessing? 1

Caller. Your number 1 was found at location 1 of the list.
Counting you, there were 3 callers.
Your winnings are $10,000.
It took 4 comparisons to check the list.
```

LAB 10.4 USING ARRAYS OF STRINGS

In ANSI/ISO Standard C++, processing a list of strings using the data type `string` is straightforward. The data in the list can be processed just like any one-dimensional array. Sorting a list of strings would be the same as sorting a list of numbers.

An array of names could be declared and processed as a two-dimensional array. Remember that a character array allows aggregate input of strings. Therefore, a two-dimensional character array can input a string into the array by designating only the subscript of the row. String processing can also be accomplished by using the subscript of the row.

Objectives

In this lab, you use the selection sort on a two-dimensional character array.

After completing this lab, you will be able to:

- Sort an unordered two-dimensional character array using the selection sort.

Estimated completion time: **40–50 minutes**

Using Arrays of Strings

1a.   *Critical Thinking Exercise:* Design a program that reads a file of names into a two-dimensional character array, sorts the array, and writes the names to an output file.

Write your design in the following space. Your design should be a list of C++ comments without any code.

1b.   Write a C++ program based on the design you created in Exercise 1a. Step through the code by hand.

In the following space, show what is displayed on the screen after executing the output message.

1c.   Enter, compile, link, and execute **sort2dimen.cpp** using **cardList.txt** as the imput file. Then copy the output and save it in a block comment at the end of your program. Save **sort2dimen.cpp** in the Chap10 folder of your Student Disk.

The following is a copy of the screen results that might appear after running your program, the file **cardList.txt**, and the file **cardList.srt**.

```
The program sort2dimen.cpp reads the file cardList.txt into an array
and sorts the array using the selection sort algorithm.
The sorted array is written to a file named cardList.srt.
```

```
Your list is sorted.
cardList.txt
Schmidt, Helga
Alvarez, Ruben
Zowkowski, Aaron
Huang, Sun Lee
Einstein, Beverly

cardList.srt

Alvarez, Ruben
Einstein, Beverly
Huang, Sun Lee
Schmidt, Helga
Zowkowski, Aaron
```

LAB 10.5 USING THE VECTOR TYPE

One of the limitations of arrays discussed so far is that once you create an array, its size remains fixed. Also, inserting or removing an element in the array at a specific position might require the program to shift the elements of the array.

In addition to arrays, C++ provides the vector type or class vector to implement a list. A variable declared using the vector type is called a vector container or a vector or a vector object or simply an object. When you declare a vector object, you must specify the type of the element the vector object stores.

Table 10-1 shows various ways to declare and initialize a vector object.

Table 10-1   Statements that declare and initialize a vector object

Statement	Effect
vector<elementType> vecList;	Creates the empty vector object, vecList, without any elements
vector<elementType> vecList(otherVecList);	Creates the vector object, vecList, and initializes vecList to the elements of the vector otherVecList; vecList and otherVecList are of the same type
vector<elementType> vecList(size);	Creates the vector object, vecList, of size size; vecList is initialized using the default values
vector<elementType> vecList(n, elem);	Creates the vector object, vecList, of size n; vecList is initialized using n copies of the element elem

The type **vector** provides various operations to manipulate data. Table 10-2 shows some of these functions and how to use them.

Table 10-2   vector functions

Expression	Effect
vecList.at(index)	Returns the element at the position specified by index
vecList[index]	Returns the element at the position specified by index
vecList.front()	Returns the first element; (does not check whether the object is empty)
vecList.back()	Returns the last element; (does not check whether the object is empty)
vecList.clear()	Deletes all elements from the object
vecList.push_back(elem)	A copy of elem is inserted into vecList at the end
vecList.pop_back()	Delete the last element of vecList
vecList.empty()	Returns true if the container vecList is empty and false otherwise
vecList.size()	Returns the number of elements currently in the container vecList; the value returned is an unsigned into value
vecList.max_size()	Returns the maximum number of elements that can be inserted into the container vecList

Objectives

In this lab, you become acquainted with the class **vector** and various functions of the class **vector** to create a list in sorted order.

After completing this lab, you will be able to:

■ Create vector variables.

■ Use various functions of the class **vector**.

Estimated completion time: **50–60 minutes**

Using the vector Type

1a.   *Critical Thinking Exercise:* Design a program that reads into a vector the file **PrizeList.txt** of unsorted numbers found in the Chap10 folder of your Student Disk. Read the list until you reach the end of file. Sort the vector. Once all values have been entered, display the contents of the vector.

Write your design in the following space. Your design should be a list of C++ comments without any code.

1b. Write a C++ program based on the design you created in Exercise 1a. Step through the code by hand.

In the following space, show what is displayed on the screen after executing the output message.

1c. Enter, compile, link, and execute **Vector.cpp**. Then copy the output and save it in a block comment at the end of your program. Save **Vector.cpp** in the Chap10 folder of your Student Disk. Compare your output to **PrizeList.srt** in the Chap10 folder of your Student Disk.

The following is a copy of the screen results that might appear after running your program, the file **PrizeList.txt**, and the file **PriceList.srt**.

This program reads a list of numbers from a file into a vector.
The vector is sorted and the sorted list is displayed.

Your sorted vector:
1
42
146
170
206
225
282
328
329
335
359
437
443
462
463
465
468
479
492
496

PrizeList.txt

42
468
335
1
170
225
479
359
463
465
206
146
282
329
462
492
496
443
328
437

PrizeList.srt

1
42
146
170
206
225
282
328
329
335

359
437
443
462
463
465
468
479
492
496

11

Records (structs)

CHAPTER 11: ASSIGNMENT COVER SHEET

Name _____   Date _____

Section _____

Lab Assignments	Assigned	Grade
Lab 11.1 Defining structs and Declaring struct Variables		
Lab 11.2 Manipulating Data Using a struct (Critical Thinking Exercises)		
Lab 11.3 Using Arrays in Structs		
Lab 11.4 Using Structs in Arrays (Critical Thinking Exercises)		
Group Project: The EmployeePay program written in Lab 11.4 can be used as a Group Project. The group should work together to establish the menu options, and then group members can be assigned different options. Some options can be further subdivided among group members.		
Total Grade		

See your instructor or the introduction to this book for instructions on submitting your assignments.

LAB 11.1 DEFINING STRUCTS AND DECLARING STRUCT VARIABLES

The array is a structured data type where all elements are of the same type. Another structured data type, called `struct` (or record) allows you to group related values that are of different types. The treatment of `structs` in this chapter is similar to the treatment of a `struct` in C. A `struct` is a collection of a fixed number of components, called members, in which the members are accessed by name. The members may be of different data types.

A `struct` is a definition, not a declaration. It defines only a data type; no memory is allocated. You may declare variables of the data type defined by the `struct` type. A `struct` is a user-defined data type that requires the keyword `struct` followed by the name chosen for the `struct`. The data members that define the `struct` are contained between a set of curly braces {}. A `struct` must end with a semicolon.

User-defined variables are declared using the same method as other variables. The declaration consists of the data type and the variable name. When the variable is a struct variable, the data type is the name of the `struct`.

Objectives

In this lab, you define `structs` and declare `struct` variables.

After completing this lab, you will be able to:

- Write `struct` definitions.

- Declare `struct` variables.

- Recognize the difference among `struct` definitions, `struct` variables, and members of `structs`.

Estimated completion time: **20–30 minutes**

Defining structs and Declaring struct Variables

Question	Answer (Circle the correct answer)	
1. The definition of a `struct` allocates memory for each member of the `struct`.	T	F
2. A `struct` is a data structure that may consists of multiple data types.	T	F
3. The definition of a `struct` must end with a semicolon.	T	F
4. Given:	T	F

```
struct animal
{
    bool mammalian;
    string habitat;
    int longevity;
};
```

The statement:

```
animal cat, dog;
```

will produce a compile time error because **dog** is not typed.

5a.   A car salesperson needs to keep track of all cars on a used car lot. The information she needs includes the type, seating capacity, price, miles per gallon, and color of each car. Define a struct named Cars that will contain all of these members.

5b.   Declare a struct variable named familyCar of the data type Cars.

LAB 11.2 MANIPULATING DATA USING A STRUCT

To access a struct member, you use the struct variable name together with the member name; these names are separated by a dot, called the dot operator, member access operator, or member selection operator. For example, in familyCar.type, the struct variable name is familyCar and type is the member name.

Unlike arrays, you can assign the value of one struct variable to another struct variable. One advantage of grouping components that are related, but of different types, is that a single variable can pass all components as parameters to a function. However, like arrays, you cannot use relational operators or aggregate input/output operations on struct variables. This must be done member by member, also called member-wise.

Objectives

In this lab, you become acquainted with manipulating data using a struct.

After completing this lab, you will be able to:

- Access struct members.

- Pass structs to functions.

- Use structs in file processing.

Estimated completion time: **90–120 minutes**

Manipulating Data Using a struct

Question	Answer (Circle the correct answer)
1. The order that struct members are defined does not affect the order in which they are accessed.	T F
2. A struct is accessed by the struct variable name, the name of the struct, and the struct member name.	T F

3. Given:

```
struct animal
{
    bool mammalian;
    string habitat;
    int longevity;
};
animal cat;
```

Which of the following correctly initializes cat?

a. mammalian = true;

   habitat = "house";

   longevity = 12;

b. cat.mammalian = true;

   cat.habitat = "house"

   cat.longevity = 12;

c. animal.cat.mammalian = true;

   animal.cat.habitat = "house";

   animal.cat.longevity = 12;

d. all the above may be used

4. Use the `struct animal` previously defined and the statements:

```
animal cat;
animal dog;
```

Which of the following statements are valid in C++?

a. `cat = dog;`

b. `cat.mammalian = dog.mammalian;`
   `cat.habitat = dog.habitat;`
   `cat.longevity = dog.longevity;`

c. both a and b

5a.   *Critical Thinking Exercise:* Design a program for a car lot. The program will prompt the user for the specifications of a car and check your inventory to see if the car is on the car lot. The inventory is found in the file **CarLot.txt** in the Chap11 folder of your Student Disk. You will read in the inventory using the `struct Cars` defined in Lab 11.1, Exercise 5a. You will read data from CarLot.txt into a `struct` variable and the user's specifications into a `struct`. Because you do not want to lose the customer, ask the customer if they want a list of all vehicles that match some specifications or only the exact car being searched. *Hint:* Because you are only reading a record at a time and you loop until the end of file flag, if you need to go through the file again, you must clear all file flags using the clear function. The following specifications apply to the cars in the lot:

- Valid car types include (C)oupe, (M)inivan, or (S)UV

- The coupe gets 25 mpg at a base cost of $15,000 and seats 4.

- The minivan gets 20 mpg at a base cost of $18,000 and seats 7.

- The SUV gets 18 mpg at a base cost of $22,000 and seats 5.

Write your design in the following space. Your design should be a list of C++ comments without any code.

5b.   Write a C++ program based on the design you created in Exercise 5a. Step through the code by hand.

In the following space, show what is displayed on the screen after executing the output message.

5c.   Enter, compile, link, and execute **CarSales.cpp**. Then copy the output and save it in a block comment at the end of your program. Save **CarSales.cpp** in the Chap11 folder of your Student Disk.

The following is a copy of the screen results that might appear after running your program, depending on the data entered. The input entered by the user is shown in bold.

```
This program prompts the user for specifications of a car.
These are then checked against a list of cars found in file CarLot.txt.
The user specifies if an exact match is required or if a list of cars that
meet some specifications is acceptable.
Enter type of car:(C)oupe, (M)inivan, or (S)UV: c
Enter the seating capacity that you want: 5
Warning: Coupes only seat 4 passengers.
Please make another selection.

Enter type of car:(C)oupe, (M)inivan, or (S)UV: s
Enter the seating capacity that you want: 5
An SUV gets 18 mpg and has a base price of $22,000.
Do you want to change your selection? (y)es/(n)o: y

Enter type of car:(C)oupe, (M)inivan, or (S)UV: m
Enter the seating capacity that you want: 7
A minivan gets 20 mpg and has a base price of $18,000.
Do you want to change your selection? (y)es/(n)o: n
Enter the color of your choice: gold
Are you only interested in an exact match? (y)es/(n)o y

I'm sorry, we do not have the exact car you want.
Do you want to try another selection? (y)es/(n)o y

Enter type of car:(C)oupe, (M)inivan, or (S)UV: m
Enter the seating capacity that you want: 7
A minivan gets 20 mpg and has a base price of $18,000.
Do you want to change your selection? (y)es/(n)o: n
Enter the color of your choice: silver
Are you only interested in an exact match? (y)es/(n)o y

Congratulations. We have the car you want in stock.


This program prompts the user for specifications of a car.
These are then checked against a list of cars found in file CarLot.txt.
The user specifies if an exact match is required or if a list of cars that
meet some specifications is acceptable.

Enter type of car:(C)oupe, (M)inivan, or (S)UV: s
Enter the seating capacity that you want: 5
An SUV gets 18 mpg and has a base price of $22,000.
Do you want to change your selection? (y)es/(n)o: n
Enter the color of your choice: any
Are you only interested in an exact match? (y)es/(n)o n

We have the following cars that you might want to consider.
A blue SUV.
A silver SUV.
A green SUV.
A black SUV.
```

LAB 11.3 USING ARRAYS IN STRUCTS

Any defined data type can be a member of a struct. Therefore, a defined struct data type can be contained within another struct. Additionally, you can use array as a member of a struct. The syntax for a struct with an array and a struct variable declaration is as follows:

```
struct structType
{
        dataType structMember[arraySize];
        dataType anotherMember;
};
structType var1;
```

The syntax to access a component in the array is as follows:

```
var1.structMember[location]
```

Objectives

In this lab, you define and use structs containing data members that are structs and arrays of structs.

After completing this lab, you will be able to:

- Design and implement in C++ a program using structs containing data members that are structs.

- Design and implement in C++ a struct containing array elements

Estimated completion time: **90–120 minutes**

Using Arrays in Structs

	Answer **(Circle the correct answer)**

1. Given the following structures and variables:
 	
``struct date
{
   int month;
   int day;
   int year;
};
struct birthStatistics
{
   date birthday;
   string citizenship;
   };
   birthStatistics student;```
 	
Which of the following statements are valid in C++?
	a. ```student.birthday.month = 12;```
	   ```student.birthday.day = 14;```
	   ```student.birthday.year = 1984;```
	   ```student.citizenship = "US";```
	
	b. ```student.birthday = {12, 14, 1984);```
	   ```student.citizenship = "US";```
	
	c. ```student.month = 12;```
	   ```student.day = 14;```
	   ```student.year = 1984;```
	   ```student.citizenship = "US";```
	
	d. None. You cannot use a struct as a data type of another struct.

2. Using the structures and variables defined above, what is the data type of `student.birthday`?	a. `int` b. `date` c. None. You cannot use a struct as a data type of another struct.

3a.   Your instructor wants to create a **struct** to keep track of student grades. The information the instructor needs includes the student's first name, last name, a six-digit ID number, ten programming assignment grades, three exam grades, and a final exam grade. Define a **struct** named **grades** that will contain all of these members.

3b.   Declare a **struct** variable named **student** of the data type **grades**.

4a.   Design a program that prepares a grade book for an instructor. Use **struct grades** and the variable **students** of data type **grades** declared in Exercise 3. Input the student information (first name, last name, six-digit ID number, ten programs, and three exam grades) from the file **GradeBook.txt**. Calculate the grade as follows: Programs total 30%, exams 15% each, and the final exam is 25%. Students with 90 and above averages earn an A, 80 to 89 earn a B, 70 to 79 earn a C, 60 to 69 earn a D, and all grades below 60 earn an F. Display each student's name and final grade.

Write your design in the following space. Your design should be a list of C++ comments without any code.

4b.   Write a C++ program based on the design you created in Exercise 4a. Step through the code by hand. The following is a copy of the file **GradeBook.txt** found in the Chap11 folder of your Student Disk.

```
George Smith 589308      100 90 80 95 85 99 98 97 89 100      90 95 85      85
Elaine Sanders 455436     85 90 80 95 89 99 100 98 97 100      96 98 84      90
Jack Cunningham 235412    72 78 97 84 83 68 85 84 83 90      70 75 80      75
Susie Brown 902568     68 85 84 83 90 80 95 85 99 98     75 92 85      87
Marvella Garcia 345432    92 78 97 98 97 89 80 95 85 99      98 89 88      95
Tony Peterson 256436     85 84 83 90 72 78 97 98 97 99      88 87 88      88
John Jones 165435     75 75 80 80 90 90 75 70 87 84     78 82 84      75
Mary Evans 879778     60 89 86 65 89 88 77 60 87 65     65 69 66      60
Nancy Drew 234234     80 75 50 60 79 89 50 45 70 50     60 58 65      45
Lola Zapeta 458741     89 98 79 97 90 96 94 100 99 98     83 78 89      88
```

In the following space, show what is displayed on the screen after executing the output message.

4c.   Enter, compile, link, and execute **CalcGrades.cpp**. Then copy the output and save it in a block comment at the end of your program. Save **CalcGrades.cpp** in the Chap11 folder of your Student Disk.

The following is a copy of the screen results that might appear after running your program, depending on the data entered.

```
This program reads a data file of student grades, calculates the final grade,
and displays the student's name and final grade.

          Final Grades
George Smith            B
Elaine Sanders          A
Jack Cunningham         C
Susie Brown             B
Marvella Garcia         A
Tony Peterson           B
John Jones              C
Mary Evans              D
Nancy Drew              F
Lola Zapeta             B
```

LAB 11.4 USING STRUCTS IN ARRAYS

When you need multiple struct variables, you can use a struct variable as an array.

The syntax for a struct with an array and a struct variable declaration is as follows:

```
struct structType
{
        dataType structMember[arraySize];
        dataType anotherMember;
};
structType var [arraySize];
```

The syntax to access the structMember component in the array is as follows:

```
var [loc].structMember[location]
```

The syntax to access the anotherMember component is as follows:

```
var[loc].anotherMember
```

Objectives

In this lab, you create programs using structs as arrays; structs containing data members that are structs; and arrays of structs.

After completing this lab, you will be able to:

- Design and implement in C++ a program using structs containing data members that are structs.

- Design and implement in C++ an array of structs.

Estimated completion time: **150–180 minutes**

Using Structs in Arrays

1a.   Define a struct named date that has year, month, and day as members.

1b.   Define a `struct` named `employee` that has string data type or character arrays for `firstName`, `lastName`, `ssn` (Social Security number), the user-defined data type `date` for `birthDate` and `startDate`, a double variable `payRate`, and a Boolean value `exempt`. The Social Security number does not include dashes.

1c.   Declare a `struct` variable array named `worker` of size 20 and of the data type `employee`.

1d.   *Critical Thinking Exercise:* Design a program for a Human Resources Department of a company. The program displays a menu for the user to select a task. The choices on the menu are the following:

1 Alphabetized listing

2 Show the record for an employee

3 Budget for employee pay increases

4 Retirement eligibility

9 End program

The program reads in the data file **employees.txt** from Chap11 of your Student Disk into a `struct` array. Option 1 requires the `struct` array to be sorted alphabetically, option 2 requires the `struct` array to be searched for a name match, option 3 requires the user to enter a percentage rate for a raise for non-exempt (salaried) employees, and a percentage rate for exempt (salaried) employees, option 4 requires the program to calculate when retirement is available. The formula for retirement is the rule of 80, meaning an employee's age and years of service must equal 80 to be eligible for retirement. Today's date must be entered to make the calculations. (You can refer to your calculations in programs LeapYear.cpp and Raises.cpp in Chapter 6 for age and raise calculations.)

Write your design in the following space. Your design should be a list of C++ comments without any code.

1e.   Write a C++ program based on the design you created in Exercise 1d. Step through the code by hand. The following is a copy of the file **employees.txt** found in the Chap11 folder of your Student Disk.

```
Richard Stamos 456897445 1980 6 12 2000 8 15 9.45 0
Val Richardson 123456543 1974 10 18 1998 6 1 28000 1
Edna Purvis 789654873 1972 8 29 1992 11 15 36000 1
Stanley Gardner 234433434 1940 1 15 1965 8 24 64000 1
Jose Garcia 455899771 1942 4 10 1965 8 24 64000 1
Luis Mendoza 654654323 1955 11 12 1974 11 3 15.50 0
Zhou Chen 453462891 1966 5 26 1990 3 4 14.00 0
Gloria Kellum 234987123 1968 9 3 1992 6 16 14.50 0
Roscoe Ivens 565643823 1945 9 16 1967 4 30 18.00 0
David Eisenberg 657342543 1970 8 14 1998 2 6 14.50 0
```

In the following space, show what is displayed on the screen after executing the output message.

1f.   Enter, compile, link, and execute **EmployeePay.cpp**. Then copy the output and save it in a block comment at the end of your program. Save **EmployeePay.cpp** in the Chap11 folder of your Student Disk.

The following is a copy of the screen results that might appear after running your program, depending on the data entered. The input entered by the user is shown in bold.

```
This program reads a data file of employee data, displays a menu of choices,
and displays the report selected.

Please make your selection from the following menu:

1 Alphabetized listing
2 Show the record for an employee
3 Budget for employee pay increases
4 Retirement eligibility
9 End program
2

Enter last name of employee: Garcia
Enter first name of employee: Joseph

Joseph Garcia is not found on the employee list.

Please make your selection from the following menu:

1 Alphabetized listing
2 Show the record for an employee
3 Budget for employee pay increases
4 Retirement eligibility
9 End program
1
```

Employee	SSN	DOB			Start Date			Pay Rate	Exemptions
Zhou Chen	453462891	1966	5	26	1990	3	4	14.00	0
David Eisenberg	657342543	1970	8	14	1998	2	6	14.50	0
Jose Garcia	455899771	1942	4	10	1965	8	24	64000.00	1
Stanley Gardner	234433434	1940	1	15	1965	8	24	64000.00	1
Roscoe Ivens	565643823	1945	9	16	1967	4	30	18.00	0
Gloria Kellum	234987123	1968	9	3	1992	6	16	14.50	0
Luis Mendoza	654654323	1955	11	12	1974	11	3	15.50	0
Edna Purvis	789654873	1972	8	29	1992	11	15	36000.00	1
Val Richardson	123456543	1974	10	18	1998	6	1	28000.00	1
Richard Stamos	456897445	1980	6	12	2000	8	15	9.45	0

```
Please make your selection from the following menu:

1 Alphabetized listing
2 Show the record for an employee
3 Budget for employee pay increases
4 Retirement eligibility
9 End program
2


Enter last name of employee: Garcia
Enter first name of employee: Jose

    Employee        SSN         DOB      Start Date     Pay Rate Exemptions
Jose Garcia      455899771   1942  4 10   1965  8 24     64000.00      1
Please make your selection from the following menu:

1 Alphabetized listing
2 Show the record for an employee
3 Budget for employee pay increases
4 Retirement eligibility
9 End program
3



The annual budget for exempt employees is        $192000.00
For non-exempt employees                         $178776.00

Enter the percent pay raise in decimal format. For example, write 5% as .05
Enter the percent pay raise for exempt employees: .025
Enter the percent pay raise for non-exempt employees: .02

It will cost $4800.00 to give a 2.50% pay raise to exempt employees.
It will cost $3575.52 to give a 2.00% pay raise to non-exempt employees.

Do you want to try other percentages (y)es or (n)o? n

Please make your selection from the following menu:

1 Alphabetized listing
2 Show the record for an employee
3 Budget for employee pay increases
4 Retirement eligibility
9 End program
4


Enter last name of employee: Garcia
Enter first name of employee: Jose
Enter today's date in the format yyyy mm: 2005 11
Employee is eligible to retire when age plus years of service total 80
Jose Garcia is 63 years and 7 months old
and has worked 40 years and 3 months.
Age plus years of service total 104 years and 35 months
You are now eligible to retire.

Please make your selection from the following menu:

1 Alphabetized listing
2 Show the record for an employee
3 Budget for employee pay increases
4 Retirement eligibility
9 End program
9
```

12

Classes and Data Abstraction

In this chapter, you will:

- ○ Learn about classes
- ○ Learn about `private`, `protected`, and `public` members of a class
- ○ Explore how classes are implemented
- ○ Examine constructors and destructors
- ○ Learn about the abstract data type (ADT)
- ○ Explore how classes are used to implement ADTs
- ○ Learn about information hiding
- ○ Explore how information hiding is implemented in C++
- ○ Learn about the `static` members of a class

CHAPTER 12: ASSIGNMENT COVER SHEET

Name _____   Date _____

Section _____

Lab Assignments	Assigned	Grade
Lab 12.1 Describing Classes Using the Unified Modeling Language (UML) Notation and Declaring Objects		
Lab 12.2 Manipulating and Accessing Data Within the class		
Lab 12.3 Designing Driver Programs (Critical Thinking Exercises)		
Lab 12.4 Invoking Default Constructors, Constructors with Parameters, and Constructors with Default Parameters		
Lab 12.5 Invoking Destructors		
Lab 12.6 Using the Abstract Data Type and Information Hiding (Critical Thinking Exercises)		
Lab 12.7 Static Members of a Class		
Group Projects: Labs 12.1, 12.2, 12.3, and Lab 12.6, Exercises 1 and 2 can be used together as a Group Project. Labs 12.4, 12.5, and Lab 12.6, Exercise 3 can be used together as a Group Project.		
Total Grade		

See your instructor or the introduction to this book for instructions on submitting your assignments.

LAB 12.1 DESCRIBING CLASSES USING THE UNIFIED MODELING LANGUAGE (UML) NOTATION AND DECLARING OBJECTS

Recall that two structured data types are arrays, which have elements of the same type, and structures, which have elements of differing types. Another structured data type is a class, which is specifically designed to combine data and functions in a single unit. A class is a collection of a fixed number of components. The components of a class are called the members of the class. If a member of a class is a variable, you define it just like any other variable, but you cannot initialize it at definition. If a member of a class is a function, you typically use the function prototype to define that member. Member functions can directly access any data member of the class without passing that data member as an argument.

No memory is allocated in a class definition. Instead, memory is allocated when the class is instantiated (an object is created). Additionally, the semicolon (;) is part of the syntax. The members of a class are classified into three categories: private, public, and protected. By default, all members of a class are private. Private members cannot be accessed outside of the class. A public member is accessible outside the class. Protected members will be discussed in Chapter 13.

A class and its members can be described graphically using Unified Modeling Language (UML) notation. A UML diagram contains three boxes stacked vertically. The top box contains the name of the class; the middle box contains the data members and their data types; and the bottom box contains the member method names, parameter list, and return types. The + (plus) sign indicates that it is a public member; the – (minus) sign indicates that it is a private member. The # (pound) symbol indicates that it is a protected member.

Objectives

In this lab, you define a class and declare objects.

After completing this lab, you will be able to:

- Use UML notation.
- Create an instantiation of the class (declare objects).
- Recognize the difference among class definitions, objects, and members of the class.

Estimated completion time: **50–60 minutes**

Describing Classes Using the Unified Modeling Language (UML) Notation and Declaring Objects

Question	Answer (Circle the correct answer)
1. A class is _____.	a. a structured data type
	b. a homogenous data type
	c. a simple data type
2. All data members of a class must be of the same data type.	T F
3. You define an object of a class in the same way that you define a variable of a data type.	T F

4. It is optional to initialize an object at declaration.   **T**   **F**

5. A data member is another term for an object.   **T**   **F**

6a.   There is no standard library for a date class. Create a UML diagram for a class named **Date** that will contain data members and member functions to allow a user to enter a date, validate the date entered, and display the date entered. Your class should meet the criteria in the following list:

- The data members named **month**, **day**, and **year** should be private members so that they cannot be directly manipulated outside of the class.

- The Boolean data member named **good** should be a public member so that it can be accessed outside of the class.

- The public **void** member method **getData** has no parameters.

- The private **void** member method **checkFormat** has an integer reference variable parameter.

- The private **void** member method **validate** has no parameters.

- The public **void** member method **display** has no parameters.

Write the class definition in the space provided.

6b.   Implement your diagram in C++ and save your code in a file named **testDate.cpp** in the Chap12 folder of your Student Disk.

6c.   Define an object named **today** of the class **Date**. Write the object definition in the space provided.

7a.   Create a UML diagram for a `struct` (if you skipped Chapter 11, define a class instead) named `Money` that will contain data members. Your `struct` (or class) should contain a `char` data member named `type` and a double data member named `amount` as public members.

7b.   Implement your diagram in C++ and save your code in a file named **Money.h** in the Chap12 folder of your Student Disk.

8a.   Create a UML diagram for a class named `Exchange` that will contain data members and member functions to allow a user to input, validate, and convert pesos, Euro dollars, and Swiss francs to U. S. dollars. Your class should meet the criteria in the following list:

- The data members `US` and those the user enters will be of the type `Money` that you defined in Exercise 7, and should be private members. (In Chapter 11, you learned that a `struct` is a user-defined data type and can be used in the data type of an array, a data member of a `struct`, and as a variable of that `struct` type. A `struct` and a class can also be a data type of a member of a class.)

- The Boolean function `getData` and the `void` functions `convert` and `displayExchange` have no formal parameters and should be public members.

- The `void` function `outputType` has no formal parameters and is a private member.

8b. Implement your diagram in C++ and save your code in a file named **testExchange.cpp** in the Chap12 folder of your Student Disk. Open your **Money.h** file and copy and paste your `struct` (or class) definition in your **testExchange.cpp** program above your Exchange class definition.

8c. Define an object named `amount` of the class `Exchange`. Write the object definition in the space provided.

LAB 12.2 MANIPULATING AND ACCESSING DATA WITHIN THE CLASS

To access another class member from a member function of the class, you use the class variable name or function name. It is not necessary to pass a class data member between the class member functions. However, if it is passed, the formal parameter is a local variable to that member function. In this case, if the change is to be reflected in the class, then the formal parameter must be passed by reference.

To access a public class member outside of the class, you use the class variable name together with the member name. The syntax is to separate the name of the class and the class variable name by a dot, called the dot operator or member access operator.

Objectives

In this lab, you become acquainted with accessing data members and member functions within a class.

After completing this lab, you will be able to:

- Access class members from member functions of the class.

Estimated completion time: **60–90 minutes**

Manipulating and Accessing Data Within the class

1a.   Using the Date class design you created in Lab 12.1, Exercise 6a, design the member functions so they meet the following criteria:

- The member function getData should call the member function checkFormat to read in the integer data member month. If month is formatted correctly, getData calls checkFormat again to read in the integer data member day. If day is formatted correctly, getData calls checkFormat again to read in the integer data member year. If year has been entered in the proper format, checkData calls the member function validate.

- The member function named checkFormat should check to see if the value to be read in is a number between 0 and 9 inclusively or is a blank. If it is a number, then the value is read in and the data member good is set to true. If it is not a number, then a message "You used the wrong format to enter the date." is displayed and the data member good is set to false.

- The member function validate should check that the month is within the limits of 1 to 12, and that the days are within the limits associated with each month. The year should be a positive integer value. If a valid date is entered, the data member good should be set to true; if invalid, good should be set to false and a message that an invalid date has been entered should be displayed.

- The member function displayDate should display the date entered.

1b.   Implement in C++ the design of your member functions. Open your **testDate.cpp** file and add the new code below your `Date` class definition. Save your **testDate.cpp** with the changes in the Chap12 folder of your Student Disk. Compile. Because there is no main function defined, you will not be able to link or execute this code. Print the source code.

2a.   Using the `Exchange` class created in Lab 12.1, Exercise 8a, design the member functions so that they meet the following criteria:

- The member function named `getData` should prompt the user for the type of currency: (p) for Mexican pesos, (d) for U. S. dollars, (f) for Swiss francs, (e) for Euro dollars, and (q) for quit, and then input the character into the data member `entered.type`. If a 'q' is entered, the value false is returned. If a valid character is entered, the program prompts the user for an amount, and inputs that amount into the data member `entered.amount`. Use a loop in the function until the user enters q to quit or enters a valid type.

- The member function named `displayExchange` displays the type of currency and the beginning amount and the amount in U. S. dollars. The amounts are displayed in six decimal places. The member function `outputType` is called from `displayExchange`.

- The member function named `outputType` displays a description for the character type of currency; for example, 'd' would display "U. S. dollars".

- The member function named `convert` assigns the exchange amount of the value entered in U. S. dollars to `US.amount` and assigns the character type of `entered.type` to `US.type`. The conversions are:

1 U. S. dollar = 0.9553 Euro dollars = 1.4054 Swiss francs = 9.815 Mexican pesos

2b.   Implement in C++ the design of your member functions. Open your **testExchange.cpp** file and add the new code below your `Exchange` class definition. Save your **testExchange.cpp** with the changes in the Chap12 folder of your Student Disk. Compile. Because there is no main function defined, you will not be able to link or execute this code. Print the source code.

LAB 12.3 DESIGNING DRIVER PROGRAMS

All C++ programs must have a `main` function. The class does not have a `main` function. To test a class, you must write a driver program (one that has a `main` function) that contains the class definition and instantiates an object of the class.

Objectives

In this lab, you become acquainted with using a class in a driver program.

After completing this lab, you will be able to:

■ Write a driver program that contains a class definition.

■ Instantiate an object of a class.

■ Access public class members through objects of the class.

Estimated completion time: **40–50 minutes**

Designing Driver Programs

1a. *Critical Thinking Exercise:* Create the design for a driver program that implements the `Date` class you implemented in **testDate.cpp**. Your `main` function should call a function `instruct` that describes the purpose and use of the program; instantiate the `today` object that you created in Lab 12.1, Exercise 6c; prompt the user with the message "Please enter today's date, month, day, and year separated by spaces:"; and call the class function `getData` using the `today` object.

Write your design in the following space. Your design should be a list of C++ comments without any code.

1b.   Write a C++ program based on the design you created in Exercise 1a. Step through the code by hand.

In the following space, show what is displayed on the screen after executing the output message.

1c.   Enter, compile, link, and execute **testDate.cpp**. Then copy the output and save it in a block comment at the end of your program. Save **testDate.cpp** in the Chap12 folder of your Student Disk.

The following is a copy of the screen results that might appear after running your program, depending on the data entered. The input entered by the user is shown in bold.

```
This program prompts the user to enter a date and validates the date
entered.
Please enter today's date (month, day, and year separated by spaces):
12/23/2005
```

With that input, the output displayed should resemble:

```
You used the wrong format to enter the date.
```

Run the program again with the following input:

```
11 23 2005
```

With that input, the output displayed should resemble:

```
You entered: 11-23-2005
```

2a.   Design a driver program that implements the Exchange class you used in **testExchange.cpp**. Your main function should call the function instruct to show the purpose and use of the program, prompt the user to enter a currency type and amount, and loop until the user enters q. Your loop control should be the return value from the class function getData using the amount object that you created in Lab 12.1, Exercise 8c. The loop should continue until the returned value is false. Within the loop the data member functions convert and displayExchange should be called.

Write your design in the following space. Your design should be a list of C++ comments without any code.

2b.   Write a C++ program based on the design you created in Exercise 2a. Step through the code by hand.

In the following space, show what is displayed on the screen after executing the output message.

2c.   Enter, compile, link, and execute **testExchange.cpp**. Then copy the output and save it in a block comment at the end of your program. Save **testExchange.cpp** in the Chap12 folder of your Student Disk.

The following is a copy of the screen results that might appear after running your program, depending on the data entered. The input entered by the user is shown in bold.

```
This program prompts the user to enter
a character to designate the type of
currency to be exchanged and the amount of money
to be exchanged.

Enter a character for currency type and an amount.
(P)esos, Swiss (f)rancs, (E)uro dollars or (q)uit: x 123.543
You entered an invalid type, please re-enter.

p 123.543
You entered 123.54 in Pesos, which is $12.59 in U.S. dollars.

Enter a character for currency type and an amount.
(P)esos, Swiss (f)rancs, (E)uro dollars or (q)uit: f 500
You entered 500.00 in Swiss francs, which is $355.77 in U.S. dollars.

Enter a character for currency type and an amount.
(P)esos, Swiss (f)rancs, (E)uro dollars or (q)uit: e 987
You entered 987.00 in Euro dollars, which is $1033.18 in U.S. dollars.

Enter a character for currency type and an amount.
(P)esos, Swiss (f)rancs, (E)uro dollars or (q)uit: q
```

LAB 12.4 INVOKING DEFAULT CONSTRUCTORS, CONSTRUCTORS WITH PARAMETERS, AND CONSTRUCTORS WITH DEFAULT PARAMETERS

C++ does not automatically initialize variables. To guarantee that the data members of a class are initialized, you use constructors. The constructor without parameters is called the default constructor.

Constructor functions have the same names as the class, have no type, and are automatically executed when a class object enters its scope. (They cannot be called directly.) When there are multiple constructors, the names are the same, but the parameter lists must differ. All constructors must be public data members.

If there is more than one constructor, the constructor called when an object is instantiated is decided by the formal parameter list and arguments. If the type of arguments does not match the formal parameters of any constructor, C++ does a type conversion and looks for the best match. Any ambiguity will result in a compile-time error.

A constructor with all default parameters is the default constructor. You should not have multiple default constructors. However, a constructor with no parameters will be ignored when a constructor with default parameters is part of the class.

If a class has constructors and you declare an array of class objects, the class must have the default constructor. It is not possible to specify different constructors for each component.

Objectives

In this lab, you define a constructor with parameters.

After completing this lab, you will be able to:

- Write a default constructor function.

- Write a constructor function with parameters.

- Write a constructor function with default parameters.

- Create an array of objects that uses the default constructor.

Estimated completion time: **60–75 minutes**

Invoking Default Constructors, Constructors with Parameters, and Constructors with Default Parameters

The Information Technology (IT) Department of a company wants to maintain consistency in the different areas dealing with employee information. To do this they need a class to keep track of employee information. In addition, their Equal Employment Opportunity (EEO) Department needs to report ethnicity statistics to the federal government. You will need to use the Date class you created in Lab 12-3, Exercise 1a.

1a.   Create a UML diagram for a class named Employee that will contain data members and member functions to allow consistency in the company programs. Your class should meet the criteria in the following list:

- The private string data members named lastName and firstName

- A private character data member named ethnicity

- The private double data member rateOfPay

- The private `Date` (created in Lab 12.1) data member `startDate`
- The default constructor `Employee` to set the base pay rate
- The constructor `Employee` with parameters to assign the pay rate
- The public member method `pay` to calculate the employee pay
- The public member method `eeo` to report the ethnic diversity
- The private member method `newHire` to add employees

Write the class definition in the space provided.

1b.   Using the `Employee` class design you created in Exercise 1a, design the member functions so that they meet the following criteria:

- The default constructor `Employee` sets the `rateOfPay` to 7.25 and calls the private member method `newHire`.
- The constructor `Employee` has a double parameter `rate` that assigns `rate` to `rateOfPay` and calls the private member method `newHire`.

- The member method newHire prompts the user for the starting date in the format mm dd yyyy; calls the Date member method getData with the startDate data member; prompts the user for first and last name; inputs the values entered into the data members firstName and lastName; prompts the user for ethnicity using the following characters (C)aucasion, (A)frican American, (N)ative American, (H)ispanic, A(s)ian, (O)ther; enters the value entered into the data member ethnicity; and converts the value entered to uppercase.

- The member method pay prompts the user by name for the number of hours worked during the week, calculates the payAmount, and displays the weekly salary. Overtime of 1.5 should be paid for all hours worked greater than 40.

- The member method eeo should display the employee's ethnicity according to the value of the data member ethnicity.

1c.   Implement in C++ the design of your class and class member functions. Save your code in a file named **testEmployee.cpp** in the Chap12 folder of your Student Disk. Compile and correct any syntax errors.

1d.   Define an object named worker of the class Employee and an object named suit with a parameter 25.0. Write the object definitions in the space provided.

1e.   Write a driver program that implements the Exchange and Date classes. Using the objects created in Exercise 1d, call the member methods pay and eeo. Enter compile, link, and execute **testEmployee.cpp**. Then copy the output and save it in a block comment at the end of your program. Save **testEmployee.cpp** in the Chap12 folder of your Student Disk.

The following is a copy of the screen results that might appear after running your program depending on the data entered. The input entered by the user is shown in bold.

```
The program testEmployee.cpp is a driver program to test the class
Employee.

Enter first name and last name separated by a space: Juanita Gonzalez
Please enter starting date mm dd yyyy for Juanita Gonzalez: 11 02 2004
Please enter your ethnicity: (C)aucasian, (A)frican American,
(N)ative American, (H)ispanic, A(s)ian, (O)ther: H

Enter first name and last name separated by a space: Gordon Chang
Please enter starting date mm dd yyyy for Gordon Chang: 09 02 1984
Please enter your ethnicity: (C)aucasian, (A)frican American,
(N)ative American, (H)ispanic, A(s)ian, (O)ther: s

How many hours did Juanita Gonzalez work this week? 42

Weekly pay for Juanita Gonzalez is $311.75
The employee ethnicity is Hispanic.

How many hours did Gordon Chang work this week? 54

Weekly pay for Gordon Chang is $1525.00
The employee ethnicity is Asian.
```

2a.   Redesign your class Employee to have one constructor with a default parameter rather than two constructors. The redesigned program will be named **testEmployee2.cpp**.

2b.   Enter, compile, link, and execute **testEmployee2.cpp**. Then copy the output and save it in a block comment at the end of your program. Save **testEmployee2.cpp** in the Chap12 folder of your Student Disk. Your output should be the same for both testEmployee.cpp and testEmployee2.cpp.

3a.   Change your **testEmployee2.cpp** program to create an array object `hourly` of the class `Employee` of size 5. Change your program to call the member method for each array element. Save the new program as **testEmployee3.cpp** in the Chap12 folder of your Student Disk.

3b.   Enter, compile, link, and execute **testEmployee3.cpp**. Then copy the output and save it in a block comment at the end of your program.

The following is a copy of the screen results that might appear after running your program depending on the data entered. The input entered by the user is shown in bold.

```
The program testEmployee.cpp is a driver program to test the class
Employee.

Enter first name and last name separated by a space: Angela Vito
Please enter starting date mm dd yyyy for Angela Vito: 1 14 2002
Please enter your ethnicity: (C)aucasian, (A)frican American,
(N)ative American, (H)ispanic, A(s)ian, (O)ther: C

Enter first name and last name separated by a space: Boubacar Zimba
Please enter starting date mm dd yyyy for Boubacar Zimba: 3 5 2003
Please enter your ethnicity: (C)aucasian, (A)frican American,
(N)ative American, (H)ispanic, A(s)ian, (O)ther: A

Enter first name and last name separated by a space: Charles Casey
Please enter starting date mm dd yyyy for Charles Casey: 5 8 2001
Please enter your ethnicity: (C)aucasian, (A)frican American,
(N)ative American, (H)ispanic, A(s)ian, (O)ther: C

Enter first name and last name separated by a space: Wanda Torres
Please enter starting date mm dd yyyy for Wanda Torres: 12 14 2000
Please enter your ethnicity: (C)aucasian, (A)frican American,
(N)ative American, (H)ispanic, A(s)ian, (O)ther: H

Enter first name and last name separated by a space: Huy Wuan
Please enter starting date mm dd yyyy for Huy Wuan: 3 22 1999
Please enter your ethnicity: (C)aucasian, (A)frican American,
(N)ative American, (H)ispanic, A(s)ian, (O)ther: s

Enter first name and last name separated by a space: Jack Smith
Please enter starting date mm dd yyyy for Jack Smith: 8 12 1998
Please enter your ethnicity: (C)aucasian, (A)frican American,
(N)ative American, (H)ispanic, A(s)ian, (O)ther: o

How many hours did Angela Vito work this week? 37

Weekly pay for Angela Vito is $268.25
The employee ethnicity is Caucasian.

How many hours did Boubacar Zimba work this week? 42

Weekly pay for Boubacar Zimba is $311.75
The employee ethnicity is African American.

How many hours did Charles Casey work this week? 14
```

Weekly pay for Charles Casey is $101.50
The employee ethnicity is Caucasian.

How many hours did Wanda Torres work this week? **47**

Weekly pay for Wanda Torres is $366.13
The employee ethnicity is Hispanic.

How many hours did Huy Wuan work this week? **28**

Weekly pay for Huy Wuan is $203.00
The employee ethnicity is Asian.

How many hours did Jack Smith work this week? **56**

Weekly pay for Jack Smith is $1600.00
The employee ethnicity is not listed.

LAB 12.5 INVOKING DESTRUCTORS

A destructor is another type of function used in a class. It is not typed, has no parameters, and there can be only one destructor per class. The name of the destructor is the same as the name of the class, but it is differentiated from the constructor by the tilde character (~). The destructor automatically executes when the class object goes out of scope.

Objectives

In this lab, you define a destructor of a class.

After completing this lab, you will be able to:

■ Write a destructor for a class.

Estimated completion time: **10–15 minutes**

Invoking Destructors

1a. Modify your `Employee` class to include a destructor. Design a destructor function that outputs the message "Employment for `Employee` has been terminated."

1b. Revise your **testEmployee3.cpp** program, saving it as **testEmployee4.cpp**. Compile, link, and execute **testEmployee4.cpp**. Then copy the output and save it in a block comment at the end of your program. Save **testEmployee4.cpp** in the Chap12 folder of your Student Disk.

The following is a copy of the screen results that might appear after running your program depending on the data entered. The input entered by the user is shown in bold.

```
The program testEmployee.cpp is a driver program to test the class
Employee.

Enter first name and last name separated by a space: Juanita Gonzalez
Please enter starting date mm dd yyyy for Juanita Gonzalez: 11 2 2004
Please enter your ethnicity: (C)aucasian, (A)frican American,
(N)ative American, (H)ispanic, A(s)ian, (O)ther: H

Enter first name and last name separated by a space: Gordon Chang
Please enter starting date mm dd yyyy for Gordon Chang: 9 2 1984
Please enter your ethnicity: (C)aucasian, (A)frican American,
(N)ative American, (H)ispanic, A(s)ian, (O)ther: s

How many hours did Juanita Gonzalez work this week? 42

Weekly pay for Juanita Gonzalez is $311.75
The employee ethnicity is Hispanic.

How many hours did Gordon Chang work this week? 54

Weekly pay for Gordon Chang is $1525.00
The employee ethnicity is Asian.

Employment for Gordon Chang has been terminated.
Employment for Juanita Gonzalez has been terminated.
```

LAB 12.6 USING THE ABSTRACT DATA TYPE AND INFORMATION HIDING

Separating the design details from their use is called abstraction. An abstract data type (ADT) is a data type that specifies the logical properties without the implementation details. Hiding the implementation details ensures that an object will be used in exactly the same way throughout the project. The implementation details are placed in a separate file, called an implementation file. The specifications are kept in a file called a header file that has the extension .h.

The implementation file contains the definitions of the functions to implement the operations of an object. There is no `main` function in the implementation file. The object code of the implementation file is linked with the object code of the program using the class (the source file). The implementation file has an extension of .cpp.

The implementation file must include the specification file (the .h file enclosed in double quotation marks) so that it will compile. When using an SDK, all files are put in the same project to be compiled, linked, and executed.

Objectives

In this lab, you create a specification file, an implementation file, and a file with a program that includes the class.

After completing this lab, you will be able to:

■ Create a specification file.

■ Create an implementation file.

■ Create a file that uses the class specified and implemented in the specification and implementation files.

Estimated completion time: **40–50 minutes**

Using the Abstract Data Type and Information Hiding

1a. *Critical Thinking Exercise:* Using the program **testDate.cpp**, place the class `Date` definition in the header file **Date.h**, the implementation of the class functions in the file **Date.cpp**, and the rest of the program in **testDateAB.cpp**. Save the files in the Chap12 folder of your Student Disk.

1b. Enter, compile, link, and execute **testDateAB.cpp** and **Date.cpp**. Copy the output for each and save it in a block comment at the end of your program. Save **testDateAB.cpp** and **Date.cpp** in the Chap12 folder of your Student Disk. Your output should be the same as your output for testDate.cpp.

2a. Using the program **testExchange.cpp**, place the `struct Money` definition in the header file **Money.h**, the class `Exchange` definition in the header file **Money.h**, the implementation of the `Money` class functions in the file **Money.h**, delete the `Date` class definition and functions, and save the rest of the program in **testExchangeAB.cpp**. Save the files in the Chap12 folder of your Student Disk.

2b. Enter, compile, link, and execute **testExchangeAB.cpp** and **Money.h**. Copy the output for each and save it in a block comment at the end of your program. Save **testExchangeAB.cpp** and **Money.h** in the Chap12 folder of your Student Disk. Your output should be the same as your output for **testExchange.cpp**.

3a.   Using the program **testEmployee2.cpp**, place the class `Employee` definition in the header file **Employee.h**, the implementation of the `Employee` class functions in the file **Employee.cpp**, delete the `Date` class definition and functions, and save the rest of the program in **testEmployeeAB.cpp**. Save the files in the Chap12 folder of your Student Disk.

3b.   Enter, compile, link, and execute **testEmployeeAB.cpp** and **Employee.cpp**. Copy the output for each and save it in a block comment at the end of your program. Save **testEmployeeAB.cpp** and **Employee.cpp** in the Chap12 folder of your Student Disk. Your output should be the same as your output for **testEmployee.cpp**.

Lab 12.7 Static Members of a Class

A class can have static members—functions or data.

- If a function of a class is static in the class definition, it is declared using the keyword `static` in its heading.

- If a data member of a class is static, it is declared using the keyword `static`.

- A public static member, function, or data of a class can be accessed using the class name and the scope resolution operator.

Objectives

In this lab, you become acquainted with static data members and static member methods of a class.

After completing this lab, you will be acquainted with:

- Static member functions of a class.

- Static data members of a class.

Estimated completion time: **10–15 minutes**

Static Members of a Class

Question	Answer (Circle the correct answer)
1. When you create objects of a class, which data members of the class become the data members of each object?	a. non-static data members b. static data members c. all data members
2. How many memory locations are allocated for static data members?	a. one for each object created b. one
3. Static data members of a class exit even when no object of the class type exists.	T F
4. To create a static data member of a class, use the keyword `static` in front of the data member declaration and define the variable in the implementation file.	T F

5. Given the following program, what is the output?

a. A compile error occurs.

b. A garbage value is displayed.

c. The value 1 is displayed.

```
#include <iostream>
using namespace std;

class exercise
{
public:
    static int number;
    void increment();
    void printNumber();
};

void exercise::increment()
{
    number++;
}

void exercise::printNumber()
{
    cout << number << endl;
}

int exercise::number;

int main()
{
    exercise first, second;
    first.increment();
    second.printNumber();
    return 0;
}
```

6. To create a static member function, put the keyword `static` in front of the function definition.

T   F

7. A static member function is used to access static data members of the class.

T   F

13 Inheritance and Composition

In this chapter, you will:

- O Learn about inheritance
- O Learn about derived and base classes
- O Explore how to redefine the member functions of a base class
- O Examine how the constructors of base and derived classes work
- O Learn how to construct the header file of a derived class
- O Become familiar with the C++ stream hierarchy
- O Explore three types of inheritance: `public`, `protected`, and `private`
- O Learn about composition
- O Become familiar with the three basic principles of object-oriented design

CHAPTER 13: ASSIGNMENT COVER SHEET

Name _____   Date _____

Section _____

Lab Assignments	Assigned	Grade
Lab 13.1 Overriding Member Functions of the Base Class		
Lab 13.2 Using Constructors of Derived and Base Classes		
Lab 13.3 Creating Header Files for the Base Class and the Derived Classes (Critical Thinking Exercises)		
Lab 13.4 Using Protected Members of a Class in Inheritance		
Lab 13.5 Relating Classes through Composition (Critical Thinking Exercises)		
Lab 13.6 Defining Object-Oriented Design (OOD) and Object-Oriented Programming (OOP)		
Total Grade		

See your instructor or the introduction to this book for instructions on submitting your assignments.

Lab 13.1 Overriding Member Functions of the Base Class

Adding members extends the definition of a class. It is not necessary to do this by changing the class directly; instead, you can inherit members of a class when designing another class. Inheritance lets you create classes from existing classes. The new classes are called derived classes, and the existing classes are called base classes.

Each derived class, in turn, could become a base class for a future derived class. In single inheritance, the derived class is derived from a single base class; in multiple inheritance, the derived class is derived from more than one base class.

The public members of a class become public members of the derived class. The private members of a class become private members of the derived class. However, public members of a base class can be inherited either as public members or as private members of the derived class.

Objectives

In this lab, you define derived classes from base classes.

After completing this lab, you will be able to:

- Write a derived class when given the base class.

- Create an instantiation of the derived class (declare objects) and the base class.

- Recognize the difference between objects of the base class and objects of the derived class.

Estimated completion time: **50–60 minutes**

Overriding Member Functions of the Base Class

1a.   Open the **Date.h** and **Date.cpp** class and implementation files from the Chap12 folder on your Student Disk. Change the private integer variables month, day, and year to be public members. Save them in the Chap13 folder of your Student Disk.

1b.   Design a base class named `Animal` to allow the following public data members:

- Integer data members named `lifeExpectancy` and `weight`

- Character data member named `gender`

- String data members called `name` and `type`

The `Animal` class must also allow a public void function named `printValues` with no parameters.

1c.   Design a derived class named `VetPatient` that inherits all the properties of the base class `Animal` as public members and has the following additional private members:

- Date values named `dateIn` and `dateOut`

- Double named `charges`

- String named `procedure`

The class must also allow a void function named `printValues` with no parameters.

1d.   Design a derived class named `Pet` that inherits all the properties of the base class `Animal` as private members and has the following additional public members:

- String value named `home`

- Boolean value named `bites`

- Public void function named `printValues`

Because the base class data members are private for the derived class `Pet`, the function `printValues` needs parameters for the `Animal` class data members.

1e.   Design three `printValues` functions—one for each class `Animal`, `VetPatient`, and `Pet`—that will display all data members for the object of that class and then call the `printValues` function of the `Animal` class when necessary to display private data members of the base class.

1f.   Design a main function to test the classes that you created. Include all comments for documentation and identification of the program in your design. Create an object named **elephant** of the type **Animal**, an object named horse as the type **VetPatient**, and an object named **dog** as the type **Pet**. For gender, use 'm' for male, 'f' for female, 'n' for a neutered male, and 's' for a spayed female. You can expect a male elephant to live 65 years and weigh around 7 tons (13,000 pounds). Depending on the breed, you can expect a dog that has been spayed to live 12 years and weigh around 20 pounds. A dog can be an indoor or outdoor pet, and may or may not bite. You can expect a female racehorse to live 25 years, weigh around 1,000 pounds, and have regular exams by a veterinarian. Using these facts, assign values to each data member in the class and call the **printValues** functions to output the values after they have been assigned.

1g. Write a C++ program based on the designs you created and name it **AnimalLife.cpp**. Step through the code by hand.

In the following space, show what is displayed on the screen after executing the output message using the following data with the following arguments:

- Animal elephant('M',65,"Jumbo",14000,"elephant")

- VetPatient horse('F', 25, "Pretty Filly", 1000, "horse", 8, 30, 2005, 8, 31, 2005, "check up", 58)

- Pet dog('S', 12, "Fifi", 20, "dog", false, "indoors")

Also call the printValues functions.

1h. Enter, compile, link, and execute **AnimalLife.cpp**. Then copy the output and save it in a block comment at the end of your program. Save **AnimalLife.cpp** in the Chap13 folder of your Student Disk.

The following is a copy of the screen results that might appear after running your program:

```
A male elephant named Jumbo should live to be 65 and weigh 13000 pounds.

A female horse named Pretty Filly should live to be 25 and weigh
1000 pounds.
The horse checked in 8/30/2005 and checked out 8/31/2005.
The procedure performed was a checkup at a cost of $58.00.

A spayed dog named Fifi should live to be 12 and weigh 20 pounds.
Your dog lives indoors and does not bite.
```

LAB **13.2** USING CONSTRUCTORS OF DERIVED AND BASE CLASSES

If the base class has a constructor function, the derived class must also have a constructor function to reach the private members of the base class. When a constructor of the base class has parameters, you specify the base class constructor name with the parameters in the heading of the derived class constructor definition.

Objectives

In this lab, you design constructor functions to initialize values sent at instantiation of the class objects.

After completing this lab, you will be able to:

- Use constructor functions in a base class.

- Use constructor funcitons in a derived class.

Estimated completion time: **30–40 minutes**

Creating Header Files for the Base Class and the Derived Classes

1a. Using the classes `Animal`, `VetPatient`, and `Pet` that you created in Lab 13.1, design constructor functions to initialize values sent at instantiation of the class objects. Design a new source program that has a main function. Your main function should instantiate the same objects that you used in **AnimalLife.cpp** with the following arguments:

- Animal elephant('M',65,"Jumbo",14000,"elephant")

- VetPatient horse('F', 25, "Pretty Filly", 1000, "horse", 8, 30, 2005, 8, 31, 2005, "check up", 58)

- Pet dog('S', 12, "Fifi", 20, "dog", false, "indoors")

Also call the `printValues` functions. Name the revised program AnimalLife2.cpp.

1b.   Enter, compile, link, and execute **AnimalLife2.cpp**. Then copy the output and save it in a block comment at the end of your program. Save **AnimalLife2.cpp** in the Chap13 folder of your Student Disk.

Compare your output to your output in **AnimalLife.cpp**. It should be the same.

LAB 13.3 CREATING HEADER FILES FOR THE BASE CLASS AND THE DERIVED CLASSES

Derived classes can be contained in header files, the same as a base class. When the derived class is in a separate file, the file containing the base class must be used in the file containing the derived class, using the preprocessor directive include.

If you try to compile a program that has more than one file that includes the same user-defined class, you will get compile errors because of the duplicated class definition. To avoid this duplication, the following preprocessor directives are used: `ifndef` (meaning if not defined), `define` (meaning define), and `endif` (meaning end of the if not defined).

The data items of a class should be private when at all possible. This is information hiding that protects the members of the class from being changed.

Objectives

In this lab, you become acquainted with using multiple header files of classes requiring the preprocessors `ifndef`, `define`, and `endif`.

After completing this lab, you will be able to:

■ Write a base class and derived classes using the preprocessors `ifndef`, `define`, and `endif`.

> Estimated completion time: **40–50 minutes**

Creating Header Files for the Base Class and the Derived Classes

1a.   Using **AnimalLife2.cpp**, break the classes into individual header files.

Save your header files as **Date.h**, **Animal.h**, **VetPatient.h**, and **Pet.h** and the implementation in C++ of the class functions in the files **Date.cpp**, **Animal.cpp**, **VetPatient.cpp**, and **Pet.cpp**.

Include the header files in your program and save the program as **AnimalLife3.cpp** in the Chap13 folder of your Student Disk.

1b.   Enter, compile, link, and execute **AnimalLife3.cpp**. Then copy the output and save it in a block comment at the end of your program. Save **AnimalLife3.cpp** in the Chap13 folder of your Student Disk.

Compare your output to the output in **AnimalLife.cpp** and **AnimalLife2.cpp**. All output should be the same

2a.   *Critical Thinking Exercise*: Design a program for a veterinarian's office. Use the **Date.h**, **Date.cpp**, **Animal.h**, and **Animal.cpp** files. Design a new header file named **VetOffice.h** and the member function implementation file **VetOffice.cpp** that is similar to the VetPatient.h header file you created in Exercise 1. Make the changes necessary to include the following requirements.

The veterinary practice is limited to dogs and cats. The procedures provided by the office include:

■ Checkups for $40

■ Spaying for $75

■ Neutering for $50

■ Anesthesia for $40

- Worming for $10

- Annual cat inoculations for $75

- Annual dog inoculations for $60

- Dog grooming for $75

- Declawing for $75

- Nail clipping for $8

- Surgery type 1 for $100

- Surgery type 2 for $200

- Surgery type 3 for $300

- Boarding for $18 per night

- Other (allows both the service and the amount to be entered)

You also need to total the charges for the day. Enter the data for each patient. Create a daily output report file named **patients.txt** with the day's procedures. Display information about the patient procedure and cost on the screen.

2b.   Write a C++ program based on the designs you created in Exercise 2a, and name it **VetReport.cpp**. Step through the code by hand.

2c.   Enter, compile, link, and execute **VetReport.cpp**. Then copy the output and save it in a block comment at the end of your program. Save **VetReport.cpp** in the Chap13 folder of your Student Disk. Print your patients.txt file and attach it to your program.

The instructions to the user should appear at execution and again when requested by the user. They should resemble the following:

```
The Healthy Pet Clinic offers services for your cats and dogs.

1        Anesthesia $40
2        Annual cat inoculations $75
3        Annual dog inoculations $60
4        Boarding per night $18
5        Checkups $40
6        Declawing $75
7        Dog grooming $75
8        Nail or claw clipping $8
9        Neutering $50
10       Spaying $75
11       Worming $10
12       Surgery type 1 $100
13       Surgery type 2 $200
14       Surgery type 3 $300
15       Other
0        Quit
```

The date prompt should occur after the first set of instructions. It should resemble the following code and continue until a valid date has been entered.

```
Please enter today's date (month, day, and year separated by spaces):
12 02 2005
```

The following prompts should appear until the user enters a 0 to end the program or until a valid procedure number has been entered.

```
Please enter the number of the service that you wish: 2
Please enter the name of your pet: Ferdinand
Please enter whether your pet is a cat or a dog: cat
Please enter the gender of your pet (m)ale, (f)emale, (s)payed,
(n)eutered: n
Would you like to see the instructions (y)es or (n)o? n
```

If an invalid number of service is entered, the following message and prompt should be displayed until a valid procedure number is entered.

```
You entered an invalid procedure.
Please enter the number of the service that you wish: 2
```

If a 15 is entered as the procedure number, the following prompt should appear.

```
Please enter the cost of this procedure: 85
```

If an invalid pet type is entered, the following message and prompt should be displayed until a valid pet type is entered.

```
This practice is limited to dogs and cats
Please enter whether your pet is a cat or a dog: cat
```

If an invalid gender type is entered, the following message and prompt should be displayed until a valid gender type is entered.

```
You did not enter a valid gender.
Please enter the gender of your pet (m)ale, (f)emale, (s)payed,
(n)eutered: n
```

If procedure 4 (boarding per night $18) is chosen, the following prompt should appear.

```
How many days do you wish to board? 1
```

If a positive number is not entered, the following message and prompt should be displayed until a positive number is entered.

```
You entered an invalid number of days
```

For each patient that visits the veterinary clinic, a message similar to the following one should appear, depending on the input data.

```
The following services were performed on your neutered cat Ferdinand:
12/02/2005      2       annual cat inoculations at a cost of $75.00.
```

The output file patients.txt should resemble the following report, depending on the data entered.

```
        The Healthy Pet Clinic Services for 12-2-2005


    Patient                 Service                     Fees

Bowser              1   anesthesia                  $ 40.00
Ferdinand           2   annual cat inoculations     $ 75.00
Fifi                3   annual dog inoculations     $ 60.00
Rover               4   boarding per night          $ 54.00
Harvard             5   checkups                    $ 40.00
Sweetie             6   declawing                   $ 75.00
Isabel              7   dog grooming                $ 75.00
Tia                 8   nail or claw clipping       $  8.00
```

```
Spot            9  neutering                 $ 50.00
Fluffy         10  spaying                   $ 75.00
Gretchen       11  worming                   $ 10.00
Heinrich       12  surgery type 1            $100.00
Lucky          13  surgery type 2            $200.00
Zachery        14  surgery type 3            $300.00
Fido           15  other                     $ 20.00


Total                                       $1182.00
```

LAB 13.4 USING PROTECTED MEMBERS OF A CLASS IN INHERITANCE

Another access to a class is called protected. The accessibility of a protected member of a class is between public and private. A derived class can directly access the protected members of a base class.

A protected member of a base class is public to the derived class, but private outside of the derived class and the base class. By using the `protected` specifier, you can create a class member that can be inherited and accessed but remain private otherwise.

Objectives

In this lab, you become acquainted with the differences among `public`, `private`, and `protected` specifiers for accessing members of a base class. You also learn about the inheritance of these specifiers.

After completing this lab, you will be able to:

- Differentiate among `public`, `private`, and `protected` specifiers of members of a class.

Estimated completion time: **20–30 minutes**

Using Protected Members of a Class in Inheritance

The following exercises are designed to demonstrate your understanding of the differences among `public`, `private`, and `protected` specifiers of members of a class so that you are better be prepared to design and write programs that use protected members of a class in inheritance.

1. Show by example how a derived class inherits a base class.

2. What members of the base class are included in the derived class?

3. Can a derived class inherit public members of the base class as private members of the derived class?

4. If so, how are these members accessed in the derived class?

5. Can a derived class inherit private members of the base class as public members of the derived class?

6. How are these members accessed in the derived class?

7. Can a derived class inherit protected members of the base class as public members of the derived class?

8. How are these members accessed in the derived class?

9. Can a derived class inherit public members of the base class as protected members of the derived class?

10. Can a derived class inherit protected members of the base class as private members of the derived class?

Lab 13.5 Relating Classes through Composition

Composition allows a class to be composed of objects of another class. When you include the string data type in your class, then you are using composition. Similarly, the first three labs of this chapter used the Date header file to allow Date data types. This, too, is composition.

When an object of a class is a data member of another class, the private data members of that class must be accessed through public or protected members of the class. When constructor functions are used for initialization, you invoke the constructor function of the class object in the class by associating that class using the colon, the class name, and arguments to the constructor function of the class object.

Objectives

In this lab, you become acquainted with accessing the constructor function of a class that has an object of that class as a data member.

After completing this lab, you will be able to:

■ Access the constructor function of a class that has an object of that class as a data member.

Estimated completion time: **50–60 minutes**

Relating Classes through Composition

In the following exercises, you redesign header files, and then create a program based on your designs. After running a program, copy the output and then paste it in a comment block at the end of your program. Submit your program with the output in the comment block.

1a.   *Critical Thinking Exercise:* Redesign the Date class in the **Date.h** header file in Chap13 folder of your Student Disk to have a constructor function that has three integer formal parameters that initialize the private data members month, day, and year. Because month, day, and year are now private, create a getDate2 function that has three integer values that are passed by reference. The function getDate2 should assign those parameters the values of the private data members month, day, and year. Rename your new Date.h file **Date2.h**.

1b.   Redesign the VetPatient class in the **VetPatient.h** header file in the Chap13 folder of your Student Disk to conform to the changes in the **Date2.h** file. Your constructor function should add six additional integer values that are passed by reference to access the private data members of the new Date class to return to the main function. You will need to create two objects, dateIn and dateOut, of the type Date2 with arguments to initialize the Date2 private data members. You need to call the getDate2 function with both objects to access the private data members. You need to change your printValues function to have six integer formal parameters for the month, day, and year values for both dateIn and dateOut.

1c.   Redesign **AnimalLife3.cpp** in the Chap13 folder of your Student Disk to use the new **Date2.h** and **VetPatient2.h** header files. You need to declare six local integer variables inMonth, inDay, inYear, outMonth, outDay, outYear to set with the dates of the private data members month, day, and year from the objects dateIn and dateOut that are created in the **VetPatient2.h** class. Include these as arguments in the list of arguments for the VetPatient2 constructor function and as arguments for the VetPatient2 printValues function.

1d.   Revise VetPatient.cpp to use the new VetPatient2.h and save the program as **VetPatient2.cpp**. Revise Date.cpp to use the new Date.h and save the program as **Date2.cpp**. Be sure to include the same versions of Pet.h, Pet.cpp, Animal.h, and Animal.cpp from previous labs.

2. *Critical Thinking Exercise:* Save the new Date.h header file as **Date2.h** in the Chap13 folder of your Student Disk. Save the new VetPatient.h as **VetPatient2.h** in the Chap13 folder of your Student Disk. Save your program as **AnimalLife4.cpp** in the Chap13 file of your Student Disk. Compile, run, and test the program. Copy the output that is displayed, and then paste it in a block comment at the end of your program. Compare your output to your output from **AnimalLife2.cpp** and **AnimalLife3.cpp**. All the output should be the same.

LAB 13.6 DEFINING OBJECT-ORIENTED DESIGN (OOD) AND OBJECT-ORIENTED PROGRAMMING (OOP)

This lab is designed to reinforce the principles of object-oriented design that you have used in the previous labs of this chapter. Object-oriented design has three basic principles:

- Encapsulation—The ability to combine data, and operations on that data, in a single unit

- Inheritance—The ability to create objects from existing objects

- Polymorphism—The ability to use the same expression to denote different operations

OOD encourages code reuse. Once an object becomes error-free, it can be reused in many programs because it is a self-contained entity. Object-oriented programming implements OOD.

Objects are created when class variables are declared. Objects interact with each other via function calls. The private members form the internal state of an object. The public members form the external state of an object.

Objectives

In this lab, you recognize the principles of object-oriented design and become acquainted with the differences between structured programming and object-oriented programming.

After completing this lab, you will be able to:

- Recognize the principles of object-oriented design.

- Differentiate between structured programming and object-oriented programming.

Estimated completion time: **15–20 minutes**

Defining Object-Oriented Design (OOD) and Object-Oriented Programming (OOP)

These questions reinforce the principles that you have applied in previous labs in this chapter.

1. What is the basic unit of encapsulation?

2. What OOD property supports the concept of hierarchical classification?

3. What OOD property allows multiple operations when using the same expression?

4. What unit allows information hiding?

5. What type of programming is also called the top-down approach to programming?

6. What type of programming separates functions and data?

7. What type of programming encapsulates functions and data?

8. Which type of programming is easier to reuse?

9. How do objects interact?

10. What is the difference between an internal state and an external state of an object?

14 Pointers, Classes, and Virtual Functions

In this chapter, you will:

- O Learn about the pointer data type and pointer variables
- O Explore how to declare and manipulate pointer variables
- O Learn about the address of operator and the dereferencing operator
- O Discover dynamic variables
- O Explore how to use the `new` and `delete` operators to manipulate dynamic variables
- O Learn about pointer arithmetic
- O Discover dynamic arrays
- O Become aware of the shallow and deep copies of data
- O Discover the peculiarities of classes with pointer data members
- O Learn about virtual functions
- O Examine the relationship between the address of operator and classes

CHAPTER 14: ASSIGNMENT COVER SHEET

Name _____   Date _____

Section _____

Lab Assignments	Assigned	Grade
Lab 14.1 Declaring Pointer Variables, the Address of Operator (&), and the Dereferencing Operator (*)		
Lab 14.2 Accessing Pointers to Classes and Structs		
Lab 14.3 Using Dynamic Variables and Dynamic Arrays (Critical Thinking Exercises)		
Lab 14.4 Understanding Shallow versus Deep Copy and Pointers		
Lab 14.5 Understanding Peculiarities of Classes with Pointer Data Members		
Lab 14.6 Using Inheritance, Pointers, and Virtual Functions (Critical Thinking Exercises)		
Total Grade		

See your instructor or the introduction to this book for instructions on submitting your assignments.

LAB 14.1 DECLARING POINTER VARIABLES, THE ADDRESS OF OPERATOR (&), AND THE DEREFERENCING OPERATOR (*)

The values belonging to pointer data types are the memory addresses (memory locations). When you declare a pointer variable, you also specify the data type of the value to be stored in the memory location pointed to by the pointer variable. The following is the general syntax of declaring a pointer variable:

```
dataType *identifier;
```

or

```
dataType* identifier;
```

In C++, the ampersand (&) is called the address of operator, and is a unary operator that returns the address of its operand.

In C++, the asterisk character (*) has multiple uses. When used as a unary operator, * is called the dereferencing operator, and refers to the object to which its operand (that is, a pointer) points. For example, consider the following statements:

```
int x = 25;
int *p;
p = &x;    // store the address of x in p
cout << *p << endl;
```

These statements print the value stored in the memory space pointed to by p, which is the value of x.

Objectives

In this lab, you use pointers, the address of operator (&), and the dereferencing operator (*).

After completing this lab, you will be able to:

- Use pointer variables.

- Use the address of operator (&).

- Use the dereferencing operator (*).

Estimated completion time: **20–30 minutes**

Declaring Pointer Variables, the Address of Operator (&), and the Dereferencing Operator (*)

In the following exercises, you design and write a program that uses pointers, the address operator, and the dereferencing operator for all input, calculations, and output.

1a.   Design a program to calculate the cost of gas for a trip. The user will be prompted for the cost of a gallon of gas, the number of miles of the trip, and the number of miles per gallon the car gets. The program should use pointers, the address operator, and the dereferencing operator for all input, calculations, and output.

1b.   Write a C++ program based on the design you created in Exercise 1a and name it **TripCost.cpp**. Step through the code by hand.

In the following space, show what is displayed on the screen after executing the output message.

1c.   Enter, compile, link, and execute **TripCost.cpp**. Then copy the output and save it in a block comment at the end of your program. Save **TripCost.cpp** in the Chap14 folder of your Student Disk.

The following is a copy of the screen results that might appear after running your program. Input by the user is shown in bold.

```
This program calculates the cost of gas for a trip when the user enters
the cost of gas, the number of miles, and the number of miles per gallon
the vehicle gets.

Enter the number of miles in your trip: 890
Enter the mpg your car gets: 23
Enter the cost of gasoline: 1.79
Your trip will cost $68.02
```

LAB 14.2 ACCESSING POINTERS TO CLASSES AND STRUCTS

To assign a value to a component of object using a pointer type, use the following syntax:

```
(*ptrVariableName).classMemberName = value;
```

The dot operator (.) has a higher precedence than the dereferencing operator, requiring the use of parentheses. C++ provides another operator, called the member access operator arrow (->). To assign a value to a component of object using the -> operator, use the following syntax:

```
ptrVariableName->classMemberName = value;
```

If you want to initialize a pointer variable, the only number that can be directly assigned to a pointer variable is 0 or NULL.

Objectives

In this lab, you declare a pointer to a class, initialize the pointer to NULL, and use pointer notation to call member methods of a class.

After completing this lab, you will be able to:

- Declare a pointer to a class.

- Initialize a pointer to NULL.

- Use pointer notation to call member methods of a class.

Estimated completion time: **30–45 minutes**

Accessing Pointers to Classes and Structs

In the following exercises, you create a UML diagram and implementation file, and then write a program that uses pointer notation.

1a.   Design a UML diagram for a class named **Grade.h** with the following private data members:

- `char letterGrade;`

- `int numericGrade;`

- `string student;`

The Grade class includes the following private member method:

- `void calcLetterGrade()` to calculate a letter grade depending on the numeric grade

The Grade class includes the following public member methods:

- `char getLetterGrade()` to return the `letterGrade`

- `int getNumericGrade()` to return the `numericGrade`

- `string getStudent()` to return the `string student`

- a constructor to prompt the user for a student name and a numeric grade, and to call `calcLetterGrade()`

Implement your design in C++ and save the class as **Grade.h** in the Chap14 folder of your Student Disk.

1b.   Write the implementation file **Grade.cpp** for the class Grade, and then compile and save the files in the Chap14 folder of your Student Disk.

1c.   Write a C++ program to test your class that uses pointer notation to the class Grade, and name the program **TestGrade.cpp**. Step through the code by hand.

In the following space, show what is displayed on the screen after executing the output message.

1d.   Enter, compile, link, and execute **TestGrade.cpp**. Then copy the output and save it in a block comment at the end of your program. Save **TestGrade.cpp** in the Chap14 folder of your Student Disk.

The following is a copy of the screen results that might appear after running your program. Input by the user is shown in bold.

```
This program uses pointer notation to the class Grade.

Enter student's name: Zelda Goldstein
Enter numeric score: 86

Zelda Goldstein has a score of 86 for a letter grade of B
```

Lab 14.3 Using Dynamic Variables and Dynamic Arrays

Variables that are created during program execution are called dynamic variables. C++ provides two operators, new and delete, to create and destroy dynamic variables, respectively. The operator new is used to allocate a single variable and to allocate an array of variables.

Consider the following statements:

```
int *p;
int *q;
p = new int;
```

These statements create a variable during program execution somewhere in memory, and store the address of the allocated memory in p.

The following statement creates an array of 16 components and stores the base address of the array in q:

```
q = new char[16]
```

An array created during the execution of a program is called a dynamic array. You can use the increment and decrement operation to access the components of the array. You can also use array notation to access these memory locations. An array name is a constant pointer. You need to copy the value of the array name to another pointer variable to perform increment and decrement operations.

A pointer variable can be passed as a parameter to a function either by value or by reference. Additionally, a function can return a value of the type pointer.

Objectives

In this lab, you create dynamic array variables and pass pointer reference variables.

After completing this lab, you will be able to:

- Call a void function with pointer reference parameters from the main function.

- Create dynamic array variables.

Estimated completion time: **20–30 minutes**

Using Dynamic Variables and Dynamic Arrays

In the following exercises, you create a UML diagram, and then design and write a program that uses dynamic variables and dynamic arrays.

1a.   *Critical Thinking Exercise*: Design a UML diagram for a class named **Vote.h** that has the following elements:

- A constructor to prompt the user for a candidate's name

- A private string data member candidate

Implement your design in C++ and save it as **Vote.h** in the Chap14 folder of your Student Disk.

1b.   Design the member method described in Exercise 1a. Your design should be a list of C++ comments without any code.

Implement your design in C++ and name it **Vote.cpp**. Step through the code by hand. Compile and correct any syntax errors.

1c.   Design a program named **declareCandidacy.cpp** that includes the following elements:

- Four pointer variables: `democrat`, `independent`, `libertarian`, and `republican` of type `Vote`.

- Function `setArray` with a pointer reference variable of type `Vote` and a `char` variable to identify the party.

- The `setArray` function should prompt the user for the number of candidates for the appropriate party and create a dynamic array of type `Vote` of that size.

In the following space, show what is displayed on the screen after executing the output message.

1d.   Enter, compile, link, and execute **declareCandidacy.cpp**. Then copy the output and save it in a block comment at the end of your program. Save **declareCandidacy.cpp** in the Chap14 folder of your Student Disk.

The following is a copy of the screen results that might appear after running your program, depending on the data entered. The input entered by the user is shown in bold.

```
How many Democratic candidates are there? 2
Enter name of candidate: Lawrence Liberal
Enter name of candidate: Lucille Left
How many Independent candidates are there? 1
Enter name of candidate: Gertrude Hopper
How many Libertarian candidates are there? 0
How many Republican candidates are there? 3
Enter name of candidate: Richard Right
Enter name of candidate: Constance Conservative
Enter name of candidate: Hector Rodriquez
```

LAB 14.4 UNDERSTANDING SHALLOW VERSUS DEEP COPY AND POINTERS

In a shallow copy, two or more pointers of the same type point to the same memory; that is, they point to the same data. If the memory is deallocated by deleting the pointer that points to that location, any other pointer that points to that location subsequently becomes invalid.

In a deep copy, two or more pointers have their own data.

Objectives

In this lab, you learn the difference between shallow versus deep copying and pointers.

After completing this lab, you will be able to:

■ Differentiate between shallow versus deep copying and pointers.

Estimated completion time: **5 minutes**

Understanding Shallow versus Deep Copy and Pointers

In the following exercises, you answer multiple-choice questions.

Question

Answer
(Circle the correct answer)

1. The following statements:

```
int *num, *value;
num = new int;
*num = 10;
value = num;
```

are an example of what?

a. shallow copying

b. deep copying

c. a compiler error

2. The following statements:

```
nt *num, *value;
num = new int;
value = new int;
*num = 10;
*value = *num;
```

are an example of what?

a. shallow copying

b. deep copying

c. a compiler error

LAB 14.5 UNDERSTANDING PECULIARITIES OF CLASSES WITH POINTER DATA MEMBERS

When an object goes out of scope, all data members of the object are destroyed. However, if a data member of that object is a pointer used to create a dynamic array, that dynamic memory must be deallocated using the operator `delete`. If the pointer p does not use the `delete` operator to deallocate dynamic memory, the memory space stays marked and cannot be accessed. A destructor can be used to ensure that all memory created by a pointer is deallocated when an object goes out of scope.

To avoid shallow copying of data for classes with a pointer data member, C++ allows the programmer to extend the definition of the assignment operator. This process is called overloading the assignment operator.

When declaring a class object, you can initialize it by using the value of an existing object of the same type. This initialization is called the default member-wise initialization. The default member-wise initialization is due to the constructor, called the copy constructor (provided by the compiler). This would result in shallow copying. To force each object to have its own copy of the data, you must override the definition of the `copy` constructor provided by the compiler; that is, you must provide your own definition of the `copy` constructor.

Objectives

In this lab, you learn the coding peculiarities of classes with pointer data members.

After completing this lab, you will be able to:

- Understand the coding peculiarities of classes with pointer data members.

Estimated completion time: **5 minutes**

Understanding Peculiarities of Classes with Pointer Data Members

In the following exercises, you answer a series of True or False questions.

Question	Answer (Circle the correct answer)	
1. Because objects are deallocated when the object is out of scope, there is no concern regarding deallocation of dynamic memory when the object goes out of scope.	T	F
2. If a class has a destructor, that destructor is automatically called when the object goes out of scope.	T	F
3. C++ allows overloading of the assignment operator.	T	F
4. A `copy` constructor is automatically executed when an object is declared and initialized to the value of another object.	T	F
5. A `copy` constructor cannot automatically be executed when, as a parameter, an object is passed by value.	T	F

LAB 14.6 USING INHERITANCE, POINTERS, AND VIRTUAL FUNCTIONS

The binding of virtual functions occurs at program execution time, not at compile time. This kind of binding is called the run-time binding. More formally, in run-time binding, the compiler does not generate the code to call a specific function; instead, it generates enough information to enable the run-time system to generate the specific code for the appropriate function call. Run-time binding is also known as dynamic binding.

In C++, virtual functions are declared using the reserved word `virtual`.

It is recommended that classes with pointer data members have destructors. The virtual destructor of a base class automatically makes the destructor of a derived class virtual.

The address of operator (&) is also used to create aliases to an object. Consider the following statements:

```
int x;
int &y = x;
```

The second statement declares `y` to be an alias of `x`. That is both `x` and `y` refer to the same memory location. Thus, `y` is like a constant pointer variable.

Objectives

In this lab, you use inheritance, pointers, and virtual functions.

After completing this lab, you will be able to:

- Write a program using inheritance and pointers.

- Understand the use of virtual functions.

Estimated completion time: **50–60 minutes**

Using Inheritance, Pointers, and Virtual Functions

In the following exercises, you design and write a program that uses inheritance, pointers, and virtual functions.

1a. *Critical Thinking Exercise*: Design a base class named `Worker` to allow the following private data members:

- A pointer to a character variable named `workerName`

- A string `SSN` in the format xxx-xx-xxxx

`Worker` should allow the following public member methods:

- A constructor to dynamically allocate enough memory to hold the employee's name setting `workerName` to 0 and `SSN` to null

- An overloaded constructor to dynamically allocate enough memory to hold the employee's name (the string length plus 1)

- A destructor to free the unused memory

- A member method `setWorkerName` to set `workerName` if `workerName` does not equal 0

- A member method `setSSN` to set the social security number

- A member method `getWorkerName` that returns the `workerName`

- A member method getSSN that returns the SSN
- A virtual void method printValues to print the data members

Write your design in the following space.

1b.   Implement your design in C++ and save it as **Worker.h** in the Chap14 folder of your Student Disk. Implement the member methods, and then compile and save your program in a file named **Worker.cpp** in the Chap14 folder of your Student Disk.

1c.   Design a derived class named `PayWorker` from the `Worker` class and allow the following private data members:

   ■ An integer `dependents`

   ■ A double `payRate`

   `PayWorker` should allow the following public member methods:

   ■ A member method `setPayRate` to set the pay rate

   ■ A member method `setDependents` to set the number of dependents

   ■ A member method `getPayRate` that returns the `PayRate`

   ■ A member method `getDependents` that returns the dependents

   ■ A member method `printValues` that displays the data members

1d.   Implement your design in C++ and save it as **PayWorker.h** in the Chap14 folder of your Student Disk. Implement the member methods, and then compile and save your program in a file named **PayWorker.cpp** in the Chap14 folder of your Student Disk.

1e.   Write a test program that creates a worker named Jesus Guerra, with a social security number 555-22-7788, a pay rate of $12.50, and 5 dependents.

1f. Enter, compile, link, and execute **TestPayWorker.cpp**. Then copy the output and save it in a block comment at the end of your program. Save **TestPayWorker.cpp** in the Chap14 folder of your Student Disk.

The Following is a copy of the screen results that might appear after running your program, depending on the data entered.

```
In base class Worker workerName is Jesus Guerra
In base class Worker SSN is 555-22-7788

In derived class PayWorker payRate is 12.50
In derived class PayWorker dependents is 5

Worker Name: Jesus Guerra
Social Security Number: 555-22-7788
Pay Rate: $12.50
Number of Dependents: 5
```

Overloading and Templates

In this chapter, you will:

- ○ Learn about overloading
- ○ Become aware of the restrictions on operator overloading
- ○ Examine the pointer `this`
- ○ Learn about `friend` functions
- ○ Explore the members and nonmembers of a class
- ○ Discover how to overload various operators
- ○ Learn about templates
- ○ Explore how to construct function templates and class templates

CHAPTER 15: ASSIGNMENT COVER SHEET

Name _____   Date _____

Section _____

Lab Assignments	Assigned	Grade
Lab 15.1 Using Operator Overloading		
Lab 15.2 Overloading Binary Operators (Critical Thinking Exercises)		
Lab 15.3 Overloading Unary Operators		
Lab 15.4 Using Templates (Critical Thinking Exercises)		
Total Grade		

See your instructor or the introduction to this book for instructions on submitting your assignments.

If you are using Visual Studio .NET to compile your C++ programs, you should disable precompiled headers before performing the exercises in the Chapter 15 labs. To do so, change the project properties so that your C++ projects do not use precompiled headers.

LAB 15.1 USING OPERATOR OVERLOADING

C++ allows you to extend the definitions of most of the operators so that they can be applied to classes, called operator overloading. However, while C++ allows you to overload operators, it does not allow you to create new operators. To overload an operator, you must write functions. The name of the function that overloads an operator is the reserved word `operator` followed by the operator to be overloaded.

The result of an operation is a value; therefore, the `operator` function is a value-returning function. Keep the following restrictions in mind when overloading an operator:

- You cannot change the precedence of an operator.

- You cannot change the associativity of an operator.

- You cannot use default arguments with an overloaded operator.

- You cannot change the number of arguments an operator takes.

- You cannot create new operators. Only existing operators can be overloaded. The operators that cannot be overloaded are:

    .   .*   ::   ?:   sizeof

- The meaning of how an operator works with built-in types, such as int, remains the same.

- Operators can be overloaded either for objects or the user-defined types, or for a combination of objects of the user-defined type and objects of the built-in type.

Objectives

In this lab, you use operator overloading for the existing addition and subtraction operators.

After completing this lab, you will be able to:

- Write a class to extend the operators for − (subtraction) and + (addition).

Estimated completion time: **50–60 minutes**

Using Operator Overloading

1a.   Design a UML diagram for a TimeClock class with the following private data members:

- `float days`

- `float hours`

The class should also have the following public member methods:

- constructor with a default that sets the data values to 0

- `getDays` to return the private data member `days`

- `getHours` to return the private data member `hours`

- `setDays` to set the private data member `days`

- `setHours` to set the private data member `hours`

- an operator + function to add hours to the private data member `hours`

- an operator − function to subtract hours from the private data member `hours`

1b.   Write the implementation file **TimeClock.cpp** for the class TimeClock. Compile the file, and save it in the Chap15 folder of your Student Disk.

1c.   Write a C++ program named **WeeklyPay.cpp** to test your class TimeClock. Your program should ask the user how many hours the user worked each day of the week. An object should be created for each day of the week with the number of hours for each day worked and an object for the weekly total. Step through the code by hand, and then enter, compile, link, and execute **WeeklyPay.cpp**. Copy the output and save it in a block comment at the end of your program. Save **WeeklyPay.cpp** in the Chap15 folder of your Student Disk.

The following is a copy of the screen results that might appear after running your program, depending on the data entered. The input entered by the user is shown in bold.

```
This program asks the user for the number of hours worked each day of
the week, totals the hours, and shows the days and hours worked.

How many hours did you work Monday? 4
How many hours did you work Tuesday? 9
How many hours did you work Wednesday? 3
How many hours did you work Thursday? 12
How many hours did you work Friday? 3
How many hours did you work Saturday? 7
How many hours did you work Sunday? 0


This week you worked in days:      and in hours:
Monday:                 0.5                 4
Tuesday:                1.125               9
Wednesday:              0.375               3
Thursday:               1.5                 12
Friday:                 0.375               3
Saturday:               0.875               7
Sunday:                 0                   0

Total for the week:     4.75                38
```

LAB 15.2 OVERLOADING BINARY OPERATORS

Every object of a class maintains a (hidden) pointer to itself, and the name of this pointer is `this`. In C++, `this` is a reserved word.

A function that is defined outside the scope of a class is called a `friend` function of the class. A `friend` function is a nonmember function of the class, but has access to the private data members of the class. To make a function be a `friend` to a class, the reserved word `friend` precedes the function prototype in the class definition, not in the definition of the `friend` function.

To overload binary operators as member functions of a class, use the following syntax:

```
returnType operator op(const className&) const;
```

In this statement, `op` stands for the binary operator, arithmetic or relational, to be overloaded; `returnType` is the type of value returned by the function; and `className` is the name of the class for which the operator is being overloaded.

To overload binary operators as nonmember functions of a class, use the following syntax:

```
friend returnType operator op(const className&, const className&);
```

The operator function that overloads the insertion operator << or the extraction operator >> for a class must be a nonmember of that class.

The assignment operator causes a member-wise copy of the data members of the class. To avoid the shallow copy of data for classes with pointer data members, you must explicitly overload the assignment operator.

Objectives

In this lab, overload the `cin` and `cout` operator using a `friend` function.

After completing this lab, you will be able to:

- Write a `friend overload cin` operator function.

- Write a `friend overload cout` operator function.

Estimated completion time: **60–75 minutes**

Overloading Binary Operators

1a.   *Critical Thinking Exercise:* Design a UML diagram for a Date class with the following private data members:

- `integer month`

- `integer day`

- `integer year`

- a two-dimensional 12 by 12 character array `names`

The class should also include the following public member methods:

- a default constructor to call the method `setNames` and to set the value month to 1, day to 1, and year to 2000

- a constructor to call the method `setNames` and to set the value `month`, `day`, and `year` to the parameter values

- a void method `setNames` to set the array `names` to the names of the month
- a void method `setMonth` to set the data member `month` to the value of the parameter
- a void method `setDay` to set the data member `day` to the value of the parameter
- a void method `setYear` to set the data member `year` to the value of the parameter
- a void method `displayDate()` to display the data members `month`, `day`, and `year` in the format name of month dd, yyyy.
- a `friend` function with an overloaded operator for the `cout` operator
- a `friend` function with an overloaded operator for the `cin` operator

1b.   Write the implementation file **Date.cpp** for the class Date. Compile the file, and save it in the Chap15 folder of your Student Disk.

1c.   Write a C++ program named **OverloadDate.cpp** to test your class Date. Your program should create an object that will call the default constructor, an object with parameters 6, 10, and 2010; another object with default parameters; and should call the function `DisplayDate` after each object is created. Your program should then test the overloaded `cin` operator and the overloaded `cout` operator. Step through the code by hand, and then enter, compile, link, and execute **OverloadDate.cpp**. Copy the output and save it in a block comment at the end of your program. Save **OverloadDate.cpp** in the Chap15 folder of your Student Disk.

For testing purposes, your program should display the date. The default constructor should initialize the date to January 1, 2000. You should also have a constructor that accepts arguments to initialize the date. The following is a copy of the screen results that might appear after running your program, depending on the data entered. The input entered by the user is shown in bold.

```
January 1, 2000
June 10, 2010
January 1, 2000
Enter the month: 11
Enter the day: 27
Enter the year: 1492
November 27, 1492
January 1, 2000
January 1, 2000
```

LAB 15.3 OVERLOADING UNARY OPERATORS

The only difference between overloading unary operators and overloading binary operators is that in the case of unary operators, the operator has only one argument. Therefore, to overload a unary operator for a class:

- If the operator function is a member of the class, it has no parameters.

- If the operator functions is a nonmember—that is, a `friend` function of the class—it has one parameter.

Objectives

In this lab, you create a class with prefix and postfix ++ and -- overloaded operators.

After completing this lab, you will be able to:

- Write a class to extend the operator -- prefix operator.

- Write a class to extend the operator -- postfix operator.

- Write a class to extend the operator ++ prefix operator.

- Write a class to extend the operator ++ postfix operator.

Estimated completion time: **50–60 minutes**

Overloading Unary Operators

1a.   Design a UML diagram for an AddSub class with a private data member named **number** of type integer. The class should also have the following public member methods:

- a default constructor that initializes **number** to 0

- a constructor that initializes **number** to the parameter value

- a **getNumber** method that returns the value of number

- an overloaded operator ++ function to perform a prefix operation

- an overloaded operator ++ function to perform a postfix operation

- an overloaded operator -- function to perform a prefix operation

- an overloaded operator -- function to perform a postfix operation

1b.   Write the implementation file **AddSub.cpp** for the class AddSub. Compile the file, and save it in the Chap15 folder of your Student Disk.

1c.   Write a C++ program to test your class AddSub and name it **testAddSub.cpp**. Your program should create six objects: minusOne, zero1, zero2, zero3, zero4, and one. Call the method getNumber with each object to show the value of each number data member of each object. Your program should then test the overloaded prefix and postfix operators and call the getNumber method to show the values after using these operators. Step through the code by hand, and then enter, compile, link, and execute **testAddSub.cpp**. Copy the output and save it in a block comment at the end of your program. Save **testAddSub.cpp** in the Chap15 folder of your Student Disk.

The following is a copy of the screen results that should appear after running your program:

```
Before operations the values are:
minus one: 0
zero1: 0
zero2: 0
zero3: 0
zero4: 0
One: 0

After prefix negation, minus one is: -1
After postfix negation, minus one is: 0

After prefix addition, one is: 1
After postfix addition, one is: 0
```

LAB 15.4 USING TEMPLATES

Templates allow you to write a single code segment for a set of related functions, called a function template, and for a set of related classes, called a class template. The syntax you use for templates is:

```
template <class Type>
declaration;
```

In these statements, `Type` is the type of data, and `declaration` is either a function declaration or a class declaration.

Similar to variables being parameters to functions, types (that is, data types) are parameters to templates.

You will no longer separate the header file and implementation file. Because the compiler cannot instantiate a function template without the actual parameter to the template, you can no longer compile the implementation file independently of the user code. Instead, put the class definition and the function definitions in the same header file.

Objectives

In this lab, you create a class with a template to accept any data type.

After completing this lab, you will be able to:

- Define a template class to accept any data type.

Estimated completion time: **40–50 minutes**

Using Templates

1a.   *Critical Thinking Exercise*: Design a UML diagram and implement in C++ the code for an Any-Type class with the following private data members:

- data type AT named `item`

- Boolean defined to indicate if the item has been set

The class should also have the following public member methods:

- a default constructor that initializes `defined` to false.

- a `getItem` method that tests to see whether `item` has been set, and if it has returns the value of `item`. If it has not, the method displays a message that the item has not been set.

- a `setItem` method that assigns the parameter the value to `item` and sets defined to true.

1b.   Write a C++ program to test your class AnyType and name it **testAnyType.cpp**. Your program should create four objects of template class AnyType. Store an integer type in object `ATint`, a character type in object `ATchar`, a string type in object `ATstring`, and a boolean type in object `ATbool`. Your program should then test the `setItem` method with the values 4, 'A', "Hello World", and false. Then call the `getItem` method to show the values of each object. Step through the code by hand, and then enter, compile, link, and execute **testAnyType.cpp**. Copy the output, including warnings, and save it in a block comment at the end of your program. Save **testAnyType.cpp** in the Chap15 folder of your Student Disk.

The following is a copy of the screen results that should appear after running your program:

```
The value of ATint is: 4
The value of ATchar is: A
The value of ATstring is: Hello World
The value of ATbool is: 0
```

Exception Handling

In this chapter, you will:

O Learn what an exception is

O Learn how to handle exceptions within a program

O See how a `try/catch` block is used to handle exceptions

O Become familiar with C++ exception classes

O Learn how to create your own exception classes

O Discover how to throw and rethrow an exception

O Explore stack unwinding

CHAPTER 16: ASSIGNMENT COVER SHEET

Name _____   Date _____

Section _____

Lab Assignments	Assigned	Grade
Lab 16.1 Catching Exceptions and Processing Exceptions During Program Execution Using `try` and `catch` Blocks (Critical Thinking Exercises)		
Lab 16.2 Using C++ Exception Classes		
Lab 16.3 Rethrowing and Throwing an Exception (Critical Thinking Exercises)		
Total Grade		

See your instructor or the introduction to this book for instructions on submitting your assignments.

If you are using Visual Studio .NET to compile your C++ programs, you should disable precompiled headers before performing the exercises in the Chapter 16 labs. To do so, change the project properties so that your C++ projects do not use precompiled headers.

LAB 16.1 CATCHING EXCEPTIONS AND PROCESSING EXCEPTIONS DURING PROGRAM EXECUTION USING TRY AND CATCH BLOCKS

Until now, you have dealt with exceptions by using an `if` statement or the `assert` function, or by simply ignoring the exception. However, with some exceptions, you don't want the program to ignore the exception and terminate.

One common way to deal with exceptions is to provide exception-handling code at the point where an error might occur. You place statements that might generate an exception in a `try` block. The `try` block also contains statements that should not be executed if an exception occurs. The `try` block is followed by one or more `catch` blocks. A `catch` block specifies the type of exception it can catch and contains an exception handler.

Keep the following guidelines in mind when you use `try` and `catch` blocks:

- If no exception is thrown in a `try` block, all `catch` blocks associated with the `try` block are ignored and program execution resumes after the last `catch` block.

- If an exception is thrown in a `try` block, the remaining statements in the `try` block are ignored. The program searches the `catch` blocks in the order they appear after the `try` block and looks for an appropriate exception handler. If the type of the thrown exception matches the parameter type in one of the `catch` blocks, the code of that `catch` block executes, and the remaining `catch` blocks are ignored.

- The last `catch` block that contains ellipses is designed to catch any type of exception.

Objectives

In this lab, you catch exceptions that should be caught and process them during program execution.

After completing this lab, you will be able to:

- Catch exceptions that should be caught.

- Process caught exceptions during program execution.

- Use multiple `catch` blocks for multiple exceptions of different types in the same program.

Estimated completion time: **40–50 minutes**

Catching Exceptions and Processing Exceptions During Program Execution Using try and catch Blocks

1a.   *Critical Thinking Exercise:* Design a program that surveys a customer to request the customer's age, state, and zip code. The program should meet the following criteria:

- Use a two-character abbreviation for the state.

- Compare the two-character abbreviation for the state to the data in a file named **states.txt** that is included in the Chap16 folder of your Student Disk.

- Display the user's age, state name, and zip code.

- Use `try` and `catch` blocks when the data does not match.

- If the user enters a character for the age, use a `catch` block to display a message.

- Call a function to enter the state abbreviation and compare it against the file list. Return the state abbreviation and the state name from the function. Also use a `catch` block in the function for any error that occurs during processing the file.

- If the user enters an invalid state abbreviation, use a `catch` block in the main function to display a message that an invalid state abbreviation was entered.

- Call a function to enter the zip code. If the user enters a character for the zip code, use a `catch` block to display a message.

- If the zip code is out of range, use a `catch` block to display a message.

- Test your program by entering the data shown in Table 16-1.

Table 16-1   Data for testing Exceptions.cpp

Data Entry Item	First Test	Second Test	Third Test	Fourth Test
Age	Character value	Integer value	Integer value	Integer value
State		Invalid two-character state abbreviation	Valid two-character state abbreviation	Valid two-character state abbreviation
Zip code			Zip code out of range	Zip code within the valid range

1b.   Write a C++ program based on the design you created in Exercise 1a, and name it **Exceptions.cpp**. Step through the code by hand.

In the following space, show what is displayed on the screen after executing the output message.

1c.   Enter, compile, link, and execute **Exceptions.cpp**. Then copy the output and save it in a block comment at the end of your program. Save **Exceptions.cpp** in the Chap16 folder of your Student Disk.

The following is a copy of the screen results that should appear after testing your program, depending on the data entered. The input entered by the user is shown in bold.

When the user enters a character for age:

```
Please enter your age: a
You entered a character for age: a
```

When the user enters a valid age and an invalid two-character state abbreviation:

```
Please enter your age: 20
Please enter your two-letter state abbreviation: WW
Your state abbreviation was invalid.
```

When the user enters a valid age, a valid two-character state abbreviation, and an invalid zip code:

```
Please enter your age: 20
Please enter your two-letter state abbreviation: TX
Please enter your zip code: 999999
Your zip code is out of range. 999999
```

When the user enters all valid data:

```
Please enter your age: 20
Please enter your two-letter state abbreviation: TX
Please enter your zip code: 78764

Thank you for participating in our survey.
Your data:
20      Age
Texas   State name
78764   Zip
```

LAB 16.2 USING C++ EXCEPTION CLASSES

C++ provides support to handle exceptions via a hierarchy of classes. Among others, this class contains the function what. All derived classes of the class exception override the function what to issue their own error messages.

C++ contains the following classes for handling exceptions:

- The class invalid_argument deals with illegal argument used in a function call.

- The class out_of_range deals with string subscript out-of-range error.

- The class length_error deals with the error that a length greater than the maximum size allowed for the object being manipulated is used.

- The class runtime_error deals with errors that can only be detected during program execution.

- The classes overflow_error and underflow_error are derived from the class runtime_error.

For exception classes that are used to handle exceptions thrown by functions of these classes, you do not include a throw statement in the try block.

Objectives

In this lab, you handle exceptions using exception classes.

After completing this lab, you will be able to:

- Test the out_of_range and bad_alloc exception handlers.

- Use the what function within a catch block.

Estimated completion time: **30–40 minutes**

Using C++ Exception Classes

In the following exercise, you design and write a program that uses exception-handling classes.

1a. Design a program to test the out_of_range and bad_alloc exception handlers. Prompt a user for a name, get the length of the name, and then try to get a substring of the name that is out of range. Use a catch block to display a message that the substring is out of range. Within the catch block, use the what function. Prompt the user for the beginning of the substring and the length of the substring to find. Run the program again with a valid substring to test for the memory allocation. Allocate an array that is too large for your computer. Make sure that you have nothing else running. Your operating system may warn you that you are running out of virtual memory and shut down before your program has a chance to handle the exception.

Write your design in the following space. Your design should be a list of C++ comments without any code.

1b.   Write a C++ program based on the design you created in Exercise 1a, and name it **ExceptClass.cpp**. Step through the code by hand.

In the following space, show what is displayed on the screen after executing the output message.

1c.   Enter, compile, link, and execute **ExceptClass.cpp**. Then copy the output and save it in a block comment at the end of your program. Save **ExceptClass.cpp** in the Chap16 folder of your Student Disk.

The following is a copy of the screen results that might appear after running your program, depending on the data entered. The input entered by the user is shown in bold.

```
Enter your first name, middle initial (no period), and last name:
Zelda A Goldstein
The length is 18
Enter the starting position and length of the substring: 20 5
In the out_of_range catch block: invalid string position


Enter your first name, middle initial (no period), and last name:
Zelda A Goldstein
The length is 18
Enter the starting position and length of the substring: 1 1
In the bad_alloc catch block: bad_alloc
```

LAB 16.3 RETHROWING AND THROWING AN EXCEPTION

When a program passes control to a `catch` block, the `catch` block handles the exception, partially processes the exception, and then rethrows the same exception, or rethrows another exception for the calling environment to handle the exception.

In some cases, it is best to let a program terminate when an exception occurs. Sometimes, you will want to handle the exception and let the program continue. If a program enters the fail state, an exception is thrown. The input stream can be restored and the program can continue when a valid number is input. Sometimes a program will report an exception and continue to run.

Objectives

In this lab, you handle exceptions and then allow the user to continue the program.

After completing this lab, you will be able to:

- Handle exceptions.

- Allow the user to continue a program after an exception has been thrown.

Estimated completion time: **40–50 minutes**

Rethrowing and Throwing an Exception

1a.   *Critical Thinking Exercise:* Redesign your **Exceptions.cpp** program from Lab 16.1 Make the following changes:

- The user enters the name of the data file.

- Your function `getZip` should rethrow an exception to be caught in the main function.

- Your program should continue until valid information is entered for each data item.

Write your design in the following space. Your design should be a list of C++ comments without any code.

1b.   Write a C++ program based on the design you created in Exercise 1a, and name it **Redo.cpp**. Step through the code by hand.

In the following space, show what is displayed on the screen after executing the output message.

1c.   Enter, compile, link, and execute **Redo.cpp**. Then copy the output and save it in a block comment at the end of your program. Save **Redo.cpp** in the Chap16 folder of your Student Disk.

The following is a copy of the screen results that might appear after running your program, depending on the data entered. The input entered by the user is shown in bold.

```
Enter the name of the input file to read: (Do not use spaces.) hello.txt
Cannot open file.
Enter the name of the input file to read: (Do not use spaces.) states.txt
Please enter your age: -4
You entered a character for age: -
Please enter your age: 20
Please enter your two-letter state abbreviation: WW
Your state abbreviation was invalid.
Please enter your two-letter state abbreviation: TX
Please enter your zip code: abc
Your zip code is out of range. -1
Please enter your zip code: 78734

Thank you for participating in our survey.

Your data:
20      Age
Texas   State name
78734   Zip
```

Recursion

In this chapter, you will:

○ Learn about recursive definitions

○ Explore the base case and the general case of a recursive definition

○ Discover what is a recursive algorithm

○ Learn about recursive functions

○ Explore how to use recursive functions to implement recursive algorithms

CHAPTER 17: ASSIGNMENT COVER SHEET

Name _____   Date _____

Section _____

Lab Assignments	Assigned	Grade
Lab 17.1 Using a Recursive Algorithm (Critical Thinking Exercises)		
Lab 17.2 Designing a Recursive Algorithm for a Power Function (Critical Thinking Exercises)		
Lab 17.3 Rewriting a Program with a Standard Loop to Use a Recursive Function		
Total Grade		

See your instructor or the introduction to this book for instructions on submitting your assignments.

If you are using Visual Studio .NET to compile your C++ programs, you should disable precompiled headers before performing the exercises in the Chapter 17 labs. To do so, change the project properties so that your C++ projects do not use precompiled headers.

LAB 17.1 USING A RECURSIVE ALGORITHM

One way to solve problems in computer programs is to use looping, or iteration. You can also use recursion, which is another method of repeating code other than looping. A recursive function is a function that calls itself. A recursive definition is one in which something is defined as a smaller version of itself. Recursion, like a loop, stops when a certain condition is met. The condition that causes the recursive function to stop is called the base case of the recursive function.

In recursion, a set of statements is repeated by having a function call itself. Moreover, a selection control structure is used to control the repeated calls in recursion.

Keep the following guidelines in mind as you work with recursive statements:

■ Every recursive definition must have one or more base cases.

■ The general case must eventually be reduced to a base case.

■ The base case stops the recursion.

A recursive function in which the last statement executed is the recursive call is called a tail recursive function.

A program design for a recursive function is similar to a program design for a loop. As a beginning student, you might find it easier to test your program design using a loop. Then, after you have determined that your design works, use the same design to implement the C++ code as a recursive function.

Objectives

In this lab, you design a program that calls a recursive function to reverse the elements of a string.

After completing this lab, you will be able to:

■ Design an algorithm to use a recursive function.

■ Use a recursive function for string processing.

Estimated completion time: 50–60 minutes

Using a Recursive Algorithm

In the following exercises, you design a program that calls a function to display a string in reverse order. For example, a string with a value "Hello" should be displayed as "olleH". To help design the algorithm, first answer a few questions. Because all program designs need to address input, processing, and output, consider how you want to accomplish these tasks.

1. How will your string be declared—as a string or as a character array? If you select a character array, what is the maximum size of the string?

2. How will the value of the string be input—as an assigned value or input by the user?

3. Do you need to know the exact length of the string or only the maximum length of the string?

4. What information (arguments) should the main program pass to the recursive function?

5. How do you know when the recursive function has reached the base case?

6. Will you display the reversed string element by element or as another string? (*Hint:* If you send the string and the length of the string to the recursive function, you always know the last element of the string. What would you do to process the string by a different last character each time?)

7a.   *Critical Thinking Exercise:* Write your program design in the space provided.

7b.   Write a C++ program based on the design you created in Exercise 7a, and name it **Reverse.cpp**. Step through the code by hand.

In the following space, show what is displayed on the screen after executing the output message.

7c.   Enter, compile, link, and execute **Reverse.cpp**. Then copy the output and save it in a block comment at the end of your program. Save **Reverse.cpp** in the Chap17 folder of your Student Disk.

The following is a copy of the screen results that might appear after running your program, depending on the data entered. The input entered by the user is shown in bold.

```
Enter your message to be reversed: Hello, how are you?
?uoy era woh ,olleH
```

8a.   *Critical Thinking Exercise:* Design a program that calls a function to input an integer and display it in reverse order. For example, if you have an integer with a value 5982, you want the integer displayed to be 2895. Do not enter the integer as a string. You must enter it as an integer.

Write your design in the following space. Your design should be a list of C++ comments without any code.

8b.   Write a C++ program based on the design you created in Exercise 8a, and name it **ReverseNum.cpp**. Step through the code by hand.

In the following space, show what is displayed on the screen after executing the output message.

8c.   Enter, compile, link, and execute **ReverseNum.cpp**. Then copy the output and save it in a block comment at the end of your program. Save **ReverseNum.cpp** in the Chap17 folder of your Student Disk.

The following is a copy of the screen results that might appear after running your program, depending on the data entered. The input entered by the user is shown in bold.

```
Enter a number greater than zero: 5982
You entered 5982. Reversed, that number is 2895.
```

LAB 17.2 DESIGNING A RECURSIVE ALGORITHM FOR A POWER FUNCTION

When designing a recursive function, you must consider that a recursive function executes more slowly than its iterative counterpart. On slow computers, especially those with limited memory space, the execution of a recursive function is visible. On new computers with a large amount of memory space, the execution of a recursive function is not noticeable.

When a statement calls a recursive function as part of an expression, it is a recursive call. Processing a value that returns a recursive function is called unwinding the recursion.

Objectives

In this lab, you design a program that uses a recursive function call to create a power function that raises a base value to a positive exponent.

After completing this lab, you will be able to:

- Design an algorithm that uses a recursive call as part of a value-returning expression to a recursive call.

Estimated completion time: **50–60 minutes**

Designing a Recursive Algorithm for a Power Function

In the following exercises, you answer questions to help design a recursive algorithm. Then you design and write a program that is a power function, which is used to raise a base value to a positive exponent. This power function should be a recursive function. You have already used the power function from the math header file. Design your own recursive function called power that takes integer arguments for base and exponent and returns an integer value. The exponent value must be greater than or equal to zero. The algorithm finds n raised to the power of x, or (n^x). To help design the algorithm, first answer the following questions to determine how your program will handle input, processing, and output.

1. How will the values for your base and exponent be input—by assignment or by interactive input?

2. The main program might restrict valid input. However, your function should accommodate all integer values. How will you accommodate negative exponents?

3. How will you accommodate zero exponents?

4. How will you accumulate the values returned from the recursive function?

5. How will you display the result from the function calls?

6a.   *Critical Thinking Exercise:* Design a program from the problem description. Write your design in the following space. Your design should be a list of C++ comments without any code.

6b.   Write a C++ program based on the design you created in Exercise 6a, and name it **Power.cpp**. Step through the code by hand.

In the following space, show what is displayed on the screen after executing the output message.

6c.   Enter, compile, link, and execute **Power.cpp**. Then copy the output and save it in a block comment at the end of your program. Save **Power.cpp** in the Chap17 folder of your Student Disk.

The following is a copy of the screen results that might appear after running your program, depending on the data entered. The input entered by the user is shown in bold.

```
Enter your base number and your exponent: 3 4
The number 3 raised to the power of 4 is 81
```

LAB 17.3 REWRITING A PROGRAM WITH A STANDARD LOOP TO USE A RECURSIVE FUNCTION

A program that has been written using a loop can usually be written using recursive function.

Objectives

In this lab, you revise a program you created in a previous lab. Instead of using a loop, you use a recursive function to perform repeated tasks.

After completing this lab, you will be able to:

■ Convert a program that uses a loop to use a recursive function.

Estimated completion time: **30–40 minutes**

Rewriting a Program with a Standard Loop to Use a Recursive Function

1a.   The **Scan1.cpp** program created in Lab 5.1 of this Lab Manual prompts the user to enter the name of a hardware item, searches a list in **invoice1.txt** for the item and its associated information, and displays the name and the price of the item. If the search item is not in the list, you reach the end of file. A compound flag-controlled `while` loop is used to search the list until either the item is found, or the end of the file is reached. A message is displayed if the item is not found. Refer to the design created for Lab 5.1, Exercise 2 to redesign the program to use a recursive function. Use the same prompts, input, and output.

Write your design in the following space. Your design should be a list of C++ comments without any code.

1b.   Write a C++ program based on the design you created in Exercise 1a and name it **RecursiveScan.cpp**. Step through the code by hand.

In the following space, show what is displayed on the screen after executing the output message depending on the data entered.

1c.   Enter, compile, link, and execute **RecursiveScan.cpp**. Then copy the output and save it in a block comment at the end of your program. Save **RecursiveScan.cpp** in the Chap17 folder of your Student Disk.

The following is a copy of the screen results that might appear after running your program, depending on the data entered. The input entered by the user is shown in bold.

```
Enter name of item for search: shovel

The item shovel costs 35.40
or
Enter name of item for search: hoe

The item hoe was not in the list
```